MAP IT

MAP IT

THE HANDS-ON GUIDE TO STRATEGIC TRAINING DESIGN

CATHY MOORE

Montesa Press

Print ISBN 978-0-9991745-0-0
Published by Montesa Press

Cover design: James T. Egan

Typesetting services by BOOKOW.COM

Contents

Introduction: Is this book for you?

"We need a course."

Does the following sound familiar?

Tina, a training designer, is meeting with Harold, who works for a big hospital.

"We need a course on sharps safety," Harold says. "It should cover how to handle needles and other sharp things. We already have 97 slides that tell people everything they need to know. Can you turn the slides into an online course?"

The next words out of Tina's mouth could doom 8,200 hospital employees to a time-sucking, soul-squashing information dump. Or, they could inspire Harold to look more closely at why he wants a course and work with Tina to actually change what people do.

What will Tina say?

What's your story?

Your story might not start with "turn these slides into a course." Maybe instead you hear, "We need training on X" or "People need to be aware of Y" or "We need a two-hour session on Z for our annual meeting."

The exact words don't matter. The message is the same: "Your job is to deliver this information."

You're supposed to assume that information will solve the problem (don't ask about the problem!). Your only responsibility is to do instructional-designy things like "chunk" the information and make it "engaging" so people will "learn" it.

Everyone seems to believe this is our role, and we obey because we don't know what else to do. So on project after project, we find ourselves sliding down a steep, slimy slope into an information dump.

This book helps you change the story from your first contact with the client. It gives you concrete steps to follow that will keep you out of the information dump. You'll steer your projects along a much more productive and pleasant path, with your client and subject matter expert by your side.

I want to help you:

- Find the simplest solution to a performance problem (it might not include training)
- Help people change what they do, not just what they know
- Create activity-rich materials that people **want** to use
- Make those materials available when people need them most
- Show how your work helps your organization meet goals that matter
- Enjoy doing fascinating work that makes a difference

Let's talk business, not education

This book walks you through a design approach I developed called action mapping. I created it for the business world after I became frustrated with applying academic models to business problems.

The goal of action mapping is to **solve business problems by changing job behavior.** Our goal isn't to prepare people for a knowledge test.

So if you want to help adults change what they do on the job, this book is for you. You might work in business, government, or an NGO. Your role might be "training designer," but we're going to expand the definition of "training" to include many types of changes and solutions.

If you're an educator, you might find some useful ideas here, but you won't be able to apply the model as it's intended. It's designed for the very different needs of business. Please don't buy the book expecting to use it easily in education.

I use the term "training design" instead of "instructional" or "learning" design to emphasize that I'm talking to people in business, not education. However, you'll see that I interpret "training" very broadly. We're really talking about performance improvement.

Who are your learners?

I'm making two important assumptions about your audience.

- They're adults with jobs in business, government, or non-governmental organizations. They aren't students in academia.

- They need to learn how to do something right now on their jobs. They're not exploring a topic for possible future use or preparing for a test.

Many of us are expected to design "someday you'll need this" training. Someday you'll need to have a difficult conversation with a team member or lead an unpopular change. Someday this stuff will be useful, so let me tell you all about it now and hope you remember it. We're not going to create that type of training.

Instead, we're going to turn vague "they should know this" training requests into **projects that solve real, clearly defined performance problems.** Our solutions will be targeted to specific groups in specific situations and provided when they're most needed. The solutions might not include conventional training at all.

By making this change, we'll stop being replaceable cogs on the wheel of the course factory. Instead, we'll show how we improve performance and help our organizations reach goals that matter.

> *This trajectory takes us on a journey from an isolated self-contained quasi-autonomous learning operation to one that is fully engaged in and aligned with the business...We move from large, extended chunks of learning, delivered infrequently, to small focused granules often delivered at the precise moment of need....*
>
> *This is so important that there really is no alternative scenario for corporate learning teams, apart from extinction.*
>
> *— Nigel Paine in The Learning Challenge: Dealing with technology, innovation and change in learning and development, 2014*

Action mapping applies to all types of workplace learning

I developed action mapping in 2008. When the model was still a toddler, it liked to play with self-paced elearning. However, action mapping is all grown up now, and it encourages you to consider all forms of workplace learning, including:

- Job aids and other references
- Face-to-face sessions
- Webinars
- Activities provided on their own, not through training events
- Discussion groups
- Mobile performance support
- Stretch assignments
- Mentoring
- Video, shared documents, emails, and a lot of other things I haven't listed here
- Any combination of the above

Quick overview of action mapping

First, the name: "Action" refers to focusing on what people need to **do**, not what they need to know. "Mapping" refers to the visual way you can show how all the elements of the solution depend on each other. It looks like a mind map but is more structured.

You'll start with a business goal and then build out from that. At the end, you'll have a map that shows what needs to happen to reach the goal. Throughout the process, your goal is to **solve the performance problem,** not just provide training.

Here's a super-high-level glance at what you'll do.

1. Write the goal for your project

By getting everyone to commit to a business performance goal, you'll show that your role is to **solve the problem,** not just provide training. You'll measure your success in a way that matters to the organization.

2. Ask, "What do they need to do, and why aren't they doing it?"

By focusing on what people need to do and asking, "Why aren't they doing it?" you'll find many ways to solve the problem. You might find that a job aid is enough. Or, you and the client might discover that you're focusing on the wrong people or problem.

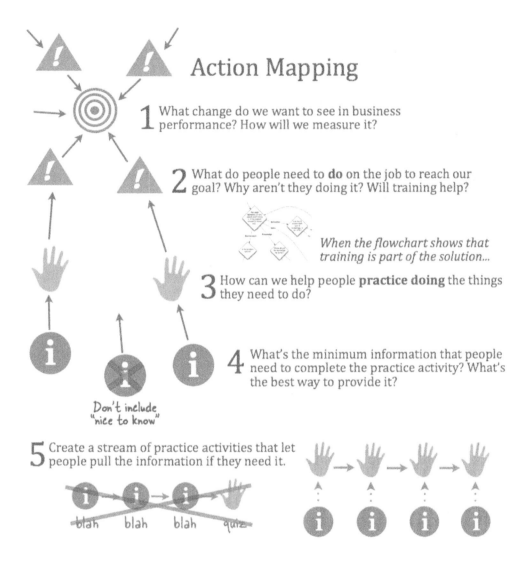

Action Mapping

1 What change do we want to see in business performance? How will we measure it?

2 What do people need to **do** on the job to reach our goal? Why aren't they doing it? Will training help?

When the flowchart shows that training is part of the solution...

3 How can we help people **practice doing** the things they need to do?

4 What's the minimum information that people need to complete the practice activity? What's the best way to provide it?

Don't include "nice to know"

5 Create a stream of practice activities that let people pull the information if they need it.

blah blah blah quiz

You won't waste time creating training for something that can't be solved through training. And if some sort of training really is part of the solution, it will be relevant and highly targeted.

3. Brainstorm practice activities

If training is part of the solution, you'll design practice activities, not presentations. You'll help people learn from the consequences of their decisions. They'll notice and fill their own knowledge gaps as they solve realistic problems. They'll practice doing what they need to do on the job, not just regurgitate information.

Practice activities are very different from the knowledge checks that we're expected to write, so we'll spend a big part of the book on them.

4. Include only the must-have information

By letting the practice activity determine what people need to know, you'll keep stakeholders from adding bloat.

5. Create a stream of activities, not a presentation

By avoiding unnecessary information presentations, you'll design more efficient, memorable materials that feel immersive. You'll have self-contained activities that can be delivered at the best time and in the best format, not necessarily as conventional training.

> **Action mapping in a nutshell**
> *Decide to improve business performance.*
> *Focus on what people need to **do**.*
> *Solve problems; don't train around them.*
> *Design experiences, not information.*
> *Training doesn't have to be an event.*

The model actually goes a lot deeper

As we'll see later, the full model has more steps and goes from setting a goal to evaluating the effectiveness of the solution. You can explore an interactive workflow of the entire process at www.map-it-book.com.

It's not a free-form mind map

Some people teach action mapping as a visual way to organize training content. They skip the analysis step and assume the content will solve the problem. A common result is training that's unfocused and unnecessary.

An action map looks like a mind map, but it has dependencies. Everything in the map has to justify its existence by directly supporting the business goal. Action mapping **eliminates** unnecessary information. It doesn't organize it.

Finally, the map should store not only your ideas for any training content, but also your notes about why the problem is happening in the first place and which non-training solutions could help. You'll see all this as we go through the book.

Benefits of action mapping

It's subversive, in a good way

Action mapping helps you change how your organization views training and your job. Here are a few common ideas you could change.

- From "We need training on X" to "We have a performance problem. Can you help?"
- From "Of course training is the best solution" to "Let's look at the problem. Hey, this tool is hard to use. Could we improve it instead of training everyone?"
- From "Tell them everything and then give them a test" to "Help them learn from realistic experience and apply what they've learned on the job."
- From "Make sure to cover my favorite information" to "Oh, they don't need to know that."
- From "Training is an event" to "How can we embed this in the workflow?"
- From "I hate taking training" to "Wait a minute, this is an interesting challenge..."

SMEs "get it"

Happy action mappers report that SMEs and clients "get" the approach quickly, making it easier to create useful training that's rich with activities instead of bloated with information.

You save money

I've seen action mapping save significant amounts of money, often by avoiding unnecessary training. The analysis doesn't take a long time, but it's powerful. It helps you identify the real cause of a problem and find the most efficient solution.

You create targeted training

When training is part of the solution, action mapping helps you create targeted, relevant activities. You'll create less "content" and more memorable experiences, and those experiences will focus on what people need to do differently.

It makes people happy

Finally, I've heard that clients and learners are happier with the solutions produced by careful action mappers. Clients enjoy seeing results and being associated with high-quality solutions, and learners appreciate being challenged instead of patronized. Training designers get the respect they deserve and tell me that they enjoy their jobs more.

Apply the book as you read it

This is a hands-on book. The first part will help you lose some cultural baggage, and then you'll start using the model with a real-life project.

So, look around now for a project that needs doing. Has someone just told you, "We need training on the new TPS procedure?" Try following the steps in this book instead of using your usual technique.

Apply action mapping from the very beginning of the project. As you're about to see, how you talk with the client in the first meeting is vitally important to getting the project on the right track.

> We're not going to "spice up" conventional training. We're going to completely overhaul how you were probably taught to do instructional design, and the change starts with the first words you speak to training requestors.

If you don't have a new project to practice on, consider redesigning a past project. This option is a distant second best, because you might have to drastically change your perspective, and that's easier to do with a new project.

Start with the end in mind

When you reach the end of this book, I hope you'll look back and see that you've achieved the following.

- You helped your client analyze their performance problem, find non-training solutions, and identify if and where training will help. You helped them see the problem clearly and feel confident that they can solve it.

- If training was part of the solution, you designed challenging activities that help people practice making the decisions they need to make on the job.

- You let people pull the information they need to solve the challenges. You showed that you respect them as intelligent adults.

- You made the practice activities available in the most effective format, whether as a training event or in a more flexible, on-demand form, and you included spaced practice to cement the changes.

- You evaluated the success of the project by looking for improvements in the performance of the team or organization, not just "I liked it!" feedback.

I'd like you to reach this happy ending:

> *Your client respects you as a performance consultant, not a training order taker. Your subject matter expert is proud of their contribution to the project. People are enjoying your challenges and confidently using what they've learned to solve problems that they care about. Your organization is seeing measurable improvements in metrics that matter.*

Chapter 1. Our cultural challenge

Quiz: Are you infected?

This chapter helps you recognize a common mindset that has limited our profession. Do you need to read it? Let's find out.

Respond to each statement without much thought, recording your natural reaction. Give each statement a score:

0 disagree
1 agree slightly
2 agree completely

_____ A. My job is to help spread knowledge.

_____ B. A training designer should start each project by writing the learning objectives.

_____ C. Sometimes people just need a job aid, not a course.

_____ D. If organizations helped their employees share knowledge, most performance problems would be solved.

_____ E. The most important skill for a training designer is the ability to explain things clearly and concisely.

_____ F. Learners shouldn't be allowed to skip material that they already know, because we often overestimate our own knowledge.

_____ G. The subject matter expert often thinks people need more information than is really necessary.

_____ H. An online course should have a knowledge check in every section.

_____ I. Designing instruction is basically the same for business or education, because learning is the same everywhere.

_____ J. The "analysis" step of instructional design refers to analyzing the audience so we can make the content more useful for them.

Your score

Throw out your scores for items C and G. Add up the numbers you assigned to the remaining statements. Here's what your total means:

- 0 to 1: You're free of infection! Feel free to skip this chapter, although you might want to skim it to understand the mindset that most people have.

- 2: You're showing some symptoms of infection. You should probably read this chapter. It won't take long, and it will help you steer clients and SMEs in the right direction.

- More than 2: Read this chapter, please. If you skip it, you'll struggle with action mapping.

Needed: A new mindset

In the introduction, we met Tina. Her client, Harold, wants her to turn 97 slides about sharps safety into an online course. If Tina is like many training designers, how will she respond?

"Sure, I can turn your slides into a course," she says.

Like thousands of designers and clients around the world, Tina and Harold have one goal: "Transfer knowledge." They've assumed that ignorance is the problem and information is the solution.

As a profession, we're obsessed with knowledge transfer. We spend our days in a cloud of knowledge that floats so high above the real world that we can't see the intelligence in the faces of the people below or the rocks they have to climb over. We just assume that they need the information we have, and we rain it down on them, not noticing that the information soon evaporates and the rocks are still there.

Tina and Harold are up in that cloud, preparing to pour slides down onto 8,200 people who deserve better.

Where did our current mindset come from?

To become a training designer, you probably had to study instructional design. You might have studied it formally, you probably read about it, and you certainly absorbed its "rules" on the job. What did you learn?

You probably learned the following rules, which are slightly disguised quotes from sites that claim to describe instructional design.

- "The most important measure in instructional design is the knowledge assessment."

- "Analysis refers to gathering information about the audience and tasks, so the content will be more useful."

- "Content should be divided into facts, concepts, processes, procedures, and principles."

- "Our focus should be on knowledge acquisition, knowledge deepening, and finally knowledge creation."

- "You should break information down into small chunks to prevent cognitive overload, and have a formative assessment for each chunk."

- "The learner should be given an assessment immediately after completing each learning objective."

I easily found these quotes in 15 minutes of poking around, because statements like this are everywhere. They're everywhere because supposedly **our job is to present information and create tests about it.**

Who else has a job that can be summarized as "present information and create tests about it?" Teachers.

"Training is teaching" — or is it?

In school, our teachers' goal was to transfer knowledge. This knowledge was supposed to be stored in our brains and then pulled out for a test. As Michael Allen summarized it in his *Guide to Elearning*, the approach is to "tell, then test." It has the stamp of approval of universities everywhere and so must be the right way to teach.

The people who ask us to develop training probably had the same schoolroom experience. Now, as adults, they assume that training is the same as teaching, because it's hard to imagine what else it could be. As a result, they expect us to deliver information and then test to make sure it got delivered right.

Let's call this the school model. There are all sorts of problems with using that model in business, but let's look at four of the biggest ones.

1. It's not a test, it's a job

The goal of a typical lesson in school is, "Get this information into their heads, and then test them to see if they know it." This "works" in schools because the goal of the system is to get good test scores. If the students score well, everyone is happy. If they score badly, everyone is upset. Even countries are ranked based on their test scores. Although teachers might want their students to become well rounded, critically thinking individuals, what gets measured is what matters, and tests are the measure.

Because most of us spent years in that tell-then-test system, it seems natural to approach training with a similar goal. The test just has a new name, "knowledge check."

Supposedly, our knowledge checks show whether people are prepared for their jobs. But does the world we create with those questions even exist?

- When was the last time you arrived at your desk to find colored blocks scrambled on its surface, each block describing a step in a process, and you had to put those blocks in order? It's a common elearning challenge. Why doesn't it happen on your job?

- How about the last time a colleague came up to you and said, "Which of the following is NOT an example of a cross-border financial transaction?"

- Or the last time you entered the breakroom and heard someone say, "Anyone could be the victim of workplace violence: True or false?" (And if you heard it, would you stick around?)

Tests are "appropriate" in schools because the whole point of conventional schooling is for kids to pass tests. But we rarely face tests on the job. What we face is far more complicated.

2. It's not just the knowledge, it's the decisions

"If they knew this information, they'd do their jobs better." This is a painfully common belief. People assume that injecting knowledge is like injecting a powerful drug. Push the knowledge into the head, and the "learner" magically changes how they do their job.

Harold and Tina believe that the hospital workers just need to know that sharp things are dangerous and be told the right ways to handle them. Then the workers will naturally change what they do.

But if it were true that people just need to "know" stuff, then everyone who scores high on the assessment should be a star performer on the job. That's not even remotely guaranteed, and we all know it. Our jobs require far more than knowledge. We have to skillfully apply that knowledge to complex situations. We have to use it to **make good decisions on the job**.

Let's say that you work as a customer service representative, answering phones all day. You were sent to a generic workshop on customer service, and as a result you "know" that you should respond to an upset customer with empathy. Then an irate caller accuses you of working for a rip-off company and says you're incompetent. You find yourself feeling anything but empathy.

What are you supposed to say? All you know is "use empathy," but you haven't practiced it except for a brief roleplay that had no structure, during which you and your partner gave up and got coffee. The workshop's final assessment had some questions about the importance of empathy, but none of them had any relation to what your job is really like.

The generic roleplay and assessment took place in Testland, a dim, formless world of intellectual abstraction up in the clouds of knowledge. Your actual job puts you in a crowded room with people who are all talking at once, where you have to use an infuriatingly slow database at the same time as you talk with customers, and you're supposed to always be helpful (and empathetic!), but you're evaluated by how quickly you get rid of each caller.

No amount of "knowledge transfer" will help unless you can use the knowledge to decide what to do in that difficult situation.

In addition, the type of knowledge imparted by most workplace training isn't like the knowledge taught in school. In school, we had to memorize a mountain of details about, seemingly, everything, ranging from Genghis Khan's birthplace to how to calculate the volume of a sphere. The amount of memorization required by school fuels a vast study-aid market ranging from cheat sheets to drugs.

In contrast, "use empathy" is typical of the "knowledge" delivered by a lot of workplace training. How many courses have you seen that deliver messages like the following?

- Be nice to the customer.
- Be nice to each other.
- When someone talks to you, listen to them.

- When something changes, don't freak out.
- Don't break the law.
- Be safe.

I've seen a ton of training, and much of it taught variations on common sense. For example, common sense says, "Salespeople should help customers see how they'll benefit by using our product." The variation taught in training is something like the Five-Step Customer Alignment Model. Often, people need to memorize only a handful of concepts and maybe a few phrases to say.

And even if our learners really do need to memorize a lot of information, we're far more interested in how they **apply** what they've learned than whether they can regurgitate it on a test. For example, it's a good sign if our engineers can answer questions on tests, but what we really want is for them to design a widget that operates well at high altitudes.

No matter what type of training we're designing, our goal isn't a good test score. Our goal is to change what people do on the job. Yet thanks to the school model, we're over-focused on memorizing information. We argue about whether a no-brainer principle like "Be nice to each other" is easier to memorize if it's a graphic accompanied by a voiceover or whether it needs to be a click-to-reveal.

If we want to argue, I'd propose we debate this: "How can we help people change what they **do**?"

3. A "course" is rarely the solution

The school model encourages our clients to think that they can solve their problems with a one-time workshop or course. "We just need a webinar for that," they'll say. "Better keep it short, no more than an hour."

As we've seen, our real goal isn't to inject knowledge but to change behavior. The typical one-hour webinar isn't very likely to change behavior. But what if we design an activity-rich webinar that helps people practice the new way to do their job? Wouldn't that work, or at least help?

Maybe.

First, we need to take the uncommon step of determining whether training will actually solve the problem. Often, it won't. Often, the client hasn't defined the problem clearly or looked closely at it. Maybe it's actually caused by an inefficient procedure, or user-hostile software, or impossible deadlines. None of those will be fixed by a webinar. In action mapping, you'll use a flowchart to find the real causes of clients' problems and avoid unnecessary training.

But even if training is an appropriate solution, no course is a cure. People develop habits over time and need time to create new ones. We especially need spaced practice to cement the new habits.

We might not need a training "event" at all. For example, could you encourage the change with just a weekly challenge and some good job aids? Does everyone really have to join a webinar or take a course?

4. Our learners aren't blank slates

In school, our teachers looked at us and saw empty heads that needed filling. In a way, they were right — at age 9 we probably couldn't name the capital of Gabon or calculate the area of a circle.

But our learners aren't kids. They're adults with a lifetime of experience. They already know plenty of stuff, including possibly the stuff we're supposed to "teach" them.

For example, if we're supposed to teach the sales staff a consultative approach to sales, we're not looking at empty heads waiting to be filled. We're looking at a diverse group of adults who have all been selling, in some cases for years, and who are now supposed to change how they do it. Some will have to change a lot and some only a little.

However, our client knows only the school model and expects us to treat all staff the same. We're supposed to present the consultative sales approach in minute detail as if it were a bizarre alien that no one could possibly have seen before, and then have everyone complete the same test.

Remember Harold? His slide deck assumes no one in the audience has ever seen how to handle sharps, even though everyone in his audience is already working in a hospital that's bristling with needles and scalpels. His decision to make a course is also based on the assumption that everyone who works in the hospital needs to know everything about handling sharps, including receptionists, paper-pushers, and the guy who keeps the furnace running.

In project after project, we're supposed to "expose them to all the information," even if it doesn't apply to their job. And instead of letting people prove that they already know something, we make them stare at it, because everyone must be equally exposed. Letting people jump in and try the technique before they've been spoon-fed every morsel of it would "set them up for failure." Their self-esteem could even be damaged!

We cling irrationally to information because, thanks to the school model, we think that training is "knowledge transfer." We feel like information is all we have, so it must be carefully presented and preserved. People can't be trusted to choose what they need to know because the information is so very precious and people are ... well, they're blank slates, right?

"But you're misrepresenting instructional design."

I realize that good instructional design goes beyond "present information and create tests about it." However, the present-and-test approach has been the dominant, and often only, technique that I've seen in the more than 30 years that I've worked in both the education and business worlds. That's why I'm writing this book.

Summary

As "instructors," we spend our days floating high above the real world in a cloud of knowledge. Information is all we have up there, so we've developed an unhealthy obsession with it. We give it magical powers. We fail to question assumptions like, "A course will solve the problem." We fail to even look closely at the problem. We follow fads that promise to "transfer knowledge." We treat adults like inexperienced children, and we design training that just puts information into short-term memory and takes it out again.

If you do just one thing...

Don't view your job as "knowledge transfer." It's much bigger than that.

To see the alternative to "knowledge transfer," let's continue the story about Harold's project.

Chapter 2.
If we don't teach, then what do we do?

Focus on performance, not information

If we dump the school model, our goal is no longer, "Tell them what they need to know and test them to make sure they know it."

Instead, we have to come down from the clouds and ask potentially scary questions, like, "What are we trying to do? What shows us that we have a performance problem? What's causing the problem? Is it really a lack of knowledge, or is something else going on? Is training even the solution? If training is part of the solution, what should it do?"

I developed action mapping in 2008 because I felt we needed a structured way to combat the school model. Let's look at how action mapping compares to the traditional approach.

Example: Same story, two approaches

Earlier, we met Tina and Harold. Harold works for a big hospital and says he needs a course on sharps safety. Tina is a training designer who's happy to convert Harold's slides into a course. However, Tina's approach isn't the only way to respond to Harold's request. We're going to compare Tina's method with another approach, using two versions of the same story.

In the first version, the designer, Tina Teachalot, thinks her job is to create a course that delivers the information that the client has provided. She'll use a conventional approach.

In the second version, the client is the same, but the designer is Anna Action von Mapp. She thinks her job is to **solve the client's problem**. She'll use action mapping.

Baby steps!

In the story, I limit the solution to elearning so you can compare the two approaches easily. In both versions of the story, training is part of the solution, but in your projects, you could find that no training is necessary. I'm using an example that includes training because that's where most of you are starting from, and I'm limiting the training aspect of the solution to elearning so you can see that even a minor change can have a big impact on the end product.

> *Like many examples in this book, this one is simple. That's because I want you to see the process clearly. Don't let the simple stories fool you — action mapping easily scales up to help you solve complex problems and deliver big projects.*

Assignment: Safety course for a hospital

The client, Harold, wants an online course about sharps safety for hospital workers. Everyone who is supposed to take the course is an adult with some experience working in a healthcare setting or who at least has seen the inside of a doctor's office.

Tina: "My job is to create a course."

Tina operates under the school model and believes her job is to create a course. Here's how she works.

Meet with the client to accept the content

"We need a course on sharps safety," Harold says. He gives Tina the slide deck that the hospital used in the face-to-face training, which they're phasing out. "Everything people need to know is in this deck. Please turn it into an online course."

"Sure, I can do that," Tina says, and she gets to work.

First, she reviews the slides and asks Harold a few questions like, "I'm not sure I understand this slide. What's the most important thing here that they need to know?"

Write a script

When Tina has all the information, she writes a script for the course. The script has separate columns showing what the narrator will say for each slide, what will appear on the slide, and how the user goes to the next slide.

The original deck has 97 slides, and some of them are dense, so Tina breaks them into smaller chunks. The final, long script describes 130 slides.

It takes Harold awhile to give his feedback on the script, but finally Tina is ready to produce.

Put it together

Welcome screen with objectives. Tina welcomes people to the course and displays a list of what it's supposed to teach them. Here's one objective:

> Identify the risks associated with improper handling of sharps

Introduction. Tina tells people why the topic is important, using scary statistics about diseases transmitted through contaminated sharps. Two million avoidable infections every year!

Presentation. First, Tina presents information on how to handle and dispose of needles correctly. She creates several screens listing do's and don'ts, with bullet points read by the narrator.

Tina wants to engage learners with interactivity, so on some screens people click images to reveal more information.

Since Tina spent money on narration, she can't afford to take custom photos of someone handling needles. Instead, she adds stock photos of no one in particular wearing a lab coat.

Knowledge check. After several screens of presentation, Tina makes sure people understand by asking a few questions. Here's one:

> True or false: To reduce the risk of a needlestick, you should recap a needle by holding the syringe in one hand and the cap in the other hand.

It's the same as asking, "Do you remember what you saw three screens ago?"

Presentation + knowledge check, over and over. Tina continues alternating between presentations and knowledge checks, adding some click-to-reveals for engagement. She spends a long time creating a clickable hypodermic needle that reveals do's and don'ts.

Assessment. Finally, Tina presents a test that uses the same kinds of questions that appeared in the knowledge checks. Here's a typical question:

Which of the following is not a method of sterilization?

a) Dry heat

b) Soaking in chemicals

c) Boiling

d) Autoclaving

Approval

Tina has Harold check everything, and she makes some changes that he requests.

Implementation

Tina puts the course on the hospital LMS, and Harold assigns it to all staff. Everyone takes the same course, whether they're a janitor or a phlebotomist.

Evaluation

Most people report that they "learned a bit" or "learned a lot" from Tina's course, and everyone passes the assessment. Success!

No one knows if people have changed their behavior on the job because no one's measuring that. Tina's done!

What was she thinking?

Tina's decisions were driven by her view of her job. Here's how she describes her job and tasks:

- "The client views me as a course producer."
- "The client identifies the information that I should cover."
- "I make an online course engaging by using narration, images, animation, and clicking."
- "I mostly design information."
- "I don't let anyone skip what they already know, because they might be wrong."

- "If people understand the information, I've done my job."

As you read the next story about another designer, Anna, consider this: How would Anna respond to Tina's beliefs?

Anna: "My job is to solve the problem."

Let's approach the same project from a different perspective. This time, the designer is Anna Action von Mapp, who views her job as "solve the client's problem."

Meet with the client to set a goal

"We need a course on sharps safety," Harold says. He gives Anna the slide deck that the hospital used in the face-to-face training, which they're phasing out. "Everything people need to know is in this deck. Please turn it into an online course."

"Thanks for the slides," Anna says. "So you're phasing out your live course?"

"Yes, it was too hard to schedule and didn't seem to be working well."

"You still had safety problems after the training?"

"Yeah, the error reports barely went down," Harold says. "I think people tuned out the course, because they have to go through so much training. They're tired of it."

"So you'd still like the errors to go down," Anna says. "Do you have a target in mind?"

"To match the hospitals with the best record, we'd need to have an 8% decrease in errors," Harold says. "Ideally, we'd reach that within a year, when a big safety report comes out."

"That sounds like a great goal," Anna says. "Let's consider that the goal for our project." She goes to the whiteboard and writes, "Errors with sharps will decrease 8% within a year as all staff correctly handle sharps."

"That looks good," Harold says, brightening. "That's what we want our course to accomplish."

Identify what people need to do

"If you have a few minutes," Anna says, "I'd like to make sure I understand what people are supposed to do and what they're doing instead."

"It's easy to list what they're supposed to do," Harold says. "It's all in our standard operating procedures. But no one looks at those."

22

"Could you send me the procedures that apply to sharps?"

"Sure," Harold says. "But they'll put you to sleep."

"Are there any other documents that tell people what to do, like job aids or signs, or anything like that?"

"Yeah, they're everywhere," Harold says. "For example, there's a sign on the wall of every room that tells you what to do if you've accidentally stuck yourself with a contaminated needle."

(Anna really should go to the hospital and follow workers around, taking pictures of the job aids and the work environment and talking with people. However, I'm limiting what she can do so you can compare her work more easily with Tina's. So...)

"Could you send me pictures or copies of that sign?" Anna says. "And copies of any other common job aids that relate to handling sharps?"

"I guess so," Harold says. "But no one pays attention to the signs. They fade into the background because you see them everywhere."

"We might be able to change that," Anna says. "Give me a little time to look at your slides and other materials, and then I'll have a few more questions and an idea on how to go forward."

Over the next few days, Harold sends Anna some standard operating procedures (SOPs) and photos of several signs about how to handle sharps. Anna looks at the training slides, noticing that they mostly present the SOP content. She also spends some time on the internet, learning about common errors in handling sharps and how other hospitals have tried to solve the problem.

Identify why they aren't doing it

Anna sets up another meeting with Harold and asks him to bring two or three future learners as well. Harold comes with a nurse who has years of experience and an aide who's just starting out.

"I've got a good idea now of what people are supposed to do," Anna says. "Could you tell me what they're doing wrong? For example, what are the most common mistakes?"

Over the next 20 minutes, Harold and the staff describe the most common mistakes, the deadliest errors, and some less common but still problematic mistakes, as Anna takes notes.

Anna focuses on the most common error, recapping a needle after use, and asks, "Why do people do this?"

"Some people don't know it's wrong," the nurse says. "For example, some nurses from other countries saw it done in their former hospitals, but it's wrong here. But most people do it because the sharps container isn't handy. It's supposed to be by the patient's bed but it can end up practically anywhere."

Harold is surprised to hear this. His job doesn't bring him into much contact with patients, and he had assumed the sharps containers were all in the right place.

Anna asks the same question — "Why do people do this?" — for the other high-priority mistakes and takes more notes.

Find the best solutions

Through Anna's questions, Harold begins to see his project differently. He decides to see if changes can be made to solve the most common problem, that of the sharps container not being in the right place.

"We should attach it to the wall by the patient's bed," he says. "I'll make sure that's done. That alone should reduce a lot of recapping errors."

> *In real life, Harold and his colleagues would identify several more non-training solutions, but we're using a simplified story to make the process clear.*

Brainstorm activities

Harold also realizes that just telling everyone what to do probably won't work. They've had training and they're surrounded by signs, but they still make mistakes. There are so many rules that staff seem to have gone into rule overload. Also, the nurse points out, many people are overconfident about their abilities.

"We could try something new," Anna says. "Instead of telling people what to do, we could give them realistic challenges and let them learn from their mistakes. In each challenge, they'd have to make the same sort of decision they make on the job, and they'd see the consequence of their choice. For example, in one activity, if I jab myself with a contaminated needle and don't clean the wound properly, I get hepatitis C."

"They'd see the consequences of their mistakes," Harold says, considering. "That would be more motivating than just being lectured at."

"That's the idea," Anna says. "Also, in each challenge they could get help by looking at the same sign that they have in the real world. We'd also include the sign in the feedback. That will remind them that those signs exist and are there to help them. The activities will model the behavior you want to see on the job — look at the sign for help and make a good decision."

Harold tentatively agrees to consider this, and while he and his colleagues get coffee and check in with their jobs, Anna quickly puts together a prototype.

Create a prototype for the client

Anna intentionally makes her prototype look like a sketch, so people will focus on what the activity asks people to do and not on its fonts or colors. Here's her prototype:

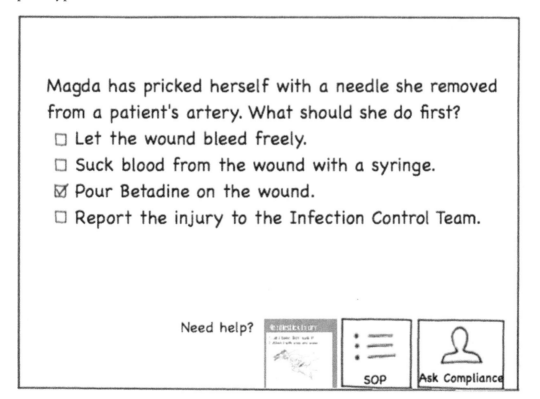

Anna shows the prototype to Harold and his colleagues. She explains that she doesn't present information before the activity. Instead, she just gives people the challenge, and they click the optional information at the bottom of the screen if they need help.

The optional information includes the real-world job aid that's on the wall of every room and that Magda could look at right now. It also includes the SOP for people who like details, and a link that opens a chat with a real or fictional compliance officer.

In Anna's mockup, an over-confident person hasn't looked at the job aid and decides to pour Betadine on the wound. Here's the feedback they get:

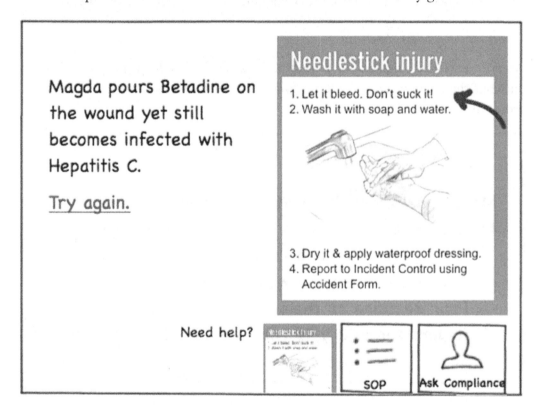

"For every choice people make," Anna explains, "we show them what happened and show the applicable part of the job aid. This reminds them that those aids exist and makes sure that they see the right procedure whether they chose correctly or not."

Harold and his team like the prototype, although Anna needs to delete the "ask Compliance" option because they don't have the budget for that. In fact, the budget is pretty limited.

"We'd need several activities like this to cover all the major mistakes," Harold says. "Wouldn't that cost more than the course I was originally planning?"

"We can keep the cost the same," Anna says. "We'll spend more time on design, but our production costs will be lower. The slide deck used in the live course had 97 slides. If we tried to turn that into a conventional online course, we'd not only have a ton of slides to produce, but we'd also have to use bells and whistles to make the information slightly interesting. Instead, we'll just design activities like this one, using the multiple-choice feature of my elearning tool. We won't have to design information slides, because we'll link to copies of the real-world job aids."

Harold considers this for a moment. "My boss will want to make sure everyone is exposed to all the information," he says. "But if we include the information in the feedback every time like you've shown, everyone is still exposed to everything. They just see it through activities, not a presentation. I like it."

> *Again, this is a super-simplified example. If you're saying, "But maybe elearning isn't the best approach to this," I heartily agree. In later chapters, we'll look at how to decide what type of solution is best. I'm sticking to elearning for this story so you can directly compare the two approaches.*

Create prototypes for learners

Harold shows the prototype to his boss, who gives the go-ahead. Then Anna talks to Harold to get the details she needs to write three realistic activities. Using word processing software, Anna writes drafts of the activities and sends them to Harold, who makes sure they're correct and realistic. He doesn't have trouble picturing the activities because he's seen the prototype.

Anna quickly develops the three typical activities as clickable slides. They look very plain, like the first prototype she developed, because she wants people to focus on the challenge and how the activity works, not the colors or fonts.

In an ideal world, she would watch some learners try the activities and ask for their feedback, but the budget is limited, so Harold runs the test on some workers during their break and passes along their feedback. With a few tweaks, Anna and Harold decide they're on the right track.

Create an outline

Anna suggests making the activities available for people to access whenever they have free time, but Harold still wants a formal online course that he can assign to people. So Anna puts together a high-level outline that shows which job roles will see which activities and the order in which the activities will be presented. She starts with the easier activities and follows them with more challenging ones. She just briefly describes each activity in the outline; she doesn't write a script.

The outline shows that there won't be any information presentation in the course. Instead, each activity will include links to optional information, and the appropriate sections of job aids will be shown in feedback.

The outline also describes the non-training solutions that were identified during the analysis and who will implement them. For example, it points out that Harold has taken responsibility for making sure the sharps containers are in the right spots.

Harold makes some changes to the outline and approves the final version.

Finish writing activities

Working in batches, Anna writes the activities identified in the outline, with Harold's help. While she waits for Harold's feedback on one batch, she develops the previous batch in her elearning tool to make sure they'll work how she and Harold want. Soon, they have a collection of challenging decision-making activities. Some of them apply only to people in specific job roles, while others apply to everyone.

Now it's time to put the activities together and create the course that Harold wants. Anna opens her elearning tool again, this time to tie everything together.

Put it together

Welcome screen. Anna presents the course as a game-like challenge: "Can you avoid infecting yourself or others in some tricky situations? Try this challenge."

There's no narration because people who work in hospitals can read, and a narration budget is better used to create challenging activities.

Choose your job. Anna lists a few job categories and asks learners to click the one that applies to them. From now on, people will see only the challenges that they'd actually face on the job. For example, people whose job is to draw blood won't waste their time deciding how to pass a scalpel in surgery.

Activities. Anna tells learners that their choices aren't being tracked. She encourages them to explore and see what happens when they make different choices. Then, **instead of presenting any information or do's and don'ts**, she plunges people into a series of activities, all designed to tempt them to make the common mistakes.

Each activity includes optional links to job aids and other real-life references, and the applicable section of the job aid appears in all feedback.

People can go back and make different decisions in any activity, whether they chose correctly the first time or not.

Debrief. After the series of activities, Anna presents a short debrief that helps people see the broader concepts that connect the activities. For example, she points out that in two scenarios, workers found it hard to follow the correct procedures because they hadn't set up their stations correctly. This highlights the concept that not following one set of procedures can cause failures in the next set. (Anna would prefer to do the debrief as a live discussion that has the learners identify the main concepts, but we're limiting the format to elearning so you can easily compare her approach to Tina's.)

Assessment. Harold's boss wants Anna to include an assessment, so now she tells learners that their choices are being tracked. Then she gives them the same kind of activities, which still link to job aids because those aids appear in real life. The only difference is that Anna is tracking everyone's choices, and they don't get to try again if they make a mistake.

Anna sets a difficult passing score. If someone fails, she sends them to more activities that cover the specific mistakes they made, and then they take the assessment again.

Anna wants people to continue to practice after the course, so she suggests that she design additional activities to be sent to people every few weeks. Harold says he'll consider that, but first he wants to deliver the conventional course that he promised to his boss.

Implementation

Anna puts the activities on the hospital's LMS, and Harold creates a simple internal marketing campaign to encourage people to try the challenge. He targets not only learners but their managers as well.

At Harold's request, maintenance staff attach the bracket of a hazardous waste container to the wall next to every bed, which should reduce the temptation to recap needles. (Again, in real life, there would be many more non-training solutions.)

Initial evaluation

Soon, Anna and Harold have their first results from the assessment that Harold's boss wanted to include. Several people fail in their first attempt, but everyone passes after going through the remedial activities.

Anna interviews some learners to find out which aspects of the materials helped them change their behavior, and which didn't help. She makes some changes to the activities as a result.

After the course has been live for a few months, Harold reports that the sharps errors have decreased. It looks like the hospital could be on track to meet the 8% reduction in errors, but it's not clear.

Spaced practice

Harold's boss is pleased with the initial results so, following Anna's recommendation, he finds additional funding for reinforcement activities. These are just like the activities in the course but are sent as links in email, one every couple of weeks.

As a result, people continue to practice making decisions and seeing the consequences, and their new behavior is reinforced.

Some staff suggest real-life cases that can be turned into activities, and when there's an outbreak of an infection at another hospital, Harold has Anna turn it into a branching scenario that causes a lot of discussion. People are paying more attention to the risks of sharps.

Ongoing evaluation

Harold's hospital continues to keep an eye on the error rate as it goes down. Encouraged by the change, the safety officers decide to crunch the data in more detail. They identify a specific mistake that they'd like to see reduced, so Harold asks Anna to make some additional activities focusing on that.

As a result, the error rate goes down more, and the hospital is in a good position for the big safety report.

The story was super-simplified

To keep the story simple, I chose a basic problem and condensed a lot. For example, I had Anna and Harold identify only one non-training solution, when normally there are many more. There were probably many other reasons why people were ignoring proper sharps handling procedures, but we skipped them to keep the story simple. I had Anna spend most of her time on training design because that's where most of you are starting from.

I had Harold play the role of both client and subject matter expert so you didn't have to keep track of more characters. Finally, I had Harold resist some of Anna's ideas, such as having no "course" and using spaced practice, so you could more directly compare Tina's and Anna's solutions. I wanted you to see that even a minor change — focusing on activities instead of an information dump — can have a powerful effect.

Even with all these restrictions, Anna's solution was more effective than the conventional one designed by Tina. I'd argue that it was also more efficient, even though there was more discussion with the client at first.

What's the difference?

Both versions of the story limited the training part of the solution to elearning. However, Tina and Anna took very different approaches.

What were they thinking?

Earlier, I asked you to consider how Anna would respond to Tina's beliefs about her job. Here's how they describe their jobs and tasks.

> **Tina:** The client views me as a course producer.
>
> **Anna:** The client might view me as a course producer in the beginning, but soon they see me as a partner in improving performance.
>
> **Tina:** The only design I do is course design.
>
> **Anna:** As I help the client identify the best solution for each aspect of the problem, I might design job aids, identify ways to help people share information, or suggest improvements to tools or procedures.
>
> **Tina:** In a course, I mostly design information.
>
> **Anna:** In a course, I mostly design practice activities.
>
> **Tina:** I push information at people by making them read or listen to it.
>
> **Anna:** I let people pull information when they need it to solve realistic problems.

Tina: My questions ask people to recall information.

Anna: My questions ask people to use information to make decisions in realistic situations.

Tina: The client identifies the information that I should provide.

Anna: The information I make available is determined by the activities, which themselves are determined by what people do on the job.

Tina: I make an online course engaging by using narration, images, animation, and clicking.

Anna: I make an online course engaging by challenging people with realistic problems that affect their jobs or lives.

Tina: I don't let anyone skip what they already know.

Anna: I challenge people with activities that show them their own knowledge gaps or prove their correct knowledge.

Tina: I evaluate the course by asking people if they liked it and giving them a knowledge test.

Anna: I evaluate the project by seeing if the performance measure we chose at the beginning has improved.

Tina: If people understand the information, I've done my job.

Anna: If the performance measure has improved, I'm happy, but I might not be done.

Tina: Once the course has been delivered, I'm done.

Anna: The client and I continue to reinforce the new behaviors by providing spaced practice. We also examine the performance measure more closely to identify ways to fine-tune the solutions.

What process did they use?

Tina used a version of the ADDIE model. She didn't follow the model as it was intended to be used, but her interpretation is common.

> Analyze: The client says they need training; therefore, they need training.

Design it all at once: Write a big script or design document that describes how you'll present and test the client's content. The document describes everything that will happen in the training, word by word, and the client understands that once they approve it, changes will be hard to make.

Develop: Turn the script into training materials.

Implement: Deliver the training as an event.

Evaluate: Ask the participants if they liked the training.

Anna followed a process that looks more like this:

Evaluate: Identify how the success of the project will be measured.

Analyze: What's the performance problem? What do people need to do differently, and why aren't they doing it? Will training help? If so, what type of training? What other solutions could we try?

Design at a high level: Brainstorm activity ideas for the training aspect of the solution. Prototype and test a few typical ideas. Change the ideas if necessary. When the prototypes are solid, write a high-level outline showing how the activities (still in idea form) will relate to each other, fit into the learners' workflow, and work with the non-training solutions.

Develop in batches: Write the full content of a few activities in a simple text document and get feedback from the SME. Develop those activities and get feedback. Refine the developed activities if necessary, and then write and develop another small batch. Maybe go back and change the outline. Maybe change the prototype or throw out some earlier ideas.

Implement: While you were designing activities, others were implementing the additional solutions that emerged during the analysis. Now that the training part seems ready, you release it, maybe to just a subset of learners, and see how it goes. Maybe you make some changes and then release it to a larger group. Maybe the training is an event or maybe it's just some on-demand activities or how-to information. Maybe it's all of the above. At least part of the release probably happens over several weeks or longer, because you've designed activities that are spaced over time.

Evaluate and tweak again: Evaluate early results by looking for progress toward the original goal, interview some learners to find out what works and what doesn't, and adjust the project as it continues.

What happened next to Tina and Anna?

Tina delivered what the client thought he needed, an online course. Her course didn't change what people did on the job, but since no one required that, it didn't matter. Tina's course was a commodity, a product that many people around the world can create for a lower price. As a result, the next time Harold needed a course, he found a less expensive provider.

Anna delivered what the client actually needed, an improvement in performance. She provided a custom service, not a commodity. She made Harold look good to his boss by helping him solve a problem, and during the process she learned how his hospital worked. As a result, the next time Harold suspected his staff had a performance problem, he called Anna.

"My clients will resist this" and other concerns

Clients, subject matter experts, and other instructional designers might resist your attempts to change what you do. If this happens, check out Appendix 2, which lists common concerns and how to respond to them.

Summary

Many designers view themselves as course producers. They think their job is to create the course that the client wants, using the information that the client provides. This often results in an ineffective information dump.

Action mapping asks you to expand that role, so your job is to solve the client's problem. When a client comes to you expecting training, you'll turn the conversation to the performance problem. You'll help the client analyze the problem and find the best solutions. If training is part of the solution, you'll create highly targeted practice activities. You'll design those activities in a way that allows for quick experimentation and confirmation, so improvements can be made at any point. As you learn more about the organization's problems, you'll become more like a performance consultant than an order taker.

If you do just one thing...

From your first contact with your client, act as if your job is to help them **solve their problem**.

What you're about to do

High-level overview

This book focuses on the tricky steps of analysis and activity design, which are done differently in action mapping. Once you've designed a typical activity to serve as a model for the others, the rest is easier and more familiar.

We'll spend most of our time in the first half of the workflow that appears on the following page. Explore an interactive version at map-it-book.com.

Meet with stakeholders and analyze the problem

First, you'll meet with your client, SME, and probably others to define and analyze the problem. This can happen in one two-hour meeting. You'll:

- Write a business goal (chapter 4)
- Answer, "What do people need to DO to reach the goal?" (chapter 5)
- Answer, "Why aren't they doing it, and what changes will help?" (chapter 6)

You'll identify different solutions to different aspects of the problem, often including improvements to procedures or tools.

Brainstorm and prototype activities

Everything that follows applies only to the training aspect of the solution, assuming that training really is part of the solution. By "training" I mean "practice activities of some sort," not necessarily a course or training event. You might decide that no course or event is necessary.

You'll brainstorm the training solution at a high level:

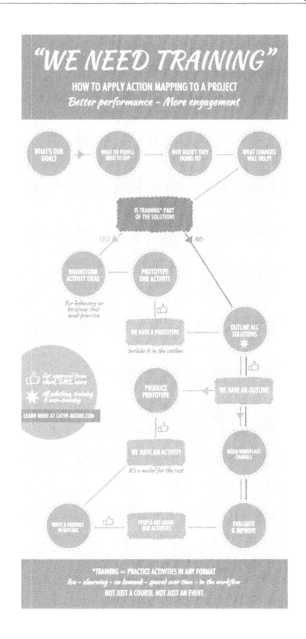

- Brainstorm activity ideas (chapter 7)
- Identify the ideal format for each activity (chapter 8)

Next, you'll design and test a prototype of a typical activity:

- Choose an activity to prototype and interview the SME (chapter 9)
- Write a stem and options for your activity (chapter 10)

- Write feedback for your activity (chapter 11)
- Add the information to your activity (chapter 12)
- Create a prototype and get feedback from your SME, client, and learners (chapter 13)

Once the prototype has been approved, you'll:

- Outline, produce, implement, and evaluate the project (chapter 14)

Job roles

In this book, I define roles in the following way.

Client: The person who requested the project. They might be part of your organization or someone from another firm. Their responsibilities:

- Help determine the business goal
- (Probably) help identify necessary actions and why they're not being taken
- Approve the outline of the solution and any prototypes
- Identify who should implement the non-training solutions
- Help make sure the new behaviors will be supported by managers
- Help market the project internally

Subject matter expert (SME): A person who **still does the job** and who has in-depth knowledge of the actions and decisions required of the audience. Another term could be "master performer." They might also be the client or even you.

It's a good idea to arrange for more than one SME. Action mapping often requires more from your SME than the usual checking of content. Having more than one SME means you can spread this work around, and you can also get good insights from their discussions or disagreements. Their responsibilities:

- Help determine the business goal
- Help identify what people need to do and determine why they're not doing it
- Help you understand the decisions required to perform the actions and the context in which those decisions take place
- Help identify the necessary information and whether it should be memorized

- Provide feedback on the prototype
- Review all content for accuracy

Future learner: A member of the intended audience for the training. Ideally, you'll talk to a lot of them. Their responsibilities:

- Help identify why people aren't performing the task to the required level
- Give you feedback about prototype activities, job aids, and other solutions

Recent learner: Someone who does the required task well enough and who learned to do it recently. Their responsibilities:

- Help identify the information you should provide and whether it should be memorized, providing a reality check to SMEs, who often overestimate this
- Provide feedback on activities and job aids if you think it will be helpful

Job aid owner: The person who designed or feels ownership of any job aids that you plan to include in the solution. Their role is likely to be minimal unless you want to change the job aid. Their responsibilities:

- Provide the current version of the job aid
- If necessary, help improve the job aid and replace the old version with the improved one

Training designer: Person who architects the solution — "you" in this book. You might also play the role of SME, developer, or other roles. Your responsibilities:

- Help identify the business goal
- Help identify what people need to do on the job to reach the goal
- Help determine why people aren't doing what's needed
- Identify training **and non-training** solutions
- When training is required, design activities and supporting information
- Create prototypes and get feedback
- Design job aids or work with the person responsible for them
- Get approval for the structure of the solution, the final activities, and other materials

- If necessary, work with the client to implement the non-training solutions
- Oversee production of the materials
- Oversee the release of the project and work with the client to get buy-in from managers and learners
- Provide ongoing reinforcement through spaced practice activities
- Help evaluate the effectiveness of the project
- Modify the project as necessary to increase its effectiveness

Developer: Person who creates the final polished materials, such as slides, video, handouts, or elearning. Their responsibilities:

- Create the final graphics, slides, and other materials
- Possibly create job aids
- Produce elearning if that's part of the solution
- Make sure everything meets internal branding standards

This book doesn't spend much time on what the developer does, because that's thoroughly covered by many other authors. Also, frankly, I don't think development should be part of your job. Analyzing and designing solutions to performance problems is enough work for one person. That same person shouldn't also be expected to create graphics, take custom photos, process audio, produce HTML5...

Chapter 3. Steer the client in the right direction

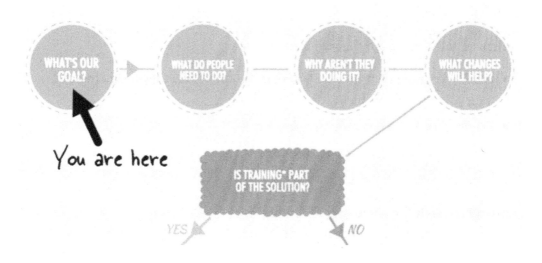

Task	Who does it	How long it might take
From the very first contact with the client, make clear you're a problem solver, not a course producer	You	10 minutes
Keep the first conversation short, just enough to get the gist of the client's problem and schedule a longer meeting	You	10 minutes
Briefly research the client and their problem	You	1-2 hours
Send a mini-agenda for the kickoff meeting that focuses everyone on the problem, not "the course"	You	10 minutes

Big idea:

- Banish "course" from your vocabulary. Your focus right now is on the performance problem.

Apply this to a real-world project

For the rest of the book, we'll walk through the steps of action mapping. I strongly recommend that you apply what you're reading to a real-world project — not just imagine it, but actually do it while you read the book.

If you don't have a project right now, consider redesigning a recent one to see how it could have been changed with action mapping. It might be easier to redesign a project that someone else created. If it was your project, it could be difficult to change your perspective.

What you'll do

1. Manage the client from the very first contact.

   - Don't accept or reject the solution that the client says they need. Instead, turn their focus to the problem they want to solve.
   - Briefly clarify the performance problem.
   - Schedule a two-hour kickoff meeting.
   - Set expectations for the meeting.

2. Briefly research the client and their employer.
3. Reverse-engineer the client's content. What does it tell you about the problem?
4. Briefly research the problem so you can propose ideas in the kickoff meeting if the client struggles.

Your job is to improve performance, not produce courses

Even though many clients say, "We need a course on X," providing a course on X is not your job. Even if your job title is "course producer," obediently cranking out a course on X is **not your job,** not as long as you're reading this book.

Think of it this way:

When your kitchen faucet starts to leak, you go to the hardware store for a washer. However, you aren't actually shopping for a washer. You're shopping for a faucet that no longer leaks.

Your client might think they're shopping for a course. But what are they really hoping to buy? Improved performance. Happier customers. Fewer complaints.

If you've misdiagnosed your leaky faucet, the new washer won't solve your problem. If your client has misdiagnosed their performance problem, your course won't solve it.

Worse, your unnecessary course will waste many hours of your time and exponentially more hours of other people's time. If thousands of people are required to take your irrelevant course, that's thousands of people who have wasted their time and who now dislike "courses" even more than they did before.

Often, the client who asks for a course hasn't diagnosed their problem. They might not even be able to clearly describe it. They just hope that throwing a course at it will help somehow. So they come to you, saying that they want to buy a course when really they're shopping for a solution.

The real solution could be a lot more compact and efficient. It might be a PDF, a help screen, or a tweak to a process. It's unreasonable and unethical for you to suffer through creating a course when a course will do nothing but waste everyone's time.

You're the last defense. You're the one remaining hero who can save thousands of innocent people from a pointless information dump. Be their hero.

> **Patient**: Hey, doc, give me some antibiotics.
> **Doctor**: Okay, here you go.
> Is this a good doctor? Of course not.
> **Client**: Hey, L&D, give me a course.
> **L&D**: Okay, here you go.
> Is this a good L&D department? Nope.

1. Manage the client from the very first contact

Many of us were taught to immediately accept the client's assumption that they need a course (or two-hour workshop or webinar or whatever they're asking for).

As a result, taking charge of the conversation might feel weird. Here's how to do it.

1.1. Banish "course" from your vocabulary.

In your very first contact with the client, don't mention "the course." Don't agree that you're building a course, don't suggest that the course might include a certain feature, and don't mention how good you are at that type of course. **Say nothing that includes the word "course."**

If instead of "course," the client said "two-hour workshop" or "webinar" or any other specific solution, ban those terms as well.

It's way too early for you to identify any solution, course or not. Your only goal at this point is to get the gist of the performance problem and set up a future meeting to learn more about it.

If it turns out that a course isn't the best solution, you want the client to see that for themselves. But that discussion happens later. Today's discussion is short, just long enough to get the client to agree to a longer meeting.

So whenever the client brings up "the course," return their focus to the performance problem.

Sound impossible? See how Anna does it below.

1.2. Clarify the performance problem. Don't talk about the course.

Remember Anna from chapter 2? She'll give us some more examples of how to talk to the client.

Notice how she avoids confirming that a course will help, while at the same time she doesn't challenge the client's faith in a course. Instead, she immediately turns the conversation to the client's problem, and then she gets a commitment for a meeting to talk in more depth.

> **Example 1**
>
> **Client**: My team needs a course on diversity. Something that focuses on respecting others' opinions, like political differences.
>
> **Anna**: I'd be glad to help. You're having issues with political statements in the workplace? Or is it strong opinions in general?
>
> **Client**: It's mostly political. You know how heated those discussions can get, and people are taking sides. It's starting to affect teamwork. Maybe a course on professionalism?

Anna: We've got a number of options. First, I'll need to understand a little better what you'd like to achieve. Are you available to get together on...?

What if the client is more firmly convinced that a course is the solution? Here's another example.

Example 2

Client: I need an online course on how to find the right foster families for children. I've got an 87-slide PowerPoint deck that tells the caseworkers what they need to know. How long would it take for you to turn that into a course? It's pretty simple, without video or anything like that.

Anna: I'm happy to talk about that. So, the issue is how to choose the best foster family? I'll bet that's complex. What's the main problem you're seeing?

Client: People aren't following the rules when it comes to matching kids culturally. For example, just because a child is Hispanic doesn't mean the best family for them is Spanish-speaking. People mean well, but they end up putting an English-speaking child in a Spanish-speaking family. It's all in the PowerPoint. Can you do those rollover things?

Anna: Rollovers are certainly something we could consider. First, please send me the PowerPoint so I can learn more about the issues you're seeing. Then I'd like to talk with you more to make sure I understand what you need people to do. Are you available for...

In the second example, Anna accepts the content, but not because she plans to turn it into a course. She says she wants to look at the PowerPoint "so I can learn more about the issues you're seeing." She didn't accept it "so I can give you an estimate" or anything like that. She keeps the focus on the client's problem, not the content.

Here's the recipe for your own conversations.

The recipe

Client: I need a course on X.

You: I'm happy to talk with you about that. *[Meaning, "I'm a happy person and I want to help you, but I'm only willing to **talk** about it at this point."]* X can cause a lot of issues in the workplace. *[You're empathizing with the client about their difficult problem even though you don't know what it is yet.]* What's the main problem you're seeing? *[Immediately get the client to talk about the problem, not the course.]*

Client: People are doing Y and Z, which is wrong. That's why we need a course. Here's the content.

You: Thank you. This will help me understand the issues you're seeing. *[Graciously accept the content and acknowledge its usefulness, but don't promise you'll turn it into a course. Instead, make clear the content will help you **understand the problem**.]* So, the main problem is that people are doing Y and Z? Why are they doing that? *[Immediately refocus the client on the problem.]*

Client: Some of them don't know any better. Others know but just don't care. So they need a course with motivational parts. I think it should have Feature A.

You: Feature A is certainly something we can consider. *[Meaning, "I hear your idea and I'm not rejecting it, but I'm not promising to implement it, either. I'm also saying 'we,' because this is going to be collaboration, not order-taking."]* First, I need to make sure I understand the problem you're seeing. *[Back again to the problem and "you."]* Are you available for a meeting on...? *[Quickly get the client to agree to a future meeting.]*

Client: I'm glad we can get started quickly. Everyone should complete the course by Date.

You: We should be able to have a solution in place before then. *[It's a solution, not a course.]* Could you tell me why that's your deadline? Is there an audit or something like that on that date? *[Relentlessly turn the client back to the problem. Deadline dates can suggest a measurement for the project goal.]*

Client: The National X Evaluation Board checks our X Factor at the end of the year. We need people to complete the course by Date so we have enough time to improve the X Factor before the board comes.

You: That's really useful to know. *[The client just identified a measurable goal, which will help focus your research before the meeting.]* I'm looking forward to learning more about it at our meeting on...

In this short conversation, you got the gist of the problem, scheduled a meeting to talk about it in more depth, and won an additional prize: you can now look up X Factor to find out what exactly it measures and how other organizations have increased it. This will give you ideas you can propose in the kickoff meeting if the client seems to draw a blank. Finally, you did all this without explicitly accepting or rejecting "the course" or any other specific solution.

You're doing this fancy stepping because you want the client to **see for themselves** whether the course they originally pictured is the best or only solution. During the analysis phase, they could easily decide to broaden their approach, and they could abandon the course idea entirely. They could even change the audience and topic. However, they'll be a lot less likely to change their mind if you immediately committed to a course or you rejected the idea and made them defensive.

Need more ideas for responses? Here are a few.

"I need a course on X."

- I'd be delighted to talk about that. X is a big issue for a lot of organizations. What exactly is happening in your organization?

- I'm happy to talk about that. X can be really problematic. What problems are you seeing?

- I'm glad you called. X can cause a lot of issues. What issues is it causing for you?

"The course should have Feature A."

- That's certainly something we could consider. So, would you say X is the main problem?

- We'll be sure to put that on the list of things to consider. First, I need to make sure I understand what you'd like to achieve. Are you available for a meeting on...?

- Feature A can certainly be useful. First, I need to understand your problem better. Are you available...

"We need the course to be ready by Date."

- Depending on the options we choose, we'll be able to have a solution in place by then. Could you tell me what happens on Date?
- We should have something by then. Why is Date significant? Is there a test or audit then?

Overall, your goal is to communicate the following, though not in these exact words:

- I care about your problem. I hear and respect your ideas, and I promise we'll discuss them when the time is right. I also recognize that the content you gave me is important to you. Maybe you put it together yourself and you're proud of it, and you think it will save me a lot of work. I'm sure it will be useful, especially because it will help me understand how you see the problem, and that's what we need to talk about first. I want to hear all about your problem.

In this first conversation, talk about the problem just long enough until you can create a decent search term out of it. How do you know if you have enough? Here are some examples.

Not enough	Enough
We need leadership training.	We've acquired another company, and their managers aren't used to being proactive. We need them to become more comfortable with making quick decisions and taking risks.
We need a course on ethics.	Our sales reps recently started working in Zekostan, where it's common to give gifts that could be misinterpreted as bribes. The sales reps are afraid of offending people, so they accept gifts that could get us into trouble.
We need a course on bedside manner.	The residents of our elder care home complain that the nurses don't listen to them or act like they care. They say the nurses just do the minimum.

What not to say

In addition to avoiding "course," avoid using any terms that reinforce the idea that some sort of training will be the inevitable result of your work or that your job is to install information in people's heads. Avoid saying the following:

- Webinar, workshop, one-day session – any term that describes a training product or event, because it's too early to assume any of these will be part of the solution

- Completion, attendance, scheduling – any term that assumes a training event or course

- Content, topic, assessment, screens, slides, interactive, LMS – any terms related to courses

- Know, understand, appreciate – any terms related to changing what happens in people's brains. The focus at this point is relentlessly on what people should do, not know.

Examples to avoid:

- "What content do you want to cover?"
- "What do they need to know?"
- "I've done several courses on that topic."
- "When would you like the workshop to take place?"
- "How long do you want the course to be?"
- "Storyline would be a great tool for this."
- "Would the content need to be translated?"
- "Do you have any materials already developed?"

1.3. Schedule a two-hour meeting. Don't mention the course.

Once you've got the gist of the problem, get the client to agree to a meeting. Two hours is usually good, but if all you can get is one hour, take it. You'll need the client and at least one SME to attend.

It can be best to meet in person, but you might be surprised at how well an online meeting can work. If you meet online, you might plan to share a whiteboard on your screen, where you'll write the draft goal and start listing behaviors.

Make sure you include the right people. It's possible that the person you're talking to right now isn't really the client. They might be someone assigned to oversee the production of "the course" and know little about the problem. In the next meeting, you need:

- The person who knows the problem, feels its pain, and wants it to stop.

- At least one subject matter expert. Two can be more useful, because you'll learn from their discussion or disagreements.

You might also ask, "Is there anyone besides you who needs to approve this project or any content?" Include them now if you can, so you get their buy-in to the goal. You don't want to invest a lot of time in analyzing a problem that someone's boss doesn't want addressed, and you definitely don't want a surprise veto when you've gotten deep into the design.

When you schedule the meeting, give yourself enough time to first look through the client's content and do about an hour of online research about them and their problem.

Find out who wrote the existing content. If the client wants to give you content to "turn into a course," casually ask who wrote it. Is it the client? The SME? If either of them was involved in creating the content, you'll want to be mindful that they could feel some ownership of it and resist changing or abandoning it.

1.4. Set expectations for the meeting. Don't mention the course.

Make the meeting sound as appealing as possible to the client.

Think of its appeal this way: You have a worrisome problem at work. You've tried to talk about it with your spouse, but they're distracted by their own issues right now. Then your pal Dominic calls, and you mention your problem to him. "That sounds rough!" Dominic says. "Let's have a long lunch on Thursday so you can tell me all about it. Will two hours be enough?"

You want to be Dominic for your client. The meeting is all about them and their problem, and they should look forward to it the way you're looking forward to Thursday's lunch.

Your goals for the meeting are to get the client and SME to do the following:

- Write a goal for the project. The goal identifies how the problem is being measured and how you'll know it's solved.

- List what people need to do on the job to reach that goal.

- Start to discuss why people aren't doing those things now.

Those are **your** goals for the meeting. Now your question is, "Will the client resist this? How can I phrase it so they'll happily participate?" The answer can depend on how committed your client appears to be to the idea that you should turn their content into a course / webinar / whatever.

- If the client isn't sure what type of solution they need and seems open to ideas, you could describe the meeting like this: "We'll consider ways to measure the problem you're seeing and identify what you'd like people to do differently. That will help us find the best ways to change what people do, and we'll be able to measure our success." Make it about collaborating to solve their problem.

- If the client seems convinced that they want a course and that it's your job to give them one, you might say that the meeting will "help make sure I understand what you need." Maybe the meeting will consist of "making sure I understand your goal for the project, what you need people to do differently, and how we'll measure the project's success." You've put yourself in a slightly subordinate position so the client doesn't get defensive. You'll rise out of that position during the meeting when the client begins to see the light, but they aren't seeing the light yet.

- Of course, if your client is already familiar with action mapping, you can just confirm what they already know: "We'll figure out the goal for the project, list what you need people to do on the job, and start to examine why they aren't doing it."

Using the kind of phrasing above, suggest that the client and SME should be prepared to:

- Describe how the problem is currently being measured

- List specifically what people need to do on the job

- Begin to examine why they aren't doing it

You might use the above list to create a mini-agenda that you email to the client and SME.

Finally, don't rely on the client to tell the SME about the meeting. Get the SME's contact details as soon as possible and send them communications yourself. Otherwise, you risk the client telling the SME that the meeting is to "decide what to include in the course."

"Wait. You really mean that I should never mention the course? That's unethical!"

"If it's obvious that the client wants a course," you might be saying, "I should give them a course. At the very least, I should warn them that I might recommend something different from what they're imagining!"

You know your clients better than I do, and only you know the expectations of your boss and organization. So exactly how thoroughly you dodge the cursed "course" is your call.

However, I strongly recommend that you learn about the client's problem before you accept or question their idea for a course (or workshop or webinar or whatever). You have to understand the problem before you can say anything about a possible solution.

Also, you're not going to "recommend something different." You're going to float a lot of ideas, and the client will see for themselves that those ideas make sense. Ideally, **the client is going to change their own mind.** You're not going to tell them what to do.

If you still don't like dodging "the course" and prefer blunt honesty, you might imagine this dialog:

> **The blunt honesty approach (not recommended)**
>
> **Client**: I need a course on X.
>
> **You**: I'm glad to help. X is pretty complex, so let me warn you right now that we might end up with a broader solution, like maybe some job aids, and a change to a process, and maybe instead of a course we might be looking at a bank of self-paced activities and a lunchtime discussion group. Would you be open to that?
>
> **Client**: Um, is one of your colleagues available instead?

You've made it sound like a lot of confusing work, and, worse, you've brought up solutions without having a clue about the problem they're supposed to solve. The more you mention specific solutions, the more likely you are to have to contradict yourself later, once you understand the problem.

If you still want to warn the client at this super-early date that the course they're picturing might not be the best solution, you might try the subtle hint approach. This avoids mentioning any specific solution but hints that it could be broader than a course.

The subtle hint approach

Client: I need a course on X.

You: I'm glad to help... [You ask about the problem, get the gist of it, schedule a meeting, and try to end the conversation, but...]

Client: I really like the course you did on Y. I'd like my course to be like that one.

You: I'm glad you liked the Y course. It's possible we could do something even more effective this time, maybe in a better format. We'll have a better sense of what will work best after our meeting on...

The subtle hint approach mentions "better formats" or "quick, effective solutions," or "we've been seeing success with a wide range of formats." And then it makes clear that the meeting will help determine that; it's too early now.

If the subtle hint is too subtle for you, you can try the slightly risky approach.

The slightly risky approach

Client: I need a course on X.

You: I'm glad to help.... [You ask a few questions to get the gist of the problem, and then you say:] In cases like this, we like to learn more about the issues you're seeing, and then we help you decide on the best solutions. You might decide that a course isn't your best or only solution.

Here, you're making clear that the client is still making the decisions, but they might decide against a course. It's slightly risky because it can inspire this:

> Client: It's not complicated. They just need to know X, so they need a course.

Or, worse:

> Client: I know my audience best, and they need a course.

In both cases, the client has gotten defensive and has doubled down on "the course," which is the last thing you want.

Your goal is to **have the client see for themselves** that the course they're picturing might not be the best or only solution. This can easily happen during the next meeting. However, they'll be open to that realization only if you haven't pushed them deeper into their "course" position.

Finally, the slightly risky approach is also risky because the client might be right. Maybe they really have analyzed the problem, and that analysis really does show that the course (or webinar or whatever they've decided) is the best solution. I put this possibility last because, frankly, a one-time training event is rarely the best or only solution. Regardless, at this point it's best to avoid accepting or rejecting any specific solution.

Why are your clients asking for a course in the first place?

Your life would be a lot simpler if all your clients said, "My department has a performance problem. Can you help me solve it?"

Why don't they say this?

I blame the school model that claims that "knowledge transfer" will fix anything, combined with the culture of "not my responsibility; I can't stick my neck out" that's common in big organizations.

I also blame L&D leaders and designers themselves.

If your department presents itself as a course factory, then it's no surprise that people expect you to crank out courses. If you're independent and you sell your services by showing people the cool courses you've made, then of course people come to you expecting a course.

We can turn "I need a course" into "Help me solve this problem" by changing how we present ourselves as described throughout this book. For more ideas on how to do this, see the appendix "Common Concerns about Action Mapping." There you'll find more steps you can take to reposition yourself or your department.

2. Briefly research the client

Now that you've scheduled the kickoff meeting, it's time to do a bit of research.

If you haven't already, spend a few minutes to look up the client in your organization's directory, on LinkedIn, or through non-intrusive internet searches. Look for answers to the following questions:

- What is their main responsibility?

- Who is their boss, and what does the boss probably want from them?

- Who else might they need to please or impress?

- How long have they been in this position or department? (How much do they know first-hand about the history of the problem?)

- If they're new, where did they work before? How might that affect how they view the problem?

If the client isn't from your organization, also look up the company they work for. Consider these questions:

- What does the company do, and who is their market?

- How much does performance matter to the company's leaders? If the company must make a profit to survive, performance should matter, and it should be relatively easy to write a measurable goal. However, if the government or generous donors fund the organization without caring about performance, prepare yourself for a difficult conversation about the goal.

- What regulatory or legal pressures is the company likely under?

- Has it been in the news lately? Are they in legal trouble that might be inspiring their interest in a course? Did they win something major that you can congratulate them for?

3. Reverse-engineer the client's content

If the client gave you content for "the course," look through it. You're searching for answers to these questions:

- What problem does the content seem designed to solve? Is it the same problem that the client described?

- Does the content refer to ways the problem could be measured? For example, does it say that there are too many complaints from patients, and that's why nurses should improve their bedside manner?

- What specific mistakes or problem areas does the content highlight? These might suggest the high-priority behaviors that need to change.

- What grey areas are missing? PowerPoint slides and similar materials tend to present simple rules: do this, don't do that. Ask yourself, "Is it really this simple? What might happen to make someone break this rule? Is it always clear what you should do?"

- What bits of content seem to have required a lot of work or expense? For example, if the material includes an expensively produced video, be prepared for the client to want the video to be included in "the course," since a lot of time and money have already been invested in it.

- Who wrote the content? If you didn't get an answer to that in the initial conversation, check the file properties, looking for the author's name.

4. Briefly research the client's problem

There are no unique problems in the business world. Some organization somewhere has faced the problem you need to solve, and maybe they've shared what worked and how they measured it.

Spend a little time searching the internet for your client's problem. For example, if the client says their managers are having trouble getting remote teams to meet project deadlines, you could start with "project management remote employees."

Your goal is to be able to show a basic understanding of the problem and, if necessary, propose some ways to measure and solve it. You might start with the standard version of Google to find the best search terms. Then you might switch to Google Scholar to find out what researchers have learned about solving the problem.

You probably shouldn't spend more than an hour, because the focus of the project could shift dramatically during the kickoff conversation.

4.1. Look for ways to measure the problem

In your upcoming meeting, your client might struggle to identify how the problem could be measured. Do a little research now so you have some ideas to propose.

You already have a basic understanding of the problem. Now add "ROI" or "how to measure" or something like that to start your search. Some examples:

- "How to measure change leadership"
- "ROI for project management training"
- "How to measure effectiveness of infection control in daycare"

- "Does improving employee engagement reduce turnover?"
- "Does diversity training work?" (Set aside some time now to enter this enlightening search before you're asked, yet again, to create diversity training.)

Not sure what search terms to use? Maybe Google has some good suggestions. For example, if the client says they want a course on bedside manner, how are they going to measure it? Is there such a thing as patient happiness? Patient engagement? Start the search and see what Google suggests.

roi patient

roi patient **portal**
roi patient
roi patient **experience**
roi **of** patient **engagement**

Google and the Google logo are registered trademarks of Google Inc. – used with permission.

Five seconds into your work, and you already have two useful search terms: "roi patient experience" and "roi of patient engagement." Following through on those, you'll find specific measures that other organizations have used.

4.2. Look for ways to solve the problem

Once you have some ideas on how others measure the problem, look for ways to solve it. Again, it's common to get useful ideas with just a few minutes of looking.

Continuing our patient experience example, you poke around for a few minutes more and decide that "patient satisfaction" has a lot of useful hits. But how could the client improve it? (see image overleaf)

It looks like there are articles about how other places improved their patient satisfaction, and Google Scholar has research that suggests someone has come up with a "caring model." Maybe that model has been proven to work, and your client might consider it.

Google and the Google logo are registered trademarks of Google Inc. – used with permission.

You spend a little more time tracking down what others have tried and what has been shown to work. You end up with a couple of models that have shown some success in research studies, some less scientific "how we did it" stories, and plenty of ideas to suggest if your client shows up idea-free.

4.3. Save the information to offer it later if the client seems to struggle

Save the useful links and some notes, but don't write up anything to give to the client. You haven't even had the kickoff meeting yet, and the client might already have a measurement and solution in mind. Also, the project can change dramatically during the meeting.

You did this preparation so you'll have something to suggest if the client struggles to come up with ideas. Your research also gives you a bit of background knowledge so you can ask smart questions.

Chapter 4.
Start the kickoff meeting and write your goal

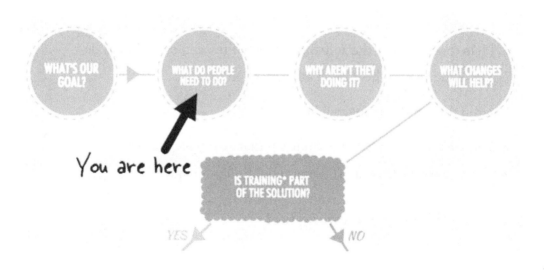

Task	Who does it	How long it might take
Lead the kickoff meeting with your client and at least one SME	You lead; client and SME will participate	You can probably cover the goal (this chapter) and at least start the analysis (next chapter) in a two-hour meeting.
Write the business goal for the project	You help the client and SME	

Result: A goal that describes how the organization will benefit from your project. Recommended format:

A measure we already use will increase / decrease number % by date as people in a specific group DO something on the job

Possible surprise: The project could change substantially. For example, the client might change the audience, or they might put the idea on hold while they do more research internally.

What you'll do

1. Choose a mapping tool
2. Put yourself in the best mindset for the meeting
3. Set up the room or screen
4. Start the meeting
5. Help the client and SME identify the measure to use and decide how it should change
6. Help them identify the audience and what the audience should do
7. Write the goal in the middle of your action map

Later in the same meeting, you'll:

- List what people need to do to reach that goal (chapter 5)
- Figure out why they aren't doing those things (chapter 6)

1. Prepare: Choose a mapping tool

You're going to start action mapping in this meeting. You'll get the goal and several actions, you'll prioritize the actions, and for the high-priority actions, you'll ask, "What makes this hard to do?"

You could end up with a map that looks like the following, although your map will probably have more actions.

Keep the map simple at this point, so it doesn't interfere with the conversation. It's just a way to record what you're talking about; it's not the focus.

Software, whiteboard, or wall?

Mind-mapping software has a lot of benefits. You can add notes from your analysis, embed documents, link to web pages – all great features, but you probably won't use any of them in this meeting.

At this point in the process, software has a major drawback: Only one person can use it (usually). If you're the one using the software, you have the advantage of controlling the map, but you also become a bottleneck, with all ideas having to go through you.

Software

If you want to use mind-mapping software in this meeting, make sure you can use it quickly and easily, and keep the graphics to a minimum. Don't spend time looking for symbols or aligning things just so. And if people present are telling you what to click on as you search for a feature, the software is getting in the way. Use a simpler tool next time.

Whiteboard

An alternative is to draw the map on a whiteboard. You might write the goal on the board but write the actions on sticky notes so they're easy to rearrange. Draw lines connecting the actions to the goal or higher-level action so the relationships are clear. Encourage the SME and client to get involved, because the physical action of moving things around can give people new insights.

Wall

Some people use a normal wall and sticky notes. The disadvantage to this is that you can't draw lines, so you can start to lose the relationships among the notes, especially as you break down big actions into sub-actions.

Sticky notes

If you plan to use sticky notes on the wall or whiteboard, get two colors. You can use one color to record what people need to do on the job, and the other to record why they aren't doing it.

Wall and whiteboard: Take a photo

If you use a physical approach to the map, plan to take a photo of the result. You'll probably want to replicate and clean up the map later in mind-mapping software. As you get deeper into the analysis and start brainstorming solutions, you'll appreciate the software's ability to link to documents, add comments, assign flags or roles, and easily move things around.

Virtual meetings

If the meeting will happen online, you'll want to share your screen. If you're a pro at managing your mind-mapping software, you might share that software on your screen.

If you're not so confident with the software, you risk having it distract from the conversation. In that case, you might use a digital pen and virtual whiteboard, or use a webinar tool that lets participants write and draw on a shared whiteboard.

Choose the tool that provides the least friction and plan to clean up the map later, on your own.

2. Prepare: Put yourself in the best mindset for the meeting

The goal of the kickoff meeting is to help the client and SME clearly define their problem and begin to solve it. Your role will be to ask good questions and, if necessary, mention the solutions that the answers seem to be suggesting. That's it.

If you've been doing conventional design for a while, you might be tempted to "present" in the meeting. For example, you might want to show them cool courses you've made or describe your work process and what you'll need from the SME.

But the meeting isn't about you, and it's definitely not about "the course." **It's all about the client and their problem.**

3. Set up the room or screen

Ideally, you'll meet in person. The room has a big dry-erase whiteboard or a wall that you can cover with sticky notes, or you'll project your computer screen and you have mind mapping or whiteboard software.

You might want to put yourself in the power seat in the room, to make clear that you'll be leading the discussion.

If you're meeting online, share your screen and, ideally, have the participants appear in video so you can read their faces. On your screen, have mind-mapping software that you handle well, a shared whiteboard in a webinar platform, or a whiteboard program and digital pen.

4. Start the meeting

Express your enthusiasm. Don't mention the course.

You did your best to set expectations for the meeting in the mini-agenda you sent earlier, but the client and SME might still be expecting to talk only about "the course" and what it should cover. So grab the reins immediately but politely.

Thank everyone for coming and make any necessary introductions. Then make clear, briefly, that you're looking forward to working on this "project" (not "course"). Identify some aspect of the problem that's interesting to you, or say that it's great to be working on something so worthwhile, or find some other way to express genuine enthusiasm for **solving the client's problem**. As before, you're not saying "course" (or "workshop" or "webinar" or whatever). The focus is on the client's problem.

Briefly outline the first two steps of the process

Next, make the following points as concisely as possible.

Say something like this	Show something like this
1. The goal of this meeting is to help me understand the problem.	
2. (optional) The content you gave me helped me see what you need people to do. Now I'd like to make sure I understand what they're doing wrong and why they're doing it.	
3. We'll use a simple, visual process to examine the problem. We often find quick and powerful solutions this way.	Maybe show a simplified action map but don't explain it in detail.

4. First we'll write a goal for the project. It will describe the change we want to see and give us a way to measure our success.	Draw a goal symbol in the middle of the whiteboard.
5. Then you'll help me understand what people need to do on the job to reach that goal.	Draw a few lines radiating out from the goal and write DO at the end of each line.
6. Finally, we'll look more closely at the most important things that people need to do. We'll try to identify why they aren't doing them or what might make it hard.	Circle one of the DOs.
7. We'll end up with a lot of ideas for how we can help people change what they do.	Draw 2-3 lines radiating out from one or two of the DOs
8. Everything we do will help bring us to the goal.	Move your hand or pointer from the last line you drew to its DO and then the goal

Let's dissect this, one statement at a time.

1. "The goal of this meeting is to help me understand..." One goal is to help you understand the problem, but the main goal is to give the problem the analysis that it deserves and that probably no one has given it. Don't say it that way, however. Instead, play the innocent outsider: "Help me understand..."

2. The content was helpful: Add some praise if someone present invested time in the content you've been given. You might say it was clear or well organized, but don't suggest it will be used as-is.

3. The "simple, visual process" is action mapping. You could call it that and say that it's used by lots of big organizations worldwide, if you think that's necessary for the client's buy-in. However, most people buy into it once they see it in action, which your client is about to do, so you might just forge ahead.

4. You'll write a goal for "the project." You're still not saying "course."

5. "You'll help me understand what people need to do..." Again, you're positioning this as "I'm a clueless outsider; help me understand" when the point is to get the client and SME to examine the problem more rigorously.

6. "We'll look more closely at the most important things..." If you suspect your client or SME is an analytical type, you might mention that you have a flowchart that makes the process easy. Some people love flowcharts (I'm one).

7. "We'll end up with a lot of ideas..." Notice again that the word "course" has yet to pass your lips. If your client seems convinced that a course is the solution to their problem, you might mention that the best solutions might come in "many formats, such as job aids or changes to processes." Continue to make clear that "we" do the analysis.

8. "Everything we do will help bring us to the goal." This is an important point that you'll probably find yourself repeating. It's common for SMEs to bring in only marginally related problems or add content that won't support the goal, so start making clear now that if it doesn't fit on the map, it doesn't belong in the project.

Stay focused on the first two steps

In the introduction, we didn't finish drawing the map. For example, we didn't explain that after we figure out what people need to do and why they aren't doing it, we identify the actions that can be helped with training, and then we brainstorm practice activities, and then... Doing all that can distract from the goal of the meeting, and, worse, it can make the client want to talk about "the course."

Instead, if you show just the first two rings, the goal and actions, you keep the client focused on the performance problem. They'll see how the map grows later.

Next step: Write the business goal. But what's a goal?

Next, you'll lead the SME and client through writing a goal. It will look simple to them, but there are so many pitfalls that we're going to put your meeting on pause for a bit so we can look closely at goals.

When a client says, "My team needs a course," they have a bigger goal in mind. That goal is the real reason the project has to happen.

Unfortunately, it's common to develop training with the wrong type of goal. Below are some typical goals. They all have a big blind spot. What are they missing?

- Salespeople will know all the product features.
- Managers will handle difficult conversations better.
- Everyone will use the new software.
- People will be aware of the dangers of the internet.
- Leaders will help people adjust to big changes.

If you had $40,000 and someone asked you to spend that money on one of the above goals, what would you say?

Here's what I'd say: "What will I get in return?"

Why should I care whether people will use the new software or handle difficult conversations better? How is that worth $40,000 to me?

A business goal is the "What's in it for me?" for the organization. **It justifies the existence of the project in business terms.** None of the goals above clearly show what's in it for the organization.

Why the goal matters

By getting everyone to commit to a performance goal, you'll show that your role is to solve the problem, not just provide training. You'll measure your success in a way that matters to the organization, and you'll help keep everyone focused on changing performance, not just delivering information.

Let's see how it works with the first goal, "Salespeople will know all the product features."

> ### A word about widgets
>
> *If English isn't your first language, you might wonder what a widget is. It's an imaginary item, usually a mechanical or technological product. The word is intentionally vague so people don't focus on a specific real-world item and instead focus on the ideas the writer is trying to convey.*
>
> *If you see other strange words and I'm using them in relation to widgets, I've probably invented those words.*

Sell it to Scrooge

Imagine that I'm a C-level type in a widget company and I'm sitting behind a tidy pile of $40,000.

A training person, let's call him Bob, comes to me and says, "Give me that $40k, and in return, salespeople will know all the product features."

"What, can't they read the product brochure?" I say, wrapping my arms protectively around the money.

"Well, yes, but they're not selling our widgets as well as they could," Bob says. "Our mystery shoppers say that the salespeople just sell the micro widget. They ignore the mega and monster widgets even when they're the best widgets for the customer. We have a reputation as cheap widget-pushers."

"So tell them to sell more mega and monster widgets," I say.

"But we don't want them to sell the mega or monster if it's the wrong widget for the customer," Bob says. "That goes against our mission and will hurt our brand."

"You want this money," I say, "so you can help salespeople identify the best widget for the customer?"

"Yes, that's it," Bob says. "I guess just knowing the features isn't enough. They have to develop the skills to identify the customer's needs and then match the features to those needs."

"And then what will happen?" I say. "How will I get my $40k back?"

"Sales of mega and monster widgets will go up," Bob says. "Since we make more profit from those than from the micro widgets, we'll make more money."

"And...?" I say in my most annoying tone, still hugging the money.

"And our reputation will improve, helping our brand," Bob says. "Overall sales could go up and we could gain market share, because we'll become the widget company that really listens. Everyone else just pushes widgets."

"All right," I say, reluctantly peeling $20k off the pile. "Here's some money. Let's see if you can show a 5% increase in mega and monster widget sales by fourth quarter. If so, we'll use the rest of the money to expand what you're doing and see if we can gain market share."

What changed during the conversation?

Bob's goal started as this:

> Salespeople will know all the product features

It ended as this:

> Mega and monster widget sales will increase 5% by Q4 as salespeople identify the best widget for each customer

Bob now has a way to measure the success of his project, at least in the short term, and it's a measure that benefits the business as a whole. His new goal **justifies the expense of the project.**

Bob's new goal also shows everyone involved in the project that he's serious and is going to measure results. It shows that "training people" like Bob play vital roles in the success of the organization.

Imagine the training that results

A good business goal helps you sell your project to Scrooges like me, but it also has a profound effect on the type of training you develop. Let's compare the training inspired by Bob's "before" and "after" goals.

First, we'll rewind the story and give Bob a happier beginning.

"Salespeople will know all the product features."

I'm out of the office and someone gives Bob all the money without question. Bob decides to spend it on elearning, because he believes it's the most efficient way to make sure that "salespeople know all the product features."

First, he creates a series of slides that present the features of each widget. He spends hours creating a clickable widget that reveals some feature information. Every five or six screens, he's careful to add a knowledge check.

While a professional narrator records the script that Bob wrote, Bob creates an impressive clickable timeline that shows when each widget was introduced and how its features have evolved since then.

When the narrator sends the audio files, Bob creates an attractive lady avatar to act as a friendly guide through the course. When the avatar speaks, her lips really move.

Then Bob buys a cool game template. He loads it up with questions like "How much does a monster widget weigh?" and assigns points for the answers.

Finally, he creates an assessment that asks more questions about features.

Bob still has budget left, so he hires a video crew to make a video of the chief of widget sales. The chief talks about how great our products are and how important it is to know everything about them.

Bob puts it all together, starting with the video and then going into the feature presentation, timeline, knowledge checks, and game. He ends with the assessment.

He publishes the course on the LMS and assigns it to all salespeople. He notes with satisfaction that 90% of the people pass the assessment on the first try, and all pass it when they try again.

Bob has met his goal. His assessment "proves" that salespeople know all the widget features.

He moves on to his next project, happily unaware that sales haven't improved and my $40k has vaporized.

What happens if we start with the other goal?

"Mega and monster widget sales will increase 5% ..."

Bob goes through the wringer in my office and emerges with only some of the money and a measurable goal:

> Mega and monster widget sales will increase 5% by Q4 as salespeople identify the best widget for each customer.

He calls his contact in sales, Luisa. She's the person who originally told him about the need for training.

"I need to understand what the salespeople are doing wrong," he says. "Can we meet?"

In the meeting, Bob shows Luisa the new goal.

"That makes me nervous," Luisa says. "We can't guarantee that our training will increase sales."

"I think it's best to consider it a goal, not a guarantee," Bob says. "And I think if we target the right behaviors, we could meet it."

Bob and Luisa spend a couple of hours listing what the salespeople should be doing, what they're doing instead, and why they're doing it. They decide that the following problems have the most influence over salespeople, and they brainstorm solutions.

Problem: Salespeople compete with each other by comparing the number of products sold, not income from sales. Since it's easy to sell something that's cheap, they try to quickly sell lots of micro-widgets.

"We could fix that easily," Luisa says. "We'll change what we show on our weekly reports. We'll show the profit that each salesperson brings in, not just the number of products sold. The profit numbers will increase as they sell more mega and monster widgets."

Problem: Salespeople are paid partly by commission, and the commission is the same for all widgets.

"I'll talk to that Scrooge at the C-level," Luisa says. "Maybe we could make the commission scale with the product."

Problem: Our main competitor, Weeber Widgets, aggressively markets their own micro-widget, which is much better-looking than ours but offers lower performance. Our salespeople want to sell more of our micro-widgets just to prove that the ugly underdog can win.

"I should start focusing more on market share in my meetings with the sales staff," Luisa says. "We should be competing for all customers, not focusing just on one product. We'll beat Weeber by stealing their market share."

Problem: Salespeople don't ask customers enough questions to identify which widget would be best for them.

"They need to practice this somehow," Luisa says. "They've been focused on one widget for so long that they've forgotten how to ask good questions."

Result: One training idea. The discussion results in several non-training changes and one opportunity for training: "They need to practice asking good questions."

Bob mulls this over and comes up with a suggestion.

"We don't have a very big budget," he says. "We can't fly all the salespeople to a face-to-face workshop, and I don't think one workshop would change them, anyway. But we could make online activities that help them practice asking good questions, and then challenge them with roleplays at the quarterly regional meetings. That way, they'll get some initial practice plus regular reinforcement, online and in person."

Luisa agrees, and Bob asks her to list the customer needs that are met by each widget.

Using the list, Bob creates profiles of fictional customers, each with a different set of needs, and Luisa makes sure they're accurate and realistic. Bob drafts a high-level plot of a sales scenario in which a salesperson has to choose the best questions to ask and, based on the answers, choose the best widget for one of the fictional customers. He creates a prototype of some typical decision points and runs the plot and prototype by Luisa and a few future learners.

After incorporating their suggestions, Bob fleshes out the scenario and creates a second one using a different customer profile. With Luisa's help, Bob creates a two-page PDF that lists examples of the types of questions that are useful for uncovering customers' needs. He adds it as an optional link to the scenarios so people can look at it for help if necessary.

Bob takes photos of some colleagues who look like typical customers and adds them to the scenarios, which are otherwise just text. Bob doesn't have the budget for audio or video, so he worries that people will complain that the production isn't slick enough.

Luisa reviews his scenarios to make sure the conversations are realistic, and she tests them on salespeople.

"They really got into it," she tells Bob. "If we can keep score, I think they'd try even harder, because they're so competitive. And they didn't notice that it was mostly text. They were too involved in the story to care."

Bob assigns scores to the scenario paths, so the player who chooses the right widget in the fewest questions gets the highest score.

Thinking of the longer-term goal — a stronger brand and increased market share — Bob also adds scenes from the future to the scenario endings. These extra scenes show whether the customer came back for more widgets, recommended the company to friends, or complained about a product mismatch.

Meanwhile, Luisa is changing how she talks about market share and how salespeople compare their performance. She also gets approval for a small increase in commission for mega and monster widget sales.

Once Bob has created several scenarios representing the most common widget customers and a few unusual ones, he embeds the scenarios on one intranet page. Luisa sends the page to regional managers first, so they experience for themselves what their teams are about to do, and then they encourage their teams to play.

Soon salespeople are visiting the page, trying scenarios in their spare time. Some of them disagree with how certain scenarios play out, which they point out on the company discussion forum. The disagreement makes other people try the scenarios and join the debate, and Luisa uses the forum to ask what the scenario should do instead, making people think more deeply about how to match features to needs.

The "training" continues each quarter at the one-day regional meetings. There, every salesperson is given a fictional customer profile that describes what they plan to do with their widget, their past experience with widgets, how much they're willing to spend, and other characteristics. At several times during the day, people are randomly paired off and have to identify their colleague's best widget by asking good questions.

As the fourth quarter starts, Luisa calls Bob.

"You can tell that Scrooge that we met our goal," she says. "Mega and monster sales are up 5%. And as far as we can tell, it looks like we've won some market share from Weeber, too."

What's the difference?

"Salespeople will know all the product features"

This typical goal inspired a forgettable and ineffective information dump. The course might have refreshed salespeople's knowledge, at least in the short term, but it had no effect on sales because it didn't solve the real problem.

"Mega and monster widget sales will increase 5% by Q4 as salespeople identify the best widget for each customer"

This goal requires people to **do something** on the job. It inspired Bob to uncover the real problems behind the request for training. Why aren't salespeople identifying the best widget for each customer? How can we encourage them to do it?

The solution was to make several non-training changes in addition to addressing one highly focused training need: "They need to practice asking good questions."

The training part of the solution helped people change what they did on the job. It gave them online and face-to-face practice, spaced over time.

5. Help the client and SME identify the measure to use and decide how it should change

Ready to lead the discussion about the goal? Here's a template that can help.

A measure we already use will increase / decrease

number % by *date*

as *people in a specific group DO something*

Start with the first blank in the template. Ask what they're currently measuring that will improve when the problem is solved. It's "a measure we already use" for two reasons: it's easier, and the fact that someone is already measuring shows that it (probably) matters.

For example, let's say our client wants "training on how to create TPS reports." Some questions to ask:

- "What are you hoping to achieve with the project?" The response often hints at something measurable, like "People need to create better TPS reports, because they keep getting rejected by Processing."

- "Is that something you normally measure? Could you say the rejection rate is a certain number?" If it's not something they currently measure, ask for something they do measure, such as the number of errors in all TPS reports, or the number of client complaints about processing delays.

- "Do you have a target in mind? How much improvement do you need?"

- "It sounds like you'd like to see this: ..." Write a partial goal on the board, for example, "The TPS report rejection rate will decrease 20%."

- "You mentioned that you needed a solution by [date]. Is there a date by which you'd like to see the rejection rate go down 20%?" Add the date to the goal, for example, "The TPS report rejection rate will decrease 20% by the end of the year."

Reassure people that the goal is for internal use

The goal you're writing is a promise made among the stakeholders to keep the project focused and measure its effectiveness. It might be shared with higher-ups when the budget is approved. It's not something you share with the learners, unless everyone is confident that it would help inspire them.

If necessary, use the research you did before the meeting

You did some quick online research to prepare for the meeting. If the client is struggling to identify a metric, pull out your notes and float some ideas.

The client might be more open if you phrase your ideas as questions and mention that other organizations are doing it. For example: "I saw in a *Widget World* article that Acme and MegaCo use an employee engagement metric. Would that be helpful for us?" and not "I think you want to measure employee engagement."

Focus on a performance metric, not a butt-covering metric

Even if you follow the template, you could write a goal that will break your analysis.

Here are three examples. One of them needs to be thrown out. Which one, and why should we throw it out?

a) "Payment errors will decrease 30% by next year as payroll staff correctly process payroll."

b) "Ethics violations will decrease 35% by next year as field staff avoid the behaviors on the Sanctioned Behaviors list."

c) "Completion rates for the new safety course will reach 90% by next year as staff complete the course."

Option **c** follows the template — it uses an observable metric, and it briefly describes who needs to do what. But it has two problems.

First, who cares about course completion rates? No one but us.

Second, and more importantly, **the goal short-circuits the analysis that would uncover why we need safety training**. It assumes that a course is the solution, which is the assumption we're trying to combat.

I call this a "training goal" because it's trapped in training-land. The only people who care about it are training people, and it assumes the solution is training.

Here are some examples of client requests turned into butt-covering Training Goals of Doom.

- "Managers need to be aware of the new law about medical leave" becomes "At least 85% of managers will complete a short course on medical leave by next month."

- "Our programmers are writing messy Xjscript code" becomes "At least 70% of programmers will complete Xjscript certification by the end of the year."

- "Sales staff need to know all the product features" becomes "All sales staff will score 90% or higher on an assessment of product features by Q4."

These goals assume that training and testing is the solution, and all they care about is how many people took the training. They don't let you clarify and analyze the problem and discover better solutions.

> *When we write a good business goal, we're not just slapping a metric on someone's decision to create training. We're challenging ourselves to solve the underlying problem and improve the performance of the business. Training probably isn't the best or only solution. Make sure your metric describes something the business cares about and helps you find the true cause of the problem.*

Tie the goal to people's values

In addition to focusing and evaluating your project, a good goal inspires people. Try to tie your goal to the organization's mission (if people care about that) or to something else that inspires.

Again, the goal is internal. You're inspiring your stakeholders. That inspiration will, ideally, express itself in the solution as a result.

For example, if your organization is proud of how it improves the lives of customers, choose a measure that reflects that. One organization I worked with processed payments owed to clients. Errors in the process could delay a payment to a person who needed it to buy groceries or pay rent. Which of the following goals is more likely to inspire a busy SME to commit time to that project?

> a) TPS records will be processed within 5 days by Q4 as all clerks follow the correct procedure.

> b) Clients will receive payment by the promised date 99% of the time by Q4 as all clerks follow the correct procedure.

You might also want to make this personal for the client. In addition to asking what the C-level people might care about, ask the client what **they** care about. How does the performance problem affect them personally? What could they achieve if the problem were solved? What do they value, and how would solving the problem help them express those values?

Create a metric yourself

In the very unlikely event that the organization doesn't measure anything related to the problem, consider measuring it yourself. Would it help to run a survey or measure a specific process before you implement the project, and then check the same measures again once the solution has been in place for a while?

The challenge of the non-profit

If the client's organization is a non-profit or government agency that receives funding regardless of its performance, you might be suffering right now. Your client might be saying things like this:

- "But we don't measure anything."

- "We don't assign monetary value to people's work."
- "We focus more on helping people than tracking numbers."

The suggestion might be that it's crass to talk about money. Even non-financial metrics like response time might be seen as inappropriate.

The irony (to me, at least) is that the organization cares about its mission, but it might not be tracking whether the mission is being achieved. For example, simply counting the number of impoverished people you advise doesn't tell you whether those people have actually improved their lives. Only tracking them will tell you that.

If the client seems open to the idea of measurement, you might encourage them to measure the issue now, and then measure it again once the project has been in place for a while. However, even if the client wants to measure something, their bosses might not agree that it's useful, so that idea might go nowhere.

As a result, it might be impossible to get a high-level metric that ties the project to the improved performance of the organization. You might need to choose a less-impressive metric that's much closer to the task, such as the percentage of forms that are completed correctly. Or, you might have to give up and accept "softer" measures, such as:

- Donors feel more included in our decision-making
- Counselors feel more confident when talking with clients from other cultures
- Volunteers in Region 3 take initiative

In case it isn't abundantly clear, I would reject these "metrics" if the client were able to identify anything (anything!) that is actually measurable. However, if the client doesn't want to measure anything and is under no pressure from anyone to measure anything, you're stuck. At this point, the best you can do is try to keep the goal somewhat focused so your analysis can examine a specific group of people and their specific behaviors.

Since you don't have a measurable goal, you won't be able to evaluate the project once it's in place. I feel ethically required to remind the client of that, but in many organizations, it isn't a problem.

Consider creating a two-level goal

You could create a good goal but find that it's too "big" for the comfort of some of your stakeholders. In that case, you might consider having two goals: the big, hairy, audacious one plus a smaller, more easily measured goal that supports the big one.

For example, your main goal might be this:

> Employee turnover will decrease 5% in two years as all managers use the Nurture Your Team management model.

Your client and SME might want this goal but worry about being able to measure it. Or, they might say that it's a good goal, but so many things affect employee turnover, such as the economy, that they won't be able to say confidently whether any improvement was due to the project.

In that case, you could keep the goal as your high-level goal, but add a more detailed layer to it, focusing on a closer, more internal metric:

> Employee engagement scores will increase 8% in two years as all managers use the Nurture Your Team management model.

It's also a good idea to identify more specific, frequent measures that will help you gauge your progress. For example, if the employee engagement score comes from an annual survey, you could set up a shorter, more frequent survey to measure aspects that are directly tied to the model you plan to teach. If the new model encourages managers to provide feedback at least once a week, your survey could include a question asking employees how often their manager provides feedback. You could send the survey to future learners before the program is in place to see what you're starting with and survey them again after the solution has been in place for a while.

A two-level goal is also a good way to provide a "hard" goal that the bean counters care about, plus a more emotionally compelling version that everyone else will buy into.

Ask the learners

If your client and SME are struggling to identify a goal, suggest asking future learners. Ask them how their work lives would improve if the issues they're struggling with were resolved. How could that improvement be measured?

Make sure the goal is achievable

You're going to use the goal to identify what staff need to do differently and to help them do it. So, your goal has to be something that can be achieved by employees. If instead you pick a goal that's subject to the whim of the market or other outside forces, you'll end up frustrated.

Here's a problematic goal: "Within two years, our company will be listed in first place in *Widget World* magazine's list of 'Best Places to Work' as managers use the Nurture Your Team model."

Obviously, that goal depends too much on an outside force, the editorial board of *Widget World*, to be useful for our analysis. How would you rephrase it to turn it into a goal that employees could achieve on their own?

Here's one possible rewrite: "Employee engagement scores will increase 20% within two years as managers use the Nurture Your Team model."

This uses an internal measurement — the employee engagement survey — and becomes much more achievable.

Goals for off-the-shelf courses

What if your client wants to create a generic, off-the-shelf course to sell to a wide audience? Action mapping isn't intended for this situation, but you can still apply it, sort of.

The client might think their goal is something like "Sell this course and profit," but that won't help your design. Instead, think of the goal from the perspective of the customer. You might include the marketing team in the discussion, because they should be asking the same questions.

Ask,

- "Who makes the decision to buy this course, and who will ultimately take it?" (They might be different people, such as employer and employee.)

- "How would the employer describe the behaviors they want to change or the skills they want to improve? How might they measure that?"

- "How will the individual personally benefit from the course? What frustrations will it relieve? How will they advance in their career?"

Look for a goal that satisfies both the employer and employee. You won't be able to measure their success very well, if at all, but you've at least focused the project on meeting their needs and are in a good position for the next steps of action mapping.

If you need a measure that applies to the client's course-selling business, consider looking for repeat sales of the same course to others in the same organization, which suggests that it worked for the first buyers and is getting recommended by them. A goal of this type might be, "Repeat sales of Persuasive Emails account for X% of that product's sales by [date] as customers achieve their goals when writing emails."

6. Help them identify the audience and what the audience should do

Here's the template again. You've got something to measure now, and you're on the "as people DO something" part.

A measure we already use will increase / decrease

number % by date

as people in a specific group DO something

Choose a specific audience

Let's say that your client is a widget manufacturer that wants to improve the quality of their widgets. Below are two goals that the client is considering. Which is more likely to inspire effective solutions to the problem?

> a) Widget returns will decrease 9% by next year as all staff ensure the quality of our widgets.

> b) Widget returns will decrease 9% by next year as inspectors eliminate poor-quality widgets.

In goal **a**, the client has assumed that all people should be addressed by the same project. However, the quality problem could have any number of causes. Maybe the widget designers have made miscalculations, leading to early failure in some parts. Maybe the widget assemblers are cutting corners, or the inspectors are missing problems, or the shippers are tossing widgets around with too much abandon.

However, rather than investigate the problem to find out its main source, the person who wrote goal **a** has decided to throw the same solution at everyone who might possibly be guilty, probably saying, "They need to be more aware of the importance of quality! Let's give them a course."

We've all seen the training that results from a one-size-fits-all approach: an information dump. If we're told to create one solution for everyone everywhere, we probably won't have time to do a decent analysis. With so many job roles that might affect quality, we can't get deep into any one of them. It becomes easiest to just succumb to the client's belief that "quality is everyone's job, so we have to address everyone."

If we decide training is part of the solution, we can't write job-specific challenges. We're stuck providing high-level information, broad lists of do's and don'ts, and preachy finger-wagging about "quality."

The second goal makes clear that we've done at least a minimum amount of investigation and have decided that lax widget inspectors are the most urgent cause of the problem. We're going to target our solution to them, and as a result our analysis will be much more useful and any activities will be specific and powerful.

What if the client still wants one solution for everyone?

If the client insists that a course is the only solution and it must be one course for everyone, you have two options. Which do you think is stronger?

> 1. Guide the analysis so it identifies the job roles that are contributing the most to the problem. Convince the client to focus on those roles and help them see targeted solutions, not just a course.
>
> 2. Accept that "everyone" is your audience and that your analysis will be shallow, but design activities that are targeted to specific job roles and send learners to the activities that apply to them.

I'd vote for option 1. You'll win in several ways: You'll identify the real cause of the problem and design a solution targeted at that cause, you won't inflict training on people who don't need training, and you'll show that you're not a course producer but someone who improves performance.

Option 2 includes a good idea — to filter by job role so people see only what applies to them — but it fails to really solve the problem. Your analysis will be broad and shallow because you won't have time to look closely at each cause of the problem, since "everyone" is supposedly causing it. You'll also reinforce the misconception that your job is to provide training on demand, regardless of whether it will solve the problem.

Often, when you start a project, you start with a vague goal like the first example ("all staff ensure the quality of our widgets"). Then, as you and the client analyze the problem and identify the main culprits, you tighten the focus to create a more specific goal like the second example ("inspectors eliminate poor-quality widgets").

Identify at a high level what they need to do

In your analysis, you'll list in specific terms what people need to do on the job. For the goal, you just need a high-level description of what they need to do.

In the example above, we said that inspectors need to "eliminate poor-quality widgets." That's focused enough to inspire a list of specific actions, such as "Determine how many widgets in each batch should be examined," "Examine the widget using the Quality Checklist," and "If Issue X is present, do Y."

What if your audience is supposed to do something more vague, like provide more useful performance reviews? In this case, models are your friend.

A model creates a standardized approach. Action mapping is a model of instructional design. The Five Whys is a model for analyzing a problem. There's a model for almost everything, and maybe it will work for your project.

For example, maybe our performance-review goal could say that "all managers apply the Actionable Advice model of performance reviews," which I just invented.

If the client or SME don't already have a model in mind, you might propose one that you found in the research you did before the meeting.

If no model will work, write a high-level description of an observable action. Avoid verbs that only happen in people's brains, like "understand," "feel more confident," or "are aware of."

7. Write the goal in the middle of your action map

If you're using mind-mapping software, you can probably fit the entire goal statement in the center node of the map. If you're using a whiteboard or wall, it's easiest to write a short version of the goal. You'll include the formal goal statement in a follow-up email, so everyone will have a copy soon enough.

Practice: Which of these goals is strongest?

You've seen how a strong goal inspires a good solution. With that in mind, which of the following statements is the best goal for a project that might include training, and why?

a) The filing backlog will decrease to 0 in eight months

b) Purchasing staff will correctly use the purchase order software, reducing calls to the help desk by 10% by Q4

c) Employee turnover will decrease 10% by next year as managers respect the diversity of their team members

d) Privacy breaches will decrease 20% by next year as all employees become aware of the risks of email and social media

Here's my take:

a) This statement doesn't mention who's responsible for the change. Instead, through no effort by anyone, the filing backlog will just disappear. This goal needs to be expanded.

b) This goal identifies who's going to be doing something and what, in general, they'll be doing: purchasing staff will use the software correctly. It also describes a measurable improvement that will result. Because we have to hire more help desk staff as calls increase, reducing the number of calls they have to answer is a good thing. This is a solid goal. It doesn't follow the template, but it has all the ingredients.

c) This one starts out well — reducing employee turnover is good because it's expensive to hire new employees. However, what exactly does "respect diversity" look like? It's hard to picture specific behaviors, which means that any training that's developed will probably be a forgettably generic presentation about diversity with no realistic practice.

d) This goal also starts out well, because privacy breaches are bad and expensive. However, we again can't picture what people will be doing. What does "become aware" look like on the job? This one is also likely to lead to a forgettable information dump.

If we use the template to rewrite the goals we looked at above, they could end up like this:

a) The filing backlog will decrease to 0 in eight months as all TPS report clerks follow our records management procedures.

b) Help desk calls about the purchasing software will decrease 10% by Q4 as purchasing staff correctly use the program.

c) Employee turnover will decrease 10% by next year as all managers follow our firm's diversity policy.

d) Privacy breaches will decrease 20% by next year as all employees follow the Responsible Internet Use policy.

Example: The entire conversation

Here's an example of the entire goal-setting conversation, using the TPS report example we used in step 5 of this chapter.

Start by asking why they've come to you, and then keep narrowing them down until you get something measurable. Let's say our client wants "training on how to create TPS reports." Some questions to ask:

- "What are you hoping to achieve with the project?" The response often hints at something measurable, like "People need to create better TPS reports, because they keep getting rejected by Processing."

- "Is that something you normally measure? Could you say [the measurable thing, in this case the rejection rate] is a certain amount?" If it's not something they currently measure, ask for something they do measure.

- "Do you have a target in mind? How much improvement do you need?"

- "It sounds like you'd like to see this: ..." Write a partial goal on the board, for example, "The TPS report rejection rate will decrease 20%."

- "You mentioned that you needed a solution by [date]. Is there a date by which you'd like to see the [rejection rate go down 20%]?" Add the date to the goal, for example, "The TPS report rejection rate will decrease 20% by the end of the year."

- "You mentioned that the project is for [the audience, like the report clerks]. They need to create more accurate reports, right?" Add that to the goal on the board: "The TPS report rejection rate will decrease 20% by the end of the year as all clerks create accurate reports."

- "How do you feel about this goal? It's a goal, not a guarantee, but do you think it's feasible?" If people feel the goal isn't achievable, ask if tweaking the numbers would help. They might also want to avoid over-promising and want to add wording that says that they hope to "contribute to" the goal.

- "Is this goal inspiring?" If people don't seem to be fired up about the goal, continue asking questions to uncover how the people in the room are personally affected by the problem. Also ask how the problem affects the ability of the organization to fulfill its mission.

Also ask these questions

Some other questions can be extremely useful at this point, including the following.

- "What has already been tried to fix this problem?" Be especially alert to any mention of previous training that failed.

- "Are there any initiatives already under way that address this problem?" It's a good idea to align your goal with existing initiatives.

Sketch a timeline for the project

This is a good time to ask when the project should be implemented. Don't phrase this as, "When do you want the training to happen?" because you might find that a training event isn't the best solution. Instead, ask something like, "When are you hoping to have a solution in place?"

Common challenges

Below are some challenges you might face when trying to get a goal out of your client, with some suggestions for things to try.

The client doesn't know the business impact of the problem.
Ask,

- "What do you see that tells you that there's a problem?"
- "What's currently being measured?"
- "If you looked at the metrics for your team a year from now, how could you tell whether the problem was solved?"
- "How is your team members' performance measured and evaluated?"

The client just wants people to "be aware" of something.
Ask,

- "If Tom is aware of the thing and Jane isn't, how can we tell by watching them do their jobs? How does that difference affect the customers? How does it affect the team? How does it affect the organization?"
- "Once everyone is aware of the thing, what will change?"

Stakeholders are nervous about saying that the project will improve business performance.

- Remind them that it's a goal, not a guarantee. While the goal should be achievable by internal staff alone, emphasize that the project is part of a larger business strategy (or it should be!). If necessary, word the goal as "Contribute to [business goal]" or agree on a percentage of the goal that the project might realistically be responsible for.

The client has a goal that they think can't be measured, such as, "Leaders will manage conflict effectively."
Ask,

- "What tells you that you have a conflict-management problem?"
- "How will you know the solution has had an effect? What will you see?"
- "What are you measuring now that you can refer to?" (employee evaluation scores? number of people leaving the organization? number of formal complaints about conflict?)
- "What else is happening in the company to improve conflict management skills, and what are they measuring?"

- If necessary, consider doing a survey before the material is developed to capture employees' perception about current conflict management. That could give you some measures that you want to change with the material and related interventions, and you could then do a follow-up survey to see if those measures really did change.

The client says it's a compliance course, so the goal is just to meet a legal requirement.
Ask,

- "What costs might the business face if people aren't compliant?"
- "If you compare two organizations, how could you tell if one was compliant and the other wasn't?"

The client wants a one-size-fits-all "welcome to our company" induction course.

- Point out that the best solution will probably be a combination of many solutions, including better distribution of information, more sharing among staff, job aids to help with decisions about benefits, some marketing-type materials about the organization's culture and history, and so forth.
- For the business metric, you might consider the costs associated with having to find replacements for new hires who fail, the amount of time it takes a new hire to reach a specific level of performance, or the impact on productivity that struggling new hires might have.

The client says there's nothing to measure because the product or policy is new.

- Help the client identify why the new product or policy was created, and then look for ways to measure that. For example, ask,
- "What sales projections were used to justify adding the product to our lineup?"
- "Is the new product supposed to reach a new market for us? If so, how big is that market?"
- "Why was the new policy created? What problem is it supposed to solve or prevent?"

The client says the training is optional and doesn't relate to a specific business need.

- If you're juggling a lot of projects, carefully suggest that you need to give priority to initiatives that support current business strategies. This could inspire the client to justify the existence of their project. It will at least make clear that your job is to improve business performance, not to produce courses on demand.

- If you can't avoid the project, ask the client to at least identify in general terms who will benefit from the training and how they'll benefit. For example, if the client wants "a mini-course on how to be creative," ask the client to help you describe the benefits of this increased creativity for the learners or their employers.

Chapter 5. What do they need to DO?

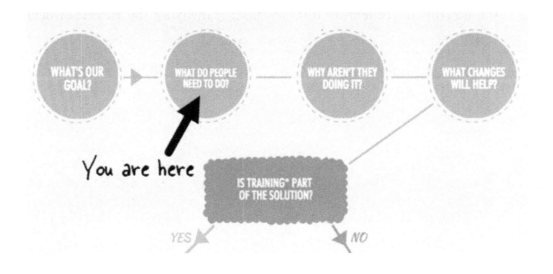

Task	Who does it	How long it might take
List what people need to do on the job to reach the business goal.	You lead; client and SME participate	This is probably part of the two-hour meeting you started in the previous chapter.
Identify the 5-10 tasks that are most important to reaching the goal.	You help the client and SME	

Result: A possibly long list of on-the-job tasks that people in your target audience need to perform, with the most important tasks highlighted. Tasks are specific, highly focused, and described in observable terms. Examples:

- Correctly label each folder
- Tell the patient how long the test will take

- When a team member expresses concerns about the merger, listen without interrupting
- Avoid commenting on religious attire

What you've done

You're still in your kickoff meeting with the client and SME. You should now have a goal that describes a measurable change in business performance. The goal mentions in broad terms who needs to change and, briefly, what they need to do differently.

What you'll do

Now you'll ask, "What do people need to do on the job for us to reach this goal?" You'll do this in four steps.

1. Help the client and SME brainstorm actions
2. Organize the items into actions and sub-actions
3. Periodically review the actions and make them more specific
4. Help the client and SME prioritize actions

In the conventional approach to training design, many people would focus now on what people supposedly need to know. For example, they might write learning objectives or start designing the content.

Instead, you're going to focus relentlessly on what people need to **do.** Some examples:

- Schedule a sales call with the appropriate person in the organization
- Steam the milk without burning it
- Respond appropriately to gifts that could be interpreted as bribes, taking local customs into account

You're adding **actions**, represented by triangles in this map.

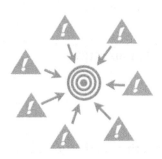

Why actions matter

Information doesn't solve problems; action does.

> Performance improves when people **do things differently**, not when they know stuff.

When you ask, "What do they need to DO?" you:

- Help the client see the performance problem clearly
- Make it possible to find the most effective solutions to the problem
- Lay the groundwork for memorable practice activities, not an information dump

Finally, this step and the next one, asking, "Why aren't they doing it?" **grounds the project in reality**. The client has come to you with an assumption that they might not have questioned: "We need training." They're floating in a cloud of knowledge and want you to make it rain. You'll use the techniques here to gently pull the client down to the real world so they can see what's really causing the problem.

What's an action?

Actions describe observable behavior. For example, let's say that we want firefighters to educate the public about preventing forest fires, and to quickly put these fires out when they occur. Our official goal is, "Fire-related losses in our region will decrease 10% by next year as firefighters prevent and extinguish brush and forest fires."

Which of the following statements do you think I'd accept as actions to reach this goal?

a) Identify the techniques used to extinguish a brush fire

b) List the principal sources of combustion in a deciduous forest

c) Describe common public misconceptions about campfires

d) Quickly extinguish a brush fire in a dry mixed forest

e) Define "incendiary device"

If you said that only **d**, "Quickly extinguish a brush fire" was an action by my standards, you've read my mind.

The ideal action is **something you see someone do on the job**. It's a normal part of their job. It doesn't take place in their head or in that abstract world I call Testland.

"But the other actions are observable!"

If you've had training in conventional instructional design, you're probably arguing with me, saying that the other statements on the list are observable objectives.

For example, we can watch a firefighter write a list of the techniques used to extinguish a brush fire, and we can point at that list and say, "See? They know it." And that's the problem — we're just measuring whether they know it. We're stuck in the school model. There's no guarantee that the firefighter will actually apply this knowledge, which is what we really want.

I'm not saying we don't want our firefighters to be able to identify the techniques. Obviously, they need to do that to complete the action we really want, which is to put out fires. "Identify the techniques" is an enabling objective. I would record it later, when we list the information people need to know to complete the on-the-job behavior — I'd list "techniques to extinguish a brush fire" as required knowledge. But that comes later, not now.

*Right now, you're focusing relentlessly on what people need to **do on the job**, because that's the only way you'll be able to determine what might be causing the problem. If you just describe what they should know, you short-circuit your analysis because you assume the only problem is ignorance.*

Actions set the stage for everything else we do

The way we write our actions can determine the success of the project. Here's why.

They help us solve real-world problems

Once we've listed our actions, we're going to choose the most important ones and ask for each one, "Why aren't they doing this?"

If an action is a test-style objective like "Identify the techniques used to extinguish a brush fire," then our only answer to "Why aren't they doing this?" is "They don't know it."

But do we **know** that they don't know it? And do we know that this alleged ignorance is the reason fires aren't getting extinguished fast enough? All we can see is that sometimes our firefighters don't extinguish fires quickly or thoroughly. We can't assume that the entire reason this happens is because they don't know the right techniques.

They might be lacking the right tools, they might have problems working together as a team, they might not be told about the fire quickly enough in the first place... There are many potential causes, and we don't want to rule them out by focusing immediately on knowledge.

So instead of writing knowledge objectives, we describe the **behavior** we want to see. If the behavior is, "Quickly and thoroughly extinguish brush fires," asking, "Why aren't they doing this?" generates a rich discussion that goes far beyond possible knowledge gaps.

You might think of actions as performance objectives that take place on the job, not on a test or in training.

They help us avoid creating information dumps

If our analysis shows that some sort of training will be part of the solution, focusing on actions performed on the job creates more memorable activities. Here's an example.

Information objective becomes information dump

Let's say that we've ignored everything I just said and one of our actions is that firefighters should "identify techniques to put out a brush fire." It becomes natural to create materials like this:

1. Information presentation:

Brush fire: Extinguishing techniques

- Pour water on it
- Throw sand on it
- Throw a wet blanket over it
- Dump snow on it

2. Quiz

Check your understanding

Which of the following is NOT a technique used to extinguish a brush fire?

A. Pour water on it
B. Throw sand on it
C. Blow it out with a fan
D. Throw a wet blanket over it
E. Dump snow on it

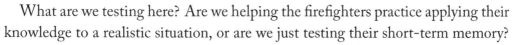

What are we testing here? Are we helping the firefighters practice applying their knowledge to a realistic situation, or are we just testing their short-term memory?

We're just testing their short-term memory. We haven't put the information in context or helped people **practice doing their job differently.**

Unfortunately, many people have been taught that the above approach is good instructional design. It starts with a "measurable" objective, presents the information in small chunks, and tests to see whether the "learner" can retrieve that information. However, that's the school model, which we're trying to escape.

Firefighters' success relies only partly on their ability to recall information. Their jobs actually require far more complex thinking and **application** of knowledge.

Real-world behavior becomes real-world simulation

Let's dump that "identify techniques" objective and instead focus on this action, which describes what the firefighters have to **do**: "Quickly extinguish brush fires."

When we use this kind of focus, it becomes natural to design materials that are based on real-world situations, such as telling a memorable story about a time when a brush fire got out of control because the firefighters failed to extinguish it quickly.

"This is the Clearwater fire of 2007. It started small but..."

Gareth Lovering Photography via Compfight; Creative Commons

This might be our SME talking, giving us ideas for realistic challenges. Or it could be a case study offered as help during a practice activity. For example, we could put our firefighters in a fictional fire that takes place near a ridge. If people ask for help when deciding what to do, they hear a firefighter describe a real situation in which a brush fire got out of control because his crew didn't prioritize the parts of the fire that were heading toward a ridge. Fire spreads faster when it goes uphill, so the situation quickly became serious.

Several case studies like this could offer examples and non-examples to help learners make decisions in the most common situations, all concrete and in context. Thanks to this focus on what people have to **do**, it becomes natural to design realistic activities like the following that simulate the decisions on the job.

It's late March in Clark County. This fire has been spreading slowly in young woods. Winds are calm. Your crew is first on the scene and determines that the fire covers about an acre. There are no structures nearby, and the land is flat.

What's the first thing you do?

bertknot via Compfight; Creative Commons

Because we've focused on what firefighters have to do, we've designed an activity that helps them practice that action. Even though it's just an imaginary situation, it requires them to go beyond simply retrieving information and apply it to a realistic situation.

1. Help the client and SME brainstorm actions

You've written a goal in the middle of your action map, or stuck it on the wall as a sticky note. Now ask, "What do people need to do on the job for us to reach this goal?"

Some people naturally start listing observable behaviors, which is what we want. Others get stuck inside people's heads.

Turn knowledge statements into observable actions

If the client or SME describes something that people should know, understand, or be aware of, don't reject the statement, but don't write it down, either. Instead, ask questions like,

- "If we watch someone do their job, how can we tell whether they understand X? What do they do or not do?"
- "If Clive understands X and Clara doesn't, what do they do differently?"

Consider calling them "tasks" or "behaviors"

If people have trouble with the concept of actions, try calling them "tasks," if that applies to the job. Another term could be "behaviors," but make sure that the behaviors are specific and observable, not vague traits like "be willing to listen to different perspectives."

2. Organize the items into actions and sub-actions

As the client and SME list actions, notice how the actions relate to each other. Some are probably high-level actions, like "Follow the X procedure." Others are sub-actions of that high-level action, such as, "In step 3 of the X procedure, be sure to do Y." When you hear a sub-action, put it on the map as a child, or subordinate, of its high-level action.

Here's an example. I've started a map that shows how I would plan materials that help designers use action mapping — the training version of this book. Here are the actions for the first few steps.

By breaking the actions down like this, I make it easier to get useful answers to "Why aren't they doing this?" and if activities will be useful, I'll be able to design highly targeted ones.

The map is organized vertically. The goal is to the left, and all the actions appear to the right, in the order in which they're completed. That's the format I like to use for procedures.

Others like to use round maps that look more like conventional mind maps, and still others turn the vertical map on its side so it looks like an organizational chart.

The organizational-chart layout might be useful if your stakeholders have trouble understanding that everything in the map has to support the business goal. However, it might get a little crowded as you add activities, notes from discussions, and ideas for information.

Don't interrupt the brainstorming

At this point, the client and SME could be listing lots of actions. Don't stop them to ask how exactly each action relates to another or to push them to be more specific. Just get their ideas down, putting the obvious sub-actions on the map below their parent actions, and let the brainstorming continue until it slows down. Then you can revisit the actions as described below.

3. Periodically review the actions and make them more specific

There will probably be an initial brain-dump of lots of actions. Then people will pause and seem to run out of ideas. That's your cue to focus on the actions that seem too broad and ask for more specific statements.

For example, you might have an action that says, "When socializing with potential clients, avoid the appearance of impropriety." This is too broad. What does "impropriety" actually look like, and how specifically do we avoid it?

A more specific action is, "When offered a gift valued at more than 100€ by a potential client in Zekostan, reject the gift using culturally sensitive methods X, Y, and Z." There should be several more of these covering the highest priority situations and most common cultures. You could list them as sub-actions under the broad "appearance of impropriety" action.

Don't skip this step! A common mistake is to stop when the actions are still too broad, and the consequences of this are grim.

For example, if you allow "Avoid the appearance of impropriety" to stand unchallenged, your analysis later on will sound like this:

> **You:** So, what makes it hard for people to avoid the appearance of impropriety?
>
> **SME:** We work in a lot of cultures where gift-giving and socializing are important for business, and no one wants to seem rude, so they accept things they shouldn't.
>
> **You:** What do you want people to do instead?
>
> **SME:** Don't do or accept anything that an outsider could interpret as improper.

You can't do anything with this. You can't identify job aids, procedures, or practice activities that could actually help people change what they do. Your only option is to create the too-common generic information dump that reminds people that they should be careful about "impropriety." The eager-to-please employee who has just been offered yak-leather gloves by a prominent Zeko businessman will still say "Thanks!" when they shouldn't.

How to tell if your actions are too broad

Below are the main symptoms of a too-broad action.

- It's a first draft. Most first-draft actions are too broad.
- You have only a few actions.
- You couldn't film someone as they perform the action (it's not observable).
- The action takes a long time to complete compared to other actions.
- You can't imagine a useful job aid or list of steps for the action (it's not concrete and specific).
- The action doesn't mention how well it should be done.

Ask if a certain standard needs to be reached

You'll probably find that the SME naturally mentions details like when or how often a behavior needs to be performed. However, they might forget to consider the standards that people need to reach.

Let's say that we've been asked to help international aid workers get more of their recommendations implemented in the field. One thing the aid workers need to do is "evaluate a rural medical clinic," which we've put on the action map and have broken down into several sub-actions.

"Once they've done the evaluation," our SME, Freja, says, "they write an improvement plan for the clinic operators to consider." So we add the following to our map:

Write a clinic improvement plan

"And then they give the plan to the operators," Freja says, but we're still mulling over the previous step. We've been hired because recommendations like the improvement plans aren't being implemented.

"Are the aid workers not writing the plan?" we ask. "Or is there a problem with the plans they write?"

"Most people write a plan," Freja says. "The main problem is that no one wants to read it. Most plans are too long and are written like an academic report. Even I don't like to read them, and I'm not trying to run an understaffed clinic during a dengue outbreak."

After some more discussion, we expand the original action to this:

> Write a clinic improvement plan of no more than six pages that achieves a score of 60 or less on the Global Readability Index

We've just gone from potentially asking, "Why aren't they writing a plan?" to asking why they aren't writing a *readable* plan. That's a huge difference. We've moved from a binary "either they do X or not" perspective into a more nuanced consideration of how to get them to do X to a useful standard.

Models can help

The following actions have issues. What's wrong with them?

- Be supportive when a team member wants to talk about a personal concern
- Prioritize sales calls each morning

These actions are hard to evaluate. If we watch someone perform the actions, we probably won't agree if they're doing them correctly. What does "supportive" look like? Prioritize calls in what way?

What if we rewrite the actions like this?

- Apply each step of the Supportive Conversation model when a team member wants to talk about a personal concern
- Each morning, prioritize sales calls according to the Call Priorities guide

The revised actions refer to models or guides. With a model, the action becomes more observable: Has Maude the manager completed step 1 of the model? Did Silas the salesman apply all the factors in the guide when he prioritized his calls?

It might become your job to create the model. For example, if the SME says, "They have to prioritize their calls better," ask, "How should they do that?" If the SME gives a long answer involving several factors and decisions, you might propose that you and the SME create a short guide standardizing how calls should be prioritized.

If you found any useful models during your research, now is the time to bring them up.

Practice: Are these actions good, or should they be rewritten?

Here are some action statements. Which do you think should be rewritten, and why? How would you rewrite them?

a) Respect employees' religious beliefs

b) Correct method for passing scalpels in surgery

c) Distribute a brief agenda at least three hours before each meeting

d) Explain how widgets are certified

e) Follow the correct procedure to pour a foundation

f) Log out of the computer at the end of the day

Here's my take on them.

a) "**Respect employees' religious beliefs**" isn't very observable. This should be rewritten to identify specific behaviors, such as, "Allow subordinates to take leave on religious holidays" and "Avoid commenting on religious attire." Your SME and client should help you identify the important behaviors, based not on abstract knowledge but on mistakes people are currently making.

b) "**Correct method for passing scalpels in surgery**" is a noun phrase, not a verb phrase. It won't help you answer, "Why aren't they doing it?" because it doesn't describe something someone does.

This is a common mistake made by people who treat action mapping as a way to organize content. They don't plan to ask, "Why aren't they doing it?" so they don't use verbs. Instead, they just list "what we should cover." Because they plan to skip the analysis, they'll create training when it's not the right solution, and their activities are likely to be generic knowledge checks.

I'd rewrite this as "Pass scalpels correctly in surgery." This gives us a good base from which to ask, "Why aren't they doing it?"

c) **"Distribute a brief agenda at least three hours before each meeting"** is clear and specific enough to be useful when you ask, "Why aren't they doing it?" If it's important for the agenda to include X, Y, and Z, I'd add those to the action statement.

d) **"Explain how widgets are certified"** is a useful action only if the learners regularly go up to someone on the job and explain how widgets are certified. For example, if the learners are expected to train new staff, this might be a useful action.

However, the statement was probably intended as an enabling objective. It's from Testland – it means, "Prove that you know how widgets are certified." The real action probably has to do with actually getting a widget certified. Maybe it's "Correctly complete widget certification form B-21" or to perform some other step of the certification process. Information on how widgets are certified would be listed later in the process, as supporting knowledge.

e) **"Follow the correct procedure to pour a foundation"** might look good at first, but the procedure has a lot of steps, and each step might have its own challenges. I'd leave this action in the map but break it down into sub-actions. Then we'll be able to ask, "Why aren't they doing this?" for each significant sub-action.

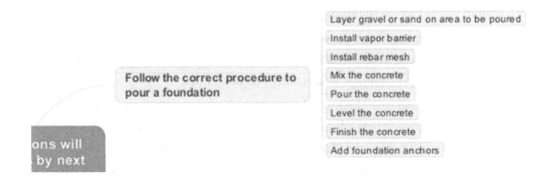

f) **"Log out of the computer at the end of the day"** is a specific, observable behavior, so it passes the test. It's a good base from which to ask, "Why aren't they doing it?"

4. Help the client and SME prioritize actions

At this point, you should have a map with a lot of specific, on-the-job behaviors that people need to perform to reach your goal. But are all behaviors equally important? Probably not.

Have the SME identify the actions that are most important. These might be actions that contribute the most to reaching your goal, are commonly performed incorrectly, or have horrible consequences if skipped.

These are the actions you'll concentrate on in the next step, when you ask, "Why aren't they doing it?" If resources are limited, these are also the actions you'll prioritize in the solution you develop.

You might aim for five to ten top-priority actions, depending on the complexity of your project.

If you're using mind mapping software, you might use a vertical layout instead of the round approach, so you can list the actions from most important to least. Another method is to label the high-priority actions, such as giving them flags.

"But they have to KNOW stuff!"

This action mapping step can be challenging for people who were taught to write traditional instructional objectives. So, let me repeat:

> *I'm not saying we should never consider what people need to know.*
> *I'm just saying that **now is not the time**. That time comes later.*

Right now, you're just trying to answer the first of these two questions:

- What do they need to do?
- Why aren't they doing it?

By focusing on what they need to **do**, not know, you'll examine all possible causes of the problem. You'll avoid assuming it's all due to a lack of knowledge. Later in the process, you'll examine what people need to know in order to complete the actions you're listing now.

Common challenges

Below are some challenges you might face at this point, with some suggestions for things to try.

You have only three or four actions.

- This is a strong sign that your actions are too broad, like "Follow the X procedure" or "Help coworkers manage change." Can you break them down? For example, consider dividing procedures into their steps, using a model to translate a vague statement into concrete actions, or limiting each action to what someone can do in a certain amount of time, such as 20 minutes.

You have a huge number of actions.

- Is your audience too diverse, covering too many different jobs? Consider breaking your project into smaller projects for different jobs.

- Are your actions so specific that one practice activity could easily cover several of them? Consider grouping them as sub-actions under the main behavior.

- Have your SME identify the most common mistakes or highest-impact behaviors and focus on those.

The actions contain words like "understand" and "appreciate."

- Encourage the stakeholders to describe how an observer could tell whether someone "understands" or "appreciates" the thing. If Mary understands X and Mario doesn't, how could we tell by watching them do their jobs? What does Mary do differently? Rewrite the action to describe that behavior.

An action is vague, like "Prepare effectively before giving a presentation."

- Ask the SME what the action looks like. For example, ask, "If I were to make a video of Sally preparing effectively for her presentation, what would the video show her doing?"

- Ask if there's a model you can use, such as "Five Steps to an Effective Presentation."

Your actions include test words like "identify" or "list."
Ask,

- "Do people have to simply 'identify X' on the job, or are you referring to knowledge that helps them do something? What is that thing they do?"
- "If we record a video of two people doing their jobs, and only one of them can identify X, how could we tell by watching the video?"
- "Does anyone literally write this list during a typical day on the job? What does knowing the list help them do?"

You have an action called "follow the procedure."

- Break it down into several actions, possibly one for each major step of the procedure.

Some actions describe basic tasks that everyone is doing without problems.

- It's often helpful to list all the steps in a procedure so there aren't any gaps, even if some of the steps are easy and don't cause problems. However, make sure the SME prioritizes the actions, giving top priority to the behaviors that are the most problematic.

The client says they can't list actions because this is "welcome to the company" training.

- As mentioned in the chapter on goals, training probably won't be your only solution to this problem. For example, making it easier to find information on the intranet is likely to reduce the need for new-hire training. Assigning newbies to mentors will give them tailored help that generic training can't provide. You might also want to question the client's decision to provide one solution for all new employees.
- With all those caveats, there probably are behaviors that the client wants to see. They could include:

  - Don't quit immediately (in other words, understand the culture, feel like part of the team)

  - Choose your health plan or other benefits before the deadline

  - Don't pester your coworkers with lots of basic questions — use the info on the intranet

  - Commit to following our rules

  - Take advantage of the training and other improvement opportunities we offer

Chapter 6. Why aren't they doing it?

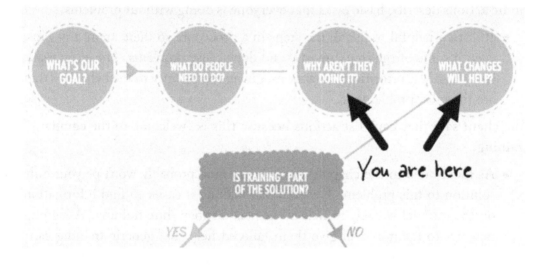

Task	Who does it	How long it might take

For each high-priority task, ask "Why aren't people doing it correctly now?" or "What might make this hard to do?"
 	
    Identify issues in the following categories:
    Environment (tools, culture)
    Skills
    Knowledge
    Motivation (probably caused by problems in the other categories)
    Note ideas for all types of solutions, not just training (job aids, new procedures, improved software...).
	You lead; client and SME participate. Future or recent learners can also be included.	This is probably part of the two-hour meeting you started two chapters ago.
		    Consider restricting the discussion of each action to 10 minutes unless it clearly reveals major issues.
		    So, if you have five high-priority actions, you could spend less than an hour on this.

Tool: Problem analysis flowchart, available at map-it-book.com
Results:

- Ideas for many ways to improve performance (not just training)
- Confirmation of whether training really is part of the solution
- Clear identification of which behaviors can be helped by training and which won't benefit

What you've done

You have a business goal and a list of the on-the-job actions that people have to perform to meet that goal. Your SME has identified the highest-priority behaviors.

You're probably still in your kickoff meeting. This could be a good time to have a break and bring in some future or recent learners. If your project is big, you might consider setting up a separate meeting for this step, depending on how long it took to complete the previous step.

What you'll do

For each high-priority action, you'll ask, "Why aren't they doing it?" or "What could make it difficult?"

You're still on the "action" ring of the map, but you're adding notes. These notes could be ideas for solutions, as shown below, and they could record why the specific behavior is problematic, such as, "The login process is confusing."

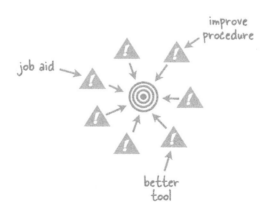

You'll follow these steps:

1. Prepare to ask, "Why? Why? Why?"
2. Consider creating a persona
3. Choose one high-priority action and make sure it's specific
4. Decide which approach to take: directive or open
5. Introduce the flowchart
6. Start with the environment category (directive approach)
7. Add notes and ideas to the map
8. Ask about skill, knowledge, and motivation
9. Repeat for the other high-priority actions
10. Review the map and help the client see solutions
11. Summarize the meeting in writing

Who's involved?

You might think that only the SME needs to be involved here, since they know the tasks better than the client. However, **try to keep the client involved.**

This step helps people see whether training will be necessary and how it could help. A course-obsessed client can lose their obsession in this step and realize that there are better, more flexible solutions.

It can also be helpful to have more than one SME at this point. Their discussion and possible disagreements will help you and the client see the possible causes of the problem more clearly.

Finally, it can be a good idea to include someone who recently learned to do the task, or a future learner who's struggling to do it. They'll help identify why the task is difficult and probably counteract the SME's or client's tendency to see every problem as a knowledge problem.

If you can't include any learners now, you could do this step with just the SME and client and then meet separately with the learners. However, it's best for the SME and client to hear what future or recent learners have to say.

How long it might take

This step could take an hour or two, assuming you have five to 10 actions to consider. You might aim to discuss each action for no more than 10 minutes, unless it becomes clear that the action has opened a can of useful worms.

Tools you'll use

You'll use the following flowchart. Download a full-sized version from map-it-book.com.

Why this matters

In this step, you'll identify the barriers between the workers and the business goal and brainstorm ways to remove the barriers. You'll make sure to design training only when training will actually help, and that training will be based on a deep understanding of the problem. You'll recommend more effective, non-training solutions for other parts of the problem.

DON'T SKIP THIS STEP!

I've seen designers skip this step. Don't join them!

This is the most important step. If you skip this and just agree that training is the only solution, you could waste huge amounts of money and time. A lot of that wasted time will be yours, because you're guaranteed to design unnecessary training. You'll also doom yourself to being an order taker.

Also, if you skip this step, you might as well throw away your goal. You can't reach a goal if you don't identify and remove the barriers in your way. You'll have no impactful way to measure the effect of your hard work.

So don't skip this. Really. It doesn't take long, and it can turn you into a money-saving, problem-solving hero.

Finally, if someone has taught you action mapping without this step, they haven't taught you the complete model. Without this step, it isn't action mapping. It's arranging content in a mind map. If you're in a conference or class and the session about action mapping doesn't include this step, you're not getting action mapping. Instead, you're getting, "How to Use a Mind Map to Create Training that Might Be Useless."

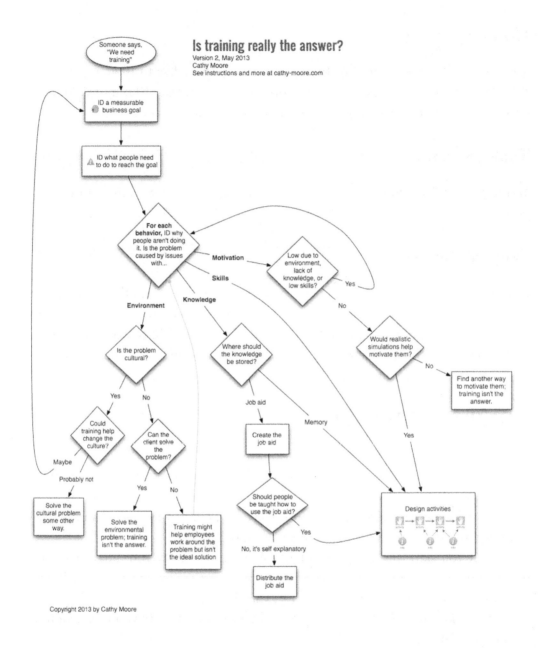

Is training really the answer?
Version 2, May 2013
Cathy Moore
See instructions and more at cathy-moore.com

Copyright 2013 by Cathy Moore

"But I can't do this step, because we're training them on something new."

If you're supposed to help people do something they've never done before, you might think this step doesn't apply to you.

For example, if you're supposed to show people how to repair the brand-new, never-seen-before widget accelerator, you might think that the only answer to

"Why aren't they doing this?" is "They don't know how, because it's new." Then, of course, the only solution is training!

But you don't get to skip ahead that easily. You're going to ask a variation of the question. Instead of asking, "Why aren't they doing this?" you'll ask, **"What might make this difficult?"**

Your goal is to identify current and **potential** barriers to performance. Even if the main barrier seems to be simple ignorance, many more barriers will be waiting for people on the job. You want to identify them now and decide how you'll deal with them, because your goal is to improve performance, not just design training.

1. Prepare to ask, "Why? Why? Why?"

Your strategy will be simple: Keep asking "Why?" for each high-priority action until you can find the real reason it's a problem. The flowchart will remind you what to ask about.

You won't settle for the first answer, because it's rarely the real answer. For example, let's say that our client says they want to reduce ethics violations. The target audience is store managers, and the highest-priority behavior is, "File accurate performance reports." Too many managers are falsifying those reports, claiming better performance than they're actually getting. We start with one "why" question about that highest priority behavior.

Q. Why are the managers falsifying their reports?

A. Because they want to look good more than they want to tell the truth.

What would happen if we stopped and accepted that answer? We might assume that the managers need some sort of corrective message: "Telling the truth is more important than filing impressive figures." That could easily spawn finger-wagging ethics training.

Instead, let's keep asking, "Why?"

Q. Why are they willing to lie just to look good?

A. Because they know that the most important goal is for them to meet all their quotas, even though they can't.

Q. Why can't they meet their quotas?

A. We have too many quotas, and they're all equally important.

Q. Why don't you reduce the number of quotas?

A. Every leader has their own favorite quota, and it's politically impossible to cut any of them.

Q. Why don't the store managers ask for help instead of filing a false report?

A. Their bosses expect them to solve their own problems. If you ask your boss for help, you'll probably hear, "Don't be a wuss. Just get it done."

At this point, would you say that the store managers need ethics training? If training has any role in helping to solve this problem, who needs the training? The report-filing managers, or their "Just get it done" bosses? Or someone else?

This is the most powerful step of action mapping, because it can break open a "simple" problem to reveal bigger issues. You could end up significantly changing the project and have a real impact on people's lives.

2. Consider creating a persona

The discussion you've had so far should have revealed a lot about the audience for your project, including their roles and tasks. Now, you might consider helping the client and SME create a persona, which is a fictional character that represents a typical performer and future learner.

For example, let's say our project is for government workers in the US who need to process claims more quickly, so people who are being helped by the agency get their money on time. The client helps us create a fictional person to represent the typical performer.

We name her Patty, and we make her a native English-speaking woman aged 47 with an associate's degree who has spent most of her career in client-facing roles in government agencies. She has two school-aged children, and her husband works for the post office. She prefers meeting face-to-face with clients, so she tends to procrastinate on her data-entry tasks and gets quickly frustrated with the poor usability of the database.

We gave Patty these characteristics because they represent the majority of the staff involved. She becomes a shorthand way to refer to the people in the job. "How could we make the data entry more appealing to Patty?" we might ask. "For example, can any part of it be more automated? Does she have to enter the same information in multiple places?"

As you create the persona, look for answers to the following questions.

- How experienced are they with the job behaviors that need improvement?

- How do they feel about this aspect of their job, and why?

- How did they respond to previous attempts to fix the problem?

- Where are they located? Do they work with colleagues in other time zones?

- Are there any cultural considerations, such as a preference for solo or group work?

3. Choose one high-priority action and make sure it's specific

You'll go through this process several times, once for each high-priority action. It doesn't take long — aim for about ten minutes for each behavior — and the payoff is great. You'll find quick non-training solutions and begin to get the understanding you need to design challenging activities.

Now, pick an action that the stakeholders have identified as high priority. It should have serious consequences or be something the client clearly cares about. Make sure it's a specific action, like, "In step 3 of the X procedure, get the customer to identify A." Don't use a broad action like "Follow the X procedure," because it won't give you useful information.

Example

Let's say we have a home construction business, and we want to decrease the complaints we've been receiving from our customers. One of the many things our workers need to do is pour a foundation and slab, and customers have been complaining that their slabs have cracks and rough finishes.

Earlier, we broke "pour a foundation" down into sub-actions. We prioritized those actions, deciding to focus only on the two that are causing the most trouble: workers aren't mixing the cement in the right proportions for the conditions, and they aren't finishing the slab well. Both of these would cause cracks and a rough finish.

Those are the only two steps of the procedure that we're going to analyze, because they're the ones that are causing the problem we're trying to solve.

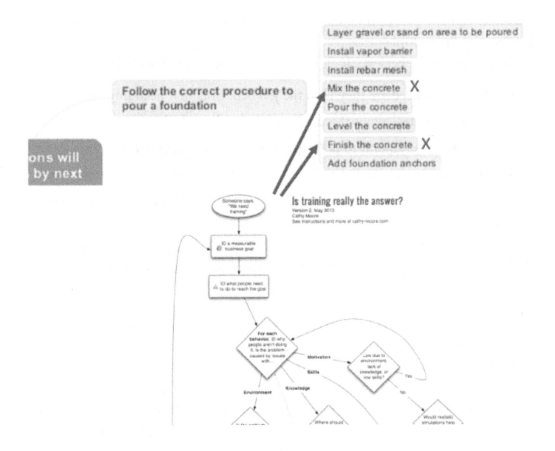

So we're going to ask, "Why aren't people using the right mix for the weather and type of slab? Do they not know what the right mix is? Do we not provide the right ingredients in the first place? Are they rushing to create the mix or doing it in bad conditions because we don't allow enough time for weather delays in the construction schedule?" and so forth.

Those questions are going to get us far more useful information than focusing on the big, vague "follow the procedure" action.

Don't ask about the entire project

Don't ask, "Why aren't they doing what we need them to do?" just once for the entire project. That won't find useful solutions because it's so broad. Instead, identify the five or six actions or sub-actions that are causing most of the trouble, and run each one through the flowchart on its own.

4. Decide which approach to take: directive or open

You're about to ask your client and SME to consider problems in four categories: environment (tools and culture), knowledge, skill, and motivation.

You need to decide whether you're going to direct them to focus on one category at a time, or you're going to be open to whatever they suggest.

Directive sounds like this: "Let's look at the environment category first." Open is, "Why aren't people doing X? Is there a problem with the tools they're supposed to use, are they under a lot of pressure, do they just not know how...?"

Use the directive approach if people seem focused on knowledge

If any of your stakeholders seems to have concluded that people aren't performing Action X simply because "they don't know how" or "they don't know any better," take the directive approach. You'll control which category to examine first, and it won't be the knowledge category.

Here are the symptoms of someone stuck on knowledge:

- They wanted to write a goal based on "understanding" or course completion.

- The actions they proposed often included test verbs like "define" or "describe."

- They had trouble describing an action in observable terms; they wanted to stay inside people's heads.

If you don't take charge, the stakeholder will zoom straight to the knowledge category, where they'll just confirm their possibly hasty conclusion that the problem is entirely due to a lack of information and that putting that information into brains will solve it.

Instead, you'll direct them to look at the environmental category first, to open their mind to other possibilities.

Use the open approach if people seem willing to talk about more than knowledge

You can take the open approach if your stakeholders have been talking about what people need to do (not know) and have mentioned tools that are possibly failing them, processes that might be too complex, or emotional or cultural pressures. You'll let their responses to your questions suggest which branch to examine first.

Your stakeholders can safely use the open approach if they:

- Easily created an observable, measurable goal

- Listed observable actions instead of describing knowledge

- Made comments that acknowledge problems in the job context, like, "They're supposed to use the X job aid, but it's a mess."

The following instructions use the directive approach. For an example of the open approach, see the example at the end of this chapter.

5. Introduce the flowchart

Project or share a printout of the flowchart.

Remind people of the action you're focusing on. Tell them you'll ask them to consider how problems in each of four categories might affect performance of the action. As you go down the path for each category, everyone will get ideas of ways to solve the problem. You'll focus on one category at a time.

Often, barriers from several categories affect each action, but it's usually possible to identify which category is causing the most trouble. This helps you decide if training will be part of the solution and uncover other solutions at the same time.

Here's how the flowchart begins. It asks people to consider four categories: environment, knowledge, skill, and motivation.

6. Start with the environment category (directive approach)

Remind people of the action you're talking about, and ask, "Is there something in the work environment or organizational culture that keeps people from performing this action well?"

This is a huge category in which I include the following:

- Missing or poor tools
- Lack of support from management
- Lack of incentives, or punishment for doing it correctly
- A physically challenging environment, such as a noisy workplace
- An emotionally challenging environment, such as having to deal with upset people
- Issues with the organization's culture, such as backstabbing coworkers or information hoarding
- Poor hiring decisions, such as putting the wrong person in the job

Examples of environmental problems

- **Bad tools:** I might know how to wrangle widgets, and I might have the skills to do it, but if the widget wrangler is old and keeps locking up, I can't perform to the required standard.
- **Hard-to-use information:** If the widget-wrangling manual is a pain to use, I'll just make things up as I go along and fail to use the correct procedure.
- **Pressure and culture:** If I'm expected to wrangle too many widgets too quickly, I'll screw up. My boss might refuse to listen to my concerns about the pressure because the company has a macho culture and the unofficial motto is "Just get it done."
- **Punished for doing it well:** If I become a good widget wrangler and my boss notices, they might actually punish me by making me wrangle even more widgets, which is boring. When my colleagues notice that, they'll make sure they don't wrangle widgets well.
- **Information hoarding:** If I figure out a good way to wrangle and I'm rewarded for it, I might not be willing to teach colleagues how to do it, because information-hoarding is the only source of power in the organization.
- **Wrong person in the job:** I might not have the manual dexterity to wrangle widgets. I actually wanted a marketing job with the company but was hired instead for widget wrangling. They've put the wrong person in the job.

Questions to ask

- Do people have the right tools to perform the task?

- Do they have enough time to do it well? If not, can we give them more time? If we can't give them more time, can we lower the required standard of performance?

- Where is the information that people need to perform the task? Is it easy to find and use? Is it up to date?

- What happens when someone does the task well? Are they rewarded, punished, or ignored by their boss? What do their colleagues do?

- What happens when someone does the task poorly? Does anyone correct them? Do their colleagues cover for them?

- Is there anything physically challenging about the context in which people perform the task? Is there a lot of noise? Are there distractions?

- What's the emotional context of the task? Are people feeling pressure, fear, or anxiety? Can we reduce the emotional load? If so, how?

- Does the organization have a "just get it done" culture that shows impatience with people who struggle, or do people feel comfortable asking for help?

- Does the culture reward people who become the lone expert, or are employees encouraged to share information?

- If an environmental factor is the major reason an action isn't being taken correctly, can we fix that factor, or do we need to help people work around it?

- If the action is brand new, is there anything we can change in the workplace to make it easier to carry out?

Emotionally tricky situations

A common mistake is to overlook the emotional challenges of a task. A classic example is having to deal with an upset customer. It's hard not just because you have to calm someone else down, but because you also have to manage your own reactions.

Some people will shut down and end the difficult conversation too quickly. Others will read disagreement as a personal affront and escalate the discussion, and still others will turn into anxious people-pleasers and give away too much. You need to understand what's happening so you can help people manage their reactions.

Even apparently mundane tasks, such as filling out a report, can be charged with emotion. Will my widget-wrangling progress report make me look good to others, or will I feel shame? Should I tweak it so I look better?

Encourage the client and SME to consider the emotional context of the task. Try to surface the common beliefs or emotional reactions that appear to trigger bad decisions. You'll also want to consider the effects of culture.

Cultural problems

Every organization has a unique culture that shapes how its employees behave, and it's probably contributing to your performance problem. But what does "culture" refer to?

One way to analyze a world culture is to identify the mental models that influence behavior. For example, one culture might believe, "Every individual should pursue what he or she wants," while another culture's model is, "The wishes of the group are more important than the desires of one member." These beliefs shape people's decisions in that culture.

The same is true of the micro-culture within an organization. The problem you're trying to solve is probably affected by beliefs that are part of the organization's culture.

For example, let's say that repeat sales of our widgets are poor because too many widgets are defective. The responsibility for the problem is probably shared by a wide range of people, from the widget designers to the makers and shippers, and including the customer support representatives, who should be reporting the common complaints they receive.

At each point, people make decisions: Should I look more closely at this widget? Should I mention this possibly minor problem? Should I share my idea for how we could make better widgets?

How might the following organizational beliefs affect people's decisions?

- "We're the low-price champions. We barely make a profit, so money is tight."

- "Our widget designers are the best in the industry. They're widget gods whose expertise should never be questioned."

- "Efficiency is everything. Our process works like clockwork and can't change."

- "You're either for us or against us. Any suggestion for improvement will be interpreted as a complaint coming from someone with a bad attitude."

- "Our widgets are just a commodity. They don't play an important role in the world."

Sheep or tiger?

As you go through the environmental branch of the flowchart asking "why" questions, notice the type of answers you're getting. Below, leadership consultant Fred Kofman identifies two types of responses. Which one are you hearing?

> *A sheep and a tiger arrive at the office, both of them wet. "Why are you wet?" we ask.*
>
> *The sheep says, "Because it rained."*
>
> *The tiger says, "Because I didn't bring my umbrella."*
>
> *Both are subject to the same reality. We're all subject to forces outside our control. The question is, are these forces something that control you, or are they information you take into account when making decisions?*
>
> *— Fred Kofman in a presentation at Universidad Francisco Marroquín, Guatemala City, in 2014; translated and paraphrased by Cathy Moore[1]*

Are you getting wet-sheep answers to your questions? If so, try rephrasing them to uncover the decisions that were made. In the example above, we could ask the sheep an additional question, like, "Is there anything you could have done to avoid getting wet?"

Simple reactive answers like, "The gaskets that I'm given are defective" or "The software is hard to use" need follow-up questions. Why are we buying defective gaskets? Why are we giving people user-hostile software? **What decisions are being made, and why are we making them?**

But can L&D fix culture?

We might not be able to turn around a problematic culture, but it's immensely helpful to identify the beliefs that shape how people make decisions. Then we can begin to create change at the root by surfacing and challenging the beliefs.

That's why I made you slog through a lot of material about mindset before we started applying action mapping. I think the biggest problem affecting our design work is our habit of blindly following the school model. The main problem is our culture, not our skills or knowledge.

How will the environment affect the success of the solution?

While you're considering the environment, look for how it might help or hurt any solutions that you suspect are necessary. Even if nothing in the environment is causing the problem, is there anything that could impede your solution? How will the context of the job support or interfere with the new behaviors you're trying to inspire? What should managers do? What changes might be necessary?

> *The key lesson here is that if you want to change someone's behavior, their context — the environment and situations in which they operate — has to act like a life-support machine for the new, desired behavior.... This is why one of the most consistent findings from research into the effectiveness of development activities such as coaching and training is that contextual factors (what happens outside the coaching or training room) are **more** important in ensuring behavior change happens than the quality of the training, development workshop, or coaching.*
>
> *— Nik Kinley and Shlomo Ben-Hur, Changing Employee Behavior: A Practical Guide for Managers (2015)*

Don't skip this branch!

It's rare to see a performance problem that doesn't have a substantial environmental component, and addressing these components can greatly reduce the need for training. For example, often a job aid or easier-to-use manual is the answer, not training, so your solution is to create or fix the job aid. You're likely to find other problems that the client can easily solve, once they see them. That's why it's a good idea to start with the environment branch.

Other times, an environmental problem won't be easily fixed, so your solution needs to work around it. For example, if people are required to wrangle widgets very quickly and that requirement can't be changed, your solution will need to help people wrangle widgets as quickly as possible to meet acceptable standards, not perfection. You'll want to identify any issues in the workplace that slow down wrangling, in addition to showing people how to do the task quickly. In that environment, any solution that says that widget wrangling as a fine art in which we should all aim for perfection will fail.

7. Add notes and ideas to the map

Add notes to the action map identifying how you plan to address each behavior. If you're using mind-mapping software, you probably have enough room to include some notes about why people aren't performing the action.

Here's an example from my map for training about action mapping. I added notes in a box connected to the high-priority actions.

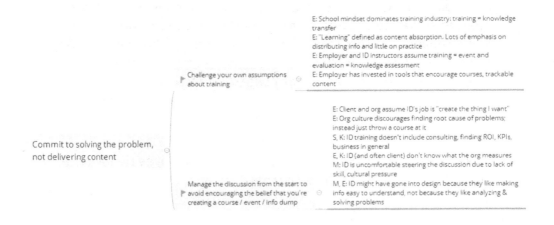

You'll notice a lot of Es representing environmental problems. In this case, they're mostly cultural. S and K represent skill and knowledge problems. An occasional M for motivation appears, but I blame it on cultural pressure and poor preparation by instructional design programs.

The "Why aren't they doing it?" or "What makes it hard?" discussion should bring up ideas for non-training solutions, which you can also add to your map. Here's how I did it for the "manage the discussion" action above.

"What makes this hard?" elicited an idea for a specific sub-action that will help designers deal with the environmental issues. It also spawned several ideas for what, in an ideal world, leadership and HR would do to make the "manage the discussion" action easier.

You're asking, "What makes this hard?" for only the high-priority actions. As a result, some actions in your map will have these notes, and others won't.

E: Client and org assume ID's job is "create the thing I want"
E: Org culture discourages finding root cause of problems; instead just throw a course at it
S, K: ID training doesn't include consulting, finding ROI, KPIs, business in general
E, K: ID (and often client) don't know what the org measures
M: ID is uncomfortable steering the discussion due to lack of skill, cultural pressure
M, E: ID might have gone into design because they like making info easy to understand, not because they like analyzing & solving problems

the start to
that you're
fo dump

Keep the initial discussion short & focused on the performance problem, not the assumed solution. Don't promise to deliver the solution that the client has assumed. Goal is to schedule kickoff meeting.

Leadership: Determine why managers are assuming that throwing a course at a problem will solve it; provide support for identifying root cause of problems

L&D leadership: Make clear designers' job is to help solve performance problems, not "turn this content into a course"

HR: Hire designers who want to consult, solve problems; prefer candidates with business experience or interest

8. Ask about skill, knowledge, and motivation

In the directive approach, you started with the environment category to get the client and SME to think about the context of the learner's jobs. They were probably over-focused on what should be installed in learners' brains, and you've helped relax that focus.

Now you'll let them talk about brains, but because they've considered the environment first, they'll be more likely to see how changes to the workplace could help.

Skill

If necessary, explain that a skill is an ability to carry out a task involving things, people, or ideas. It gets better with practice.

Some people confuse cognitive skills with knowledge. For example, people learning Spanish need to know the patterns used to conjugate verbs for the familiar and formal versions of "you." But just knowing the rules isn't enough. Spanish learners also need to quickly choose the correct level of formality for each person who talks to them and conjugate verbs correctly on the fly while speaking a sentence. Simply knowing the formulas isn't enough. They need lots of practice applying them in the real world.

Questions to ask:

- Do people lack the mental or physical skills to do the action correctly?
- Does the task make them feel awkward or clumsy?

123

- Can they do the task, but not quickly or fluently enough?

- Do they freeze up in difficult situations?

- Would they get better with practice?

- Would it help for them to develop some metacognitive skills, such as recognizing and managing their emotions?

- Could people build the necessary skill on the job? For example, can they practice and make mistakes on the job without causing serious damage, or should they practice in a safe place?

Examples

If I know how to wrangle widgets but I'm clumsy at it, dropping widgets and holding the wrangler wrong, I need to improve my skills.

Or if I'm supposed to use "active listening" when customers call me to complain about miswrangled widgets, I might know what "active listening" is and be able to describe it on a test, but I still need to practice actually **doing it** during a conversation, or I'll just stammer awkwardly. I need to develop a skill, not just knowledge.

Keep asking "Why?"

Even if it's clear that lack of skill is a component of the problem, don't stop your "why?" questions. For example, why can't the widget wranglers we hire actually wrangle widgets? Are we hiring the wrong people? If so, why are we hiring the wrong people? (Hello again, environment branch!)

Knowledge

Most people who came to you looking for "a course" will try to put everything in this branch. Make sure you keep asking "why" to uncover whether the problem really is so simple.

Questions to ask:

- Do people know that they're supposed to perform the action?

- Do they know how to do it?

- Do people know how to do it, but they don't know how well they're supposed to do it?

- Do they know why they're doing it? Do they know how the quality of their work affects their colleagues or customers?

- Do people think they know it, but they have the wrong information in their heads?

- Do they actually know the necessary information but fail to apply it? Why?

- If they don't know something, **why don't they know it?** For example, is there a manual they're ignoring? If so, why are they ignoring the manual? Is it too hard to use or filed somewhere that's too hard to get to?

- Were they "taught" the necessary information before? If so, why didn't the teaching work?

- Once they know the information, will they be able to apply it?

Keep asking "why?" until you're sure you see the root of the problem. You could easily end up back on the environmental branch, because many "knowledge" problems can be solved by improving resources or communication. You might also end up revisiting the skill branch as stakeholders realize that just installing the information in people's brains might not be enough.

Job aids often reduce training

If the information can just be distributed as a PDF, supplied as a reference on mobile phones, or delivered through a help screen, there's often no need for training activities. You design the information, make sure it's self-explanatory by testing it on some future learners, and you're done.

If your job aid is complex, you might end up designing activities. However, they won't be memorization drills; instead, they'll be practice activities that help people use the job aid.

Memory or job aid?

If the problem really does seem to be caused by a lack of knowledge, SMEs often assume that the knowledge should be memorized, not stored in a job aid or other resource. Being an expert, they've got that knowledge in their head, so they assume others should also store it in their heads. But is it really necessary for newbies to memorize it?

125

Here's a little flowchart that you might use with a memorization-happy SME. It will help you make sure that people really need to memorize the information to complete the task.

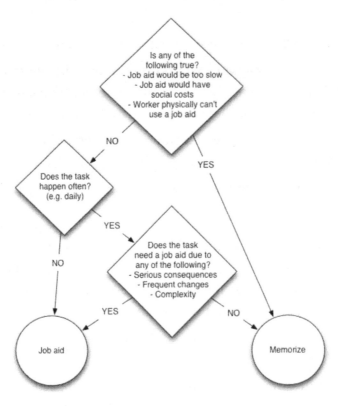

At the first decision point, the flowchart has you consider the social costs of using a job aid. That refers to how the person's use of a reference could affect their credibility or trustworthiness.

For example, imagine you've gone to an orthopedist. "My knee hurts," you say. "It's worst in the morning and when I'm climbing stairs."

"Hmm," the doctor says. "Wait a sec while I look that up."

How would you feel about that doctor? That's the social cost of their reliance on job aids.

If the worker "physically can't use a job aid," they're too busy doing the task to refer to something. For example, an emergency responder in the middle of performing CPR on a patient won't be able to look at a long checklist.

The central decision point has you consider whether a frequent task has high consequences. If so, the chart says you should use a job aid. An example would be the procedures an airplane crew goes through to prepare for takeoff. They do the same procedures many times each day, but they still might be required to use a checklist because the consequences of missing a step could be fatal for everyone.

Have people share their work

If people could be encouraged to share their knowledge informally, you might remove the need for training.

In *Show Your Work* (2014), Jane Bozarth gives many examples of ways that staff can share knowledge, skills, and, importantly, the elusive "how I think as I do this thing." It's most useful to share a work in progress, showing how it's done, than to just show the final product.

People can share their work through blog posts, quick videos, and any other fast, informal method. It should be as easy as possible. "Sharing work should be an organic activity in the everyday workflow," Jane writes, "not some separate overengineered process that eventually proves to be nothing but more work."

Some options include:

- Create a quick video of a top performer completing the task while thinking aloud
- Connect experts and novices through simple technology, such as a Skype video call
- Help people create a collection of lessons learned
- Find a tool that makes it easy for people to share how-to information and tips

It's especially useful to share mistakes. For example, your client might already perform after-action reviews or have a collection of lessons learned that could be shared more widely so everyone can learn from the misadventures of a few.

These lessons are also rich fodder for more formal training activities. For example, when I worked on a project with the US Army, the design team had access to a collection of short stories from the field, called "critical incidents." Each incident was a true event in which the people involved discovered an especially good or bad way to do things.

We used some of those incidents to create branching scenarios. In the scenarios, learners faced the same challenge that happened in the incident, and their options included the same good or bad decisions that people made in real life.

Aim for acceptable performance, not expertise

Finally, it can help to remind your SME that people need to perform to an **acceptable** level. They don't all need to be experts like the SME for the organization to reach its goal.

If you haven't already, it can help to identify a good-but-not-expert performer and use them as an example. "We need more people to be like Sonia," you might say. "She hasn't memorized X and still does a good job, so we don't need to make everyone else memorize it."

Motivation

I actually don't like this category. I'm including it because it's common to hear someone say, "Oh, they can do it. They just don't **want** to." It's all their fault, not ours.

Hmm, really?

If at first "low motivation" appears to be keeping people from performing the required action, take another look at the other categories. "Low motivation" is usually a side effect of problems with knowledge, skills, or the environment.

Knowledge and skills affect motivation

If I don't know how to wrangle widgets or my skills are poor, I won't want to do the wrangling. I'll procrastinate, and then I'll wrangle only a few widgets, slowly and badly, and I'll complain to my coworkers.

Environment affects motivation

Poor tools, poor management, and other issues with the environment are probably the biggest causes of "low motivation."

- **Bad tools:** If the wrangler is old and stiff, I won't want to use it.
- **No big picture:** If my job is so specialized that I never see the effect that my widgets have on people down the line and my leaders never mention it, I won't care how well I wrangle them.
- **Punished for doing it well:** If I see colleagues get punished for developing their skills, I won't show any interest in developing mine.

- **No reward:** If no matter how well I wrangle widgets, I'm never given more authority, autonomy, or recognition, I won't see any reason to improve.

- **Clash of values:** If the organization has expressed no values that I care about, I won't care about supporting its mission with my widget-wrangling.

- **No voice:** If I propose a better way to wrangle widgets and I'm ignored, I'll wonder why I'm working there at all.

- **Anti-achievement culture:** If the entire culture of the organization has become one of resentment and my coworkers are crabs in a bucket that pull each other down, I'll avoid showing any motivation because motivation would cause me to be shunned or even attacked.

Sometimes, "low motivation" can be surprisingly easy to fix. For example, if people can't see how their work affects others, you could take literally five minutes help them find out.

> *In a 2007 study at the University of Michigan, paid call-center workers had a five-minute conversation with scholarship students who had been directly helped by the school's past fund-raising efforts. They then called potential donors. The interaction with the beneficiaries of past giving was brief, but the effect was profound. One month later, these call-center workers were spending 142 percent more time on the phone with donors than before the study, and donations jumped by 171 percent.*
>
> *— Tracy Maylett and Paul Warner in MAGIC: Five Keys to Unlock the Power of Employee Engagement (2014)*

Solve the original problem to improve motivation

If the "low motivation" is caused by problems in other categories, as it probably is, then solving the original problem should solve the motivation problem. For example, if you give me a new, smoothly working wrangler and reward me with recognition and interesting new duties as my skills improve, my low motivation magically goes away.

If you really can't find any other cause for the apparent lack of motivation, then you might have the wrong person in the job. I'd file that under "environmental problem," because there's a mismatch between the person and the position.

Questions to ask

- If people appear to be unmotivated, could it be caused by weak knowledge, poor skills, or a problem in the environment? (Revisit those branches if necessary.)

- If there does seem to be a genuine problem with motivation, might incentives help? (Incentives include recognition, more autonomy, flexible hours, better pay, etc.)

- If incentives aren't possible, what types of messages might motivate people?

- Are these messages best delivered through training, or are there better ways to deliver them? For example, should they come from leadership and not trainers?

- Would it be useful to ask the marketing department for help with the messages?

9. Repeat for the other high-priority actions

Do the same for the other high-priority actions. It might take about 10 minutes each, unless you uncover major problems that inspire a lot of discussion.

10. Review the map and help the client see solutions

You've been taking notes all this time, probably in the action map. After you've gone through the high priority behaviors, take a step back and help the client and SME see what's happening in the map.

Point out the quick wins that reduce or eliminate the need for training

First, point out the ideas that will reduce or eliminate the need for training and that people in the room can quickly implement or oversee. These could include:

- New or improved job aids, such as tip sheets, help screens in software, or signs on the wall

- Improvements to processes, such as removing unnecessary steps

- Improvements to tools, such as making a form easier to complete or making in-house software easier to use

- Bringing together existing content, such as already-existing videos, and giving people time to use it on the job instead of creating new materials
- The elimination of an action from consideration, for example when a stakeholder realizes that the task isn't really a problem or the client decides the task should be outsourced

With the client and SME, identify who will be responsible for overseeing each change and how long it might take.

The client and SME should see for themselves that these solutions reduce or eliminate the need for training, but you might want to point that out to make sure it's clear.

Point out the slower changes that reduce or eliminate the need for training

Next, look at the ideas for changes that are bigger or politically more challenging and that reduce the need for training. For example, the organization might:

- Set up an incentive system to reward better performance
- Reduce time pressure by adjusting the typical milestones for a project
- Improve the organization's intranet so it's easy to find answers to questions
- Encourage managers to provide a specific type of support
- Add filters to the hiring process to create a better fit between the employee and the job
- Give people "stretch" assignments: Have them apply the new skill or knowledge in a non-vital situation with support
- Have learners shadow more experienced colleagues
- Set aside some time each week for more experienced people to mentor others
- Distribute a list of experienced people who are willing to answer questions
- Create a community of practice, such as an online chat group that meets in person each month, so people can easily share knowledge and tips
- Recommend to leadership that they steer the company's culture in a direction that will reduce the problems you've identified

These bigger changes are probably the client's responsibility, not yours. Ideally, the client helped think of these changes, so they already feel ownership of them.

They should decide which ones have some hope of succeeding and set the changes in motion.

Clarify the role that training will have

Ideally, you've eliminated some actions from training by addressing them through the changes listed above. For the tasks that remain, clarify how training could help, and make clear that **"training" means "practice activities," not an information presentation**.

In general:

- If you see a genuine, confirmed **skill** problem, training could be part of the solution, especially if it helps people practice tricky things in a safe place.

- If you see a genuine, confirmed **knowledge** problem, training might be part of the solution. However, a job aid or other simple information delivery might be a better choice, especially if it provides the information when and where it's needed. If applying the information is tricky, training could help people practice using the job aid.

- If you see an **environmental** problem, fix the problem. If you or the client can't fix the problem, consider whether you could show people how to work around it, in which case training might help.

- If you see a **motivational** problem, fix the problem that's affecting motivation. Training is unlikely to help unless it solves a knowledge or skill problem that's killing motivation.

In all of these cases, by "training" I mean, "practice activities delivered in whatever way works best." I don't mean "a training event," like a one-time workshop or online course. As you'll see in later chapters, we're not designing events. We're designing activities that are part of larger solutions. These activities might be packaged as a training event and they might not.

11. Summarize the meeting in writing

Plan to send a concise email to the participants after the meeting, summarizing what was discovered and what actions will be taken. Clean up the map if necessary and include it.

The discussion probably identified solutions that are beyond the reach of L&D, which you should make clear in your summary. For example, you could say, "For us to meet our goal, in addition to the training we plan to develop, X will need to provide ThisThing, and Y will need to do ThisOtherThing."

If you're required to submit a formal proposal, you might send the meeting summary now but wait to create the formal proposal until you've developed a prototype activity. Then create an outline as described in chapter 14. It will describe how much training will probably be required, what the other solutions include, and who might need to participate in implementing the solution.

Example of the open approach: Grace and the TPS records

We've just seen the directive approach: you direct the client and SME to the flowchart branches in a specific order. Now let's walk through the same process but use the "open" approach.

This example is available as a video on my site. Follow the link to the flowchart at map-it-book.com.

Initial client meeting

Let's say that a client, Grace, comes to us and says, "My organization provides legal help to people around the country. The government requires us to file TPS records. My staff need training on how to complete the records, which are forms in a database. I think an online course would be best, because our offices are spread all over the country and, after all, this is software training."

As often happens, we have a client who has already decided what the solution should be. However, we don't want to design training when there could be a more effective solution. We don't actually tell Grace that. Instead, we're going to let her discover those other solutions through this process.

Set a goal

"Help me understand the problem," we say. "What are you trying to change with the training? How will the performance of your department improve?"

"The records that we complete go to another department for processing," Grace says. "That department says that too many of the records have errors, and they send them back. Right now, 20% of the records are being sent back to us. I want to reduce that to 5% in the next six months."

That's a solid, measurable goal, so we're off to a good start.

List what people need to do

Next, we ask Grace to help us identify the behaviors that people need to perform on the job to reach that goal.

"What do they need to do to reduce the errors?" we ask.

Grace lists several behaviors she'd like to see. The most important ones are:

- Enter the appropriate XR code based on the client's age
- Correctly fill out the fields for the client's name
- Determine whether the record should be flagged

Next, we focus on one behavior at a time and ask Grace, "Why aren't people doing this?"

For each high-priority action, identify why they aren't doing it

Enter the appropriate XR code

Let's start with, "Why aren't they entering the right XR code?"

"There are a lot of codes," Grace says. "People have to go to the code lookup sheet that's on the shared server, and it's a pain to log in. Some people print out the sheet but the codes change every month and they forget to print out the new one, so they enter old codes."

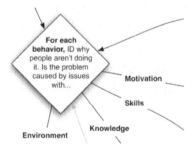

Has Grace described a problem with the staff's environment, such as their tools or management style? Is it a knowledge problem — do they not know where the sheet is? Do people lack the skills to find the sheet, or maybe the motivation?

It sounds like it's mostly environment, with a side effect of low motivation. It's tedious to go into the shared server to get the current code sheet. Workers try to get around this environmental problem by printing out the sheet, and then it gets outdated.

Some environmental problems are caused by company culture. Is the XR code issue a cultural problem, like heavy-handed management or impossible standards? Probably not. It sounds like a simple workflow problem with a technical solution.

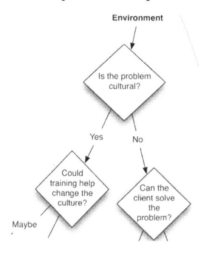

Since they're filling out the forms using software, maybe the software could at least link to the current XR code sheet or, better, display the table in a popup right when the worker needs it. Grace says she thinks that's possible, so for that behavior we end up solving the tool problem.

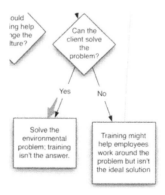

So far, we're not designing any training. We're changing the environment instead by making the current XR code table pop up in the software.

Correctly fill out the fields for the client's name

Earlier, Grace said that people weren't filling out the name fields correctly.

"Why not?" we ask. It sounds like it should be straightforward.

"Most of our staff are native English speakers," Grace says, "but many of the client names are Hispanic, with more than one last name. If a client is named María Lorena Rosas García, some staff will say that her last name is García, but actually we should enter Rosas. The database accepts only one last name, and that's the one we should use."

What type of problem is this? Is it a problem in the environment, a lack of knowledge, a skill that needs to be developed, or a lack of motivation?

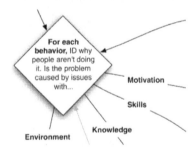

You could argue that it's caused by a factor in the environment, because many client names are Spanish while staffers mostly speak English.

However, the problem isn't really that big. You don't have to learn Spanish to learn how to identify a Spanish speaker's last name for the database. There's a pattern to it, and it's really basic. You just need to know the pattern. It looks like we've got a knowledge problem.

As we go down the knowledge branch, the flowchart asks, "Where should this knowledge be stored?" Should this pattern be stored in each worker's head, or could we put it in a job aid, like a little reminder right there in the software under the name field?

Grace votes for putting it in people's heads. "Staff don't use the names just in the database," she says. "They also need to be able to go out into the waiting room and say, 'Come in, Ms. Rosas,' rather than 'Come in, Ms. García.'"

So, we decide to put this basic information in memory so people will be able to quickly and easily apply it everywhere. This sends us to the "design activities" end node.

We decide that people need just a tiny bit of training. We'll show them the pattern for identifying the last name and give them some practice applying it with a variety of names. It will probably take 10 minutes.

We end up designing a short activity that could be done online, as part of a larger face-to-face event, in a quick webinar — whatever works best for Grace and her team.

Determine whether the record should be flagged

Earlier, Grace said that staff need to determine whether the record should be flagged. It's not as simple as it sounds. There are a lot of conditions to consider.

For example, if the client is employed but is making less than $60,000 and has more than two children, the record would be flagged. However, if the client is unemployed and has the same income from investments or a pension, the record would also be flagged, regardless of children. Got it?

Experienced staff know most of the reasons to flag a record, but new people don't. What's the problem, then? Is it environment, knowledge, skills, or motivation?

We've got another knowledge problem.

Where should this knowledge be stored? It's pretty complicated and only applies to filling out the TPS record. It's not something people have to know all the time, so a job aid sounds like a good idea.

With Grace's help, we draft a decision table that makes it easy to decide whether to flag a record. We run it by some new hires and they show us that they can use it without coaching. It looks like it's self-explanatory and needs no training. We'll just have it pop up at the appropriate place in the software screen.

We've solved another problem with just a job aid.

Final result: Very little training

Grace came to us believing that her team needed training. But we've identified only one behavior that needs to be changed through training, and it's such an easy pattern to learn that the activity will take about 10 minutes.

We've solved the two other problems with job aids. In addition to being less expensive to create, the job aids are likely to be more effective. They help people while they complete the task, standardizing performance without relying on possibly faulty memory.

What if we used the conventional approach instead?

Let's avoid the "work" of going through the flowchart and just give Grace the course she originally envisioned. What does that look like?

We spend many expensive hours creating an online course that starts with "Welcome to the course on completing TPS records." We list objectives like, "At the completion of this course, you will be able to enter the correct XR code."

We "motivate" the learners by talking about the importance of completing the record properly and describing the costs of having our records rejected.

Then we tell people what they already know — that they have to log in to the annoying server to see the XR codes. We walk them through the login process "to make sure everyone knows how" and lecture them on the importance of using the current sheet.

To "teach" the rules for flagging records, we display several slides full of rules, give some examples, and then quiz the learners on whether they can remember the information that they saw ten seconds ago and which they will forget by tomorrow if not later today.

Finally, we include a little activity to help them practice identifying last names.

The 3,000 TPS report creators in Grace's organization obediently spend 30 minutes each going through the course. That's 1,500 hours of staff time.

Within a month, we'll discover that people are still printing out the XR code sheet and failing to flag records properly.

Practice: Which branch of the flowchart is most appropriate?

Which type of problem do you think each of the following statements is describing? Is it mostly a problem with knowledge, skill, environment, or motivation?

a. "People don't want to enter records in the database, so they just send emails, which is wrong."

b. "People make a lot of mistakes when they complete the form."

c. "This policy is new, so no one has had to follow it before."

d. "They're not used to doing it this way, so they need to practice."

e. "They don't care how well they do it, because they never see how it affects customers."

a. "People don't want to enter records in the database, so they just send emails, which is wrong."

Some people might put this in the "motivation" category, but what's causing the motivational problem? If we look at the database, I'll bet we'll see a user-hostile system that's clumsy and slow. That's why people want to send emails. If we make the database easier to use, people will be more willing to enter records. It's an environmental problem because the problem is caused by a poor tool.

b. "People make a lot of mistakes when they complete the form."

The most common reaction to this is to give them training on how to complete the form. This assumes it's a knowledge or skill problem.

But stop that train for a minute and look at the form. Does it make clear what you're supposed to put in each field? If it's common for people to make mistakes filling out a form, the problem is the form. Make it easier to complete and you've solved the problem. This is another environmental problem — it's a bad tool.

c. "This policy is new, so no one has had to follow it before."

This looks at first like a straightforward knowledge problem. Something new has appeared that they don't know about, so we should help them "know."

But take a closer look. Will it be easy to apply the policy, or will it require a lot of interpretation and judgment calls? If it's easy to apply, then yes, they probably just need to "know" about the policy. Before we assume that they need training, we should consider whether just telling them about it is enough. How about an email?

If the policy will be tricky to apply, we need to consider how skills come into play. The skills could include recognizing situations in which the policy applies, interpreting the policy, and applying that interpretation in the appropriate way. We're also likely to spend time in the environment category, because a nuanced and complex policy will probably bump into cultural issues and other workplace barriers.

d. "They're not used to doing it this way, so they need to practice."

They've been doing it the old way, and now they've been shown a new way, but it feels awkward. This sounds like a simple problem with skills, and it goes in the "skills" category.

But before we assume that the best way to improve their skills is through formal training, we should also consider other solutions. Maybe people could be given more time on the job to complete the task as they adjust to the new way, or a more experienced colleague could take 20 minutes to help them practice.

If they're using software, maybe we could give them access to a sandbox, a part of the program where they can't do any damage, and let them practice the new skills without worrying about breaking anything. A "course" might not be necessary at all.

e. *"They don't care how well they do it, because they never see how it affects customers."*

Many people are tempted to label this as a motivational problem, but what's causing the low motivation? It's caused by the fact that they don't know the effects of their work, which points to the knowledge category. However, what's keeping them from knowing the effects? It's the isolated nature of their job and management's lack of communication, both of which are environmental problems.

I'd be tempted to consider this a leadership problem and therefore environmental. The company's leaders should know that there are many cogs that never see anything but their wheel. It's the leaders' job to draw the big, inspiring picture for everyone.

If we can light a fire under the leadership and get them to do their job, that would help solve the problem. Unfortunately, that might not be possible. Instead, this is the kind of problem that really should be solved one way but might have to be imperfectly addressed another way.

If it looks like you'll be creating training for other actions in your map, you could toss this action into the training, too, and, for example, create motivational scenarios in which people finally see the end results of their job decisions.

If you're not going to be creating training, your client might talk to someone with good marketing skills about communicating the big picture throughout the firm, and jump through the necessary political hoops to make that happen.

What about KSAs?

If you've had conventional training in instructional design, you might be used to working with three categories: knowledge, skill, and (usually) attitude, or KSA. Often these are lumped together and referred to as KSAs.

"Knowledge" and "skill" are the same as I've described above. Can you guess why I don't use the "attitude" category?

If you said, "Attitude is shaped by our experiences in the environment and HEY, PEOPLE, WHAT ABOUT THE ENVIRONMENT?" you've spoken my thoughts.

The KSA model lives in the remote clouds of the education world, where the goal is to pour information into brains. As a result, the model focuses on what's happening inside people's heads. It ignores the biggest, ugliest cause of performance problems: the workplace, with all its unwieldy tools and malfunctioning managers.

If we're trapped in learners' heads examining their KSAs, we don't notice and solve a simple environmental problem. Instead, we laboriously train people to work around it.

For example, let's apply the KSA model to this problem: "People aren't completing the form correctly." We immediately zoom into the users' heads to examine the knowledge, skills, and attitudes that live there. We compare those to the optimal KSAs that we need to elicit for successful form completion. Then we design training that's supposed to elicit those KSAs. It doesn't occur to us to simply spend an hour improving the form.

I'm not saying that examining attitudes is useless. For example, it's very helpful to know people's attitude about a task before we encourage them to try it, and the deeper we get into "soft skills," the more that attitudes come into play.

However, there's an entire world out there. It presents very real barriers to performance, and we can't ignore it. Also, it's often easier to change the environment than to climb into people's heads and try to install new attitudes.

A more complete analysis

I've just described the quickest way to do this analysis —go through the flowchart with your SME, the client, and maybe a future learner, asking them about each of the high-priority behaviors.

The order-taking approach to training design does no analysis at all, so you've already taken a big step, even though it didn't take long. However, like every quick solution, this approach has drawbacks:

- You depend on only a few people's opinions.

- Cultural or interpersonal issues might keep participants from raising important problems.
- You miss many contextual cues because you're not seeing the workplace.

To do a more thorough analysis, you have several options.

Go to the workplace and see for yourself

My favorite approach is this:

- Go to the people who are struggling to do the job.
- Watch them work.
- Non-judgmentally ask them what they're doing and why.
- Notice the job aids that they use and the notes that they've made for themselves.
- Notice if they ever open the manual or refer to the standard operating procedure.
- Ask them what would make the task easier. Encourage them to identify all possible changes, not just training. You should get an earful, especially if you're an outsider.
- When you see something that seems difficult or inefficient, ask them non-judgmentally why it's done that way.
- Notice all the barriers to easy, correct work.
- Ask to be introduced to someone who does the task well, and watch them. What are they doing differently than the people who struggled? Is anything different in their environment?

A lot of questions will naturally come up during your visit, such as questions about how easy it is to find information. Here are some additional questions you might ask workers:

- What standard are you supposed to reach as you complete this task? What's acceptable and what isn't? (Look for vague or conflicting standards.)
- Do you get any feedback about how you've done the work? Where does it come from? Is it helpful? (Look for missing or vague feedback, or feedback only about poor performance.)

- What happens to your work product down the line? Where does it go next? (Look for low motivation due to lack of communication about the big picture.)

- What do you like about your job? Why do you do it? (Look for values that you can highlight to help motivate everyone involved.)

In addition to giving you a clearer idea of the problem and possible solutions, your personal experience with the workers will make any activities you design more realistic. You'll have seen the job context, heard the jargon, seen the common challenges, and met people whom you can picture as you design activities.

Gather more information

Also look for additional sources of information, especially any reports that quantify the issue or give you real-life examples of problems. Ask for documents such as:

- Customer complaints
- Staff evaluations
- Audits
- Reports from the help desk listing the most common questions
- Collections of "lessons learned" or after-action reviews
- Examples of people's current work

Consider setting up a quick survey of workers. You could use a simple tool like SurveyMonkey to learn from employees themselves what the barriers are.

If you suspect that the problem is mostly caused by imperfect knowledge and weak decision-making skills, you could create a diagnostic branching scenario to reveal the gaps. You could design a scenario that closely mimics the situation that people face on the job and send it to a large number of people. Treat it as an assessment scenario, meaning players don't have the chance to go back and change their choices. Then you could analyze their choices to see where the gaps lie. What common mistakes do they make?

Let the client do a more thorough analysis

During the quick analysis with the flowchart, the client might realize that they need to learn more about the problem before they continue with the project.

For example, during the flowchart discussion, one of my clients began to suspect that a cultural problem was more severe than they had originally thought. They formed an internal team to investigate with a survey and in-depth interviews. A month later they returned with a much better understanding of the problem and we continued our work with a more effective focus.

Avoid analysis paralysis

Taking five or six actions through the flowchart can take just an hour. Doing the more in-depth analysis described above could take a lot longer. While it's good to dig deeper, make sure you're getting information that **directly applies to the high-priority actions** in your map. In other words, don't research, "How do our employees feel about their jobs?" Instead, you want to answer questions like, "Why do people seem to resist wrangling widgets to the standards we've established?"

Common challenges

Below are some challenges you might face at this point, with some suggestions for things to try.

There are multiple reasons why people aren't performing a task.

- This is normal. If you need to prioritize or narrow down the reasons, ask:
- "If we solved this aspect of the problem, would people still not perform the task?"
- "Which of these reasons can we affect?"

A stakeholder insists that the cause of a problem is laziness or a bad attitude and wants you to motivate people through training.

- Revisit the knowledge, skills, and environmental branches to make sure the alleged laziness isn't a reaction to a separate problem.
- If the problem does appear to be low motivation that isn't a side effect of something else, ask the stakeholder if incentives could be used.

- If no incentives are possible, consider carefully whether training could motivate people. For example, it's possible that you could motivate people with scenarios that show in an emotionally compelling way what happens when the action isn't performed to the necessary standard. However, it might be better to involve marketing staff to build a campaign rather than relying on training to change attitudes. Marketers are experts at influencing people.

The main cause of the problem is a factor in the environment that the client says they can't change.

- Ask around to make sure that you have no power to solve the problem. For example, L&D staff are sometimes surprised to find that they can request changes to a software interface or online reference.

- If the problem is cultural, consider whether training could help change the culture and whether you're targeting the right audience. For example, the cultural issue might be created by the managers of your original audience members, so you might change the focus of the project to those managers.

- If you can't affect the environmental problem, identify how high performers are working around it, and help others use those techniques.

It's taking too long to do this analysis.

- For most projects, this discussion really shouldn't take long. For example, I've seen a team of four people who were new to action mapping analyze six high-priority actions in about an hour, working remotely with a shared screen. If it's taking significantly longer for you, consider the following:

- Did you prioritize your actions? If time is short, analyze only the highest priority actions.

- Are you including too many people in the discussion? Consider limiting it to the subject matter expert, the client, and a current practitioner (recent or future learner).

- Are you trying to analyze multiple audiences at once? Your project should focus on one audience, such as people who all have the same job. If you're supposed to "fix" people who are in vastly different jobs, step back and refocus your goal so each project addresses one audience.

- Who says it's taking too long? If it's a SME who's used to just approving content, it's possible they didn't leave any time in their calendar for this kind of discussion. One option is to politely suggest that having an additional (or different) SME might be helpful since "this is a lot of work for one person."

A stakeholder is concerned that you'll create too many job aids and cause "death by job aid."

- Make clear that the only information that will go into job aids is required to perform the task. History, interesting but nonessential facts, and other optional information won't be included. Job aids will have only the minimum information necessary to guide performance, formatted for quick scanning.

- Show how you intend to organize the job aids, centralizing them if possible. For example, all job aids related to the task go in the same folder on the intranet, or are all under the "help" menu in software.

You can solve the problem with just a job aid, but you're still required to produce training.

- If possible, show the person who requires training how you can solve the problem less expensively, and ask them to move the budgeted funds to another project.

- If it's somehow politically impossible to avoid the requirement for training, design an interesting, challenging activity in which people practice using the job aid to perform the task, or consider turning the "training" into a session in which the learners themselves design the necessary job aid.

Meta-challenge: "It's hard to think this way."

Action mapping as a process is pretty easy. Once you've got a good goal, it's all downhill from there. But changing your mindset — and the mindset of your stakeholders — is another story.

The common "knowledge transfer" approach to training design seems easy because we as designers aren't expected to think very much. We're just supposed to use the client's content, make design decisions based on myths, and follow rules of thumb that came out of nowhere but that everyone treats as truth. In contrast, action mapping can seem hard. You might be struggling with this now.

I'd encourage you to ask yourself, "Is this actually hard, or is it just new? In the long run, will it make my life easier or harder? Which approach, easy or hard, actually supports my values?"

Below, I compare the common "easy" approach and the supposedly "hard" action mapping alternative. The irony is that the "hard" approach can find much simpler solutions and make you and your colleagues happier in your jobs.

If we propagate this "hard" mindset, our jobs will actually become more satisfying. We'll spend less time following irrelevant rules to crank out boring materials that have no effect, and we'll spend more time exploring and solving interesting problems.

Easy?	Hard?
"Please give the invoicing staff some time-management training. There's a backlog of invoices."	"What might be causing the invoicing backlog? Let's follow a typical invoice through the process."
"Convert these slides about proper widget wrangling into a 30-minute online course, and use this template."	"Too many widgets are getting miswrangled. Why?"
"I'd like you to provide a half-day workshop on Leadership Fundamentals at our quarterly gathering."	"We think our managers could be stronger leaders. What's the best way to develop their skills?"
"People complain that this course is boring. Please spice it up with some scenarios and more pictures."	"People complain that this course is boring. Why?"
"People aren't motivated enough to do the task correctly. We need a snazzy video to motivate them."	"People don't seem motivated to do the task correctly. Why?"
"Add pictures for the visual learners, and use a narrator for the audio learners."	"What's the most memorable and effective way to design activities for this topic and audience?"

Chapter 7. Brainstorm activity ideas

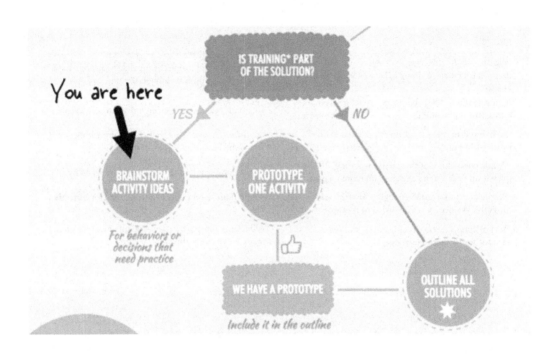

Task	Who does it	How long it might take

For each on-the-job behavior that will benefit from practice, note at least one high-level idea for a practice activity.
    Don't let the client's assumptions influence you. Identify the best activities for the learners, not the client.
	You should do this on your own, though you might ask the SME for help.	You might spend 10 minutes brainstorming for each action that requires practice, possibly more if you need help from the SME.
		    If you're used to creating knowledge checks, consider giving yourself more time until you're used to this approach.

Result: High-level ideas for realistic activities that will help people practice the difficult aspects of the behavior. These are just notes, not scripts. Example: "Parent says they don't want you to give their child the X vaccine, but it's required for school."

What you've done

You've finished your analysis meeting with the client and SME. So far, you've done the following.

- You identified a goal that describes how the performance of the organization will improve.
- You asked what people need to do on the job to reach that goal.
- You had the SME and client identify the most important or problematic behaviors.
- For each important behavior, you asked, "Why aren't they doing it?" or "What makes it hard?"
- For each behavior, you identified non-training solutions, such as job aids or improvements to processes.

You've recorded the non-training solutions in your action map. Maybe you're responsible for creating them, or maybe someone else will do it.

But right now, you'll focus on the actions that you've decided require some sort of training. This is a big step, so I'm spreading it out over several chapters.

What you'll do

Here's what you'll do next:

1. Brainstorm ideas for activities (this chapter)
2. Identify the best format for each activity (the next chapter)
3. Write a typical activity
4. Create a prototype of it and have the client, SME, and learners give you feedback

This chapter focuses on the first step, brainstorming ideas for activities, which are represented by the hand icon in the map below.

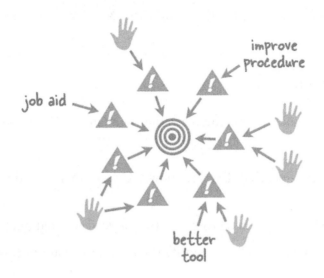

Who's involved?

You should be in charge of brainstorming activities and will probably do this on your own. An enthusiastic SME might help you brainstorm, but avoid letting a fan of fact checks participate, or they'll keep pulling you toward test-style activities. Your goal is to design practice activities, not knowledge checks.

Since you're just working with high-level ideas now, you don't need lots of details from the SME. That comes later. However, if you can't picture clearly what people do on the job, you might ask the SME for help at this step. Make clear you need help understanding the common challenges that people face, not what they need to know.

> **Brainstorm and prototype first!**
>
> In the common approach to training design, you'd now go off to write the "course," sending the content to the SME for correction.
>
> Instead, we're going create **ideas** of activities and determine their best format. Then we'll make prototypes of a few typical activities and test them. We won't actually write many activities until the client, SME, and future users have given their feedback on our prototypes.

Ignore what the client wants, for now

Your client might have assumed a certain type of training would work best, such as an online course or face-to-face workshop. **For now, ignore what the client wants.**

In this chapter and the next, your job is to identify the best type of activity for the learners, not for the client. You'll focus on what will help people most realistically practice what they need to practice, regardless of format and regardless of the client's assumptions.

Once you've identified the best type and format of activities for the learners, you'll convince the client that those ideas will be more effective than, for example, the one-shot course the client is picturing.

If you're required to use a specific format and really, truly have zero power to argue against it (really? you can't even make a suggestion?), you'll at the very least look for ways to reconcile the best approach with the required approach.

What's a "practice activity?"

I've been using the term "practice activity" a lot. But what does that mean?

Let's consider a data privacy course. Does the following question help people practice making the decisions they need to make on the job, or is it more like a test question?

> Tanya wants to work on the salary data on her home computer. On her drive home, she needs to pick up her kids at school and stop for groceries. How should she get the data home?

If you said, "That's a practice activity," I agree. We're asking people to make a decision similar to the decisions they have to make on the job. They're not just recalling information; they're using it to make a realistic decision. The fact that it's text instead of, say, video is irrelevant. It's the decision that matters.

How about this question? Is it a test question or practice activity?

> What's the most secure way to transfer sensitive data to another PC?

That's a test question, because it simply asks people to retrieve abstract information from the clutter in their brain. It's not asking them to also **apply** that information to a realistic situation.

> A test question asks people to recall information. It takes place in an abstract world.
>
> A practice activity asks people to not only recall information but also **apply** it to a specific, realistic situation.

The decision drives the activity

Everything we do consciously is preceded by a decision. I turn on the light because I've decided to do so. I waste money on the powdered-eggplant diet because I decided that the people who sell it were telling the truth.

On the job, our decisions can range from "Which button should I push?" to "What's the best way to set up the scaffolding on this hill?" to "How can I help my team handle the merger?" **Every behavior on your action map is based on a decision.** (If instead you've recorded things they should "understand" or "appreciate," go back and revise your map so it includes only the **actions** that your learners take on the job.)

Practice activities help people practice making those decisions in a safe place, where they can learn from the consequences. These activities break out of the school model because they require people to make realistic decisions, not just store and retrieve information.

What happens after they make a decision?

Earlier, we asked how Tanya should bring the salary data home. Let's say that a learner decides that Tanya should email the data to her home address, tanya445@wowzamail.com, to avoid the risk of carrying it around town. Here's one type of feedback we could provide. Who's speaking in this feedback, and what does your brain do in response?

> Incorrect. Tanya's home email address might not be secure. For example, Tanya may have been the victim of a phishing campaign. She might have given a hacker her email password without realizing it. Try again.

That's the voice of the all-knowing teacher jumping in to correct a child: "No, that's not right. And since you can't think for yourself, I'll tell you why you're wrong." Your brain does nothing but receive correction.

How about this feedback? What effect does it have on your brain?

> Tanya emails the salary file to herself and later deletes it from her home computer. Two weeks later, a colleague forwards her an email that has been going around the firm.
>
> "Look what I bought from a guy online," the email says, with the salary file attached. "Does your manager deserve what they're being paid? I'm disgusted."
>
> That night, a tech-savvy friend, Sophie, examines Tanya's home email. "Look," Sophie says, pointing at an access log. "Someone has been logging into your email from a town in Zekostan. I think you've been phished."

This feedback shows people the consequence of their choice and lets them **conclude for themselves** whether they've made a good decision. It's the antithesis of the school model because it trusts people to think — in fact, it **requires** them to think.

It's all part of "show, don't tell"

You'll see a pattern in my recommendations: "show, don't tell."

The feedback above that stopped the story and said, "Incorrect" is "telling" feedback by my definition, because it tells people what to think: "You're wrong, and here's why."

In contrast, the feedback that continued the story and showed what happened to the salary data is "showing" feedback because, well, that's what it does. It shows the consequence, and then it shuts up and lets the learner interpret what they're seeing.

On a bigger scale, I'll also recommend that you organize your activities in a "show, don't tell" way. I'll suggest that you not tell people every little thing that they might possibly need to know before giving them an activity. Instead, I'll suggest you send people into an activity before they're 100% prepared, encourage them to make a choice while you stand by with optional help, and then show them the consequences of their choice.

This technique lets people challenge themselves as much as they feel comfortable and pull the information that they need when they need it. The conventional, school-influenced approach is to push information at people whether they need it or not.

Four requirements of a practice activity

A practice activity as I'm defining it meets these criteria:

- **Decision**: The activity asks people to decide what to do, not show what they know.

- **Context**: The activity has people with names in a specific place, doing specific things.

- **Realism**: The context is the same as the learner's job. It's not a fantasy land or game show. The decision is one that the learner takes on the job.

- **Consequences**: The feedback shows the realistic consequence of the learner's decision and lets the learner draw conclusions. It doesn't say "incorrect" or preach, though it might provide tips after showing the consequence.

No special technology required

You can probably create the type of practice activity described in this book with the same tools you're using now.

For example, if you decide online activities would be useful, you can probably create them with the same tool that you currently use to make multiple-choice questions. If you decide to have a live session, the question for a practice activity can be displayed or just read aloud, and participants can debate it. You can print activities out on paper and have people complete them in small groups.

The only time you'll need to consider a new tool is if you decide a branching scenario is necessary. Some people use conventional elearning software, but that can be cumbersome. I use a free tool (Twine), but you can also buy tools.

Why should we care?

It's easy to design a fact check. It's much harder to design a realistic practice activity. So why should we make the effort?

It's a job, not a test

As I pointed out earlier, tests don't happen on our jobs. We want people to know stuff, but knowing isn't enough. We need them to also apply that knowledge to their jobs. Practice activities help people practice applying their knowledge in a safe place.

Practice activities are interesting

Practice activities are far more interesting than test questions. That's because the real world is far more interesting than Testland. Testland is a dim, formless place where there are no Tanyas, no children to pick up, and no groceries.

They inspire more thought and discussion

Practice activities are more likely to generate in-depth thought and discussion than fact checks.

For example, if you ask participants in a live session, "What's the most secure way to transfer sensitive data to another PC?" you'll get short, shallow answers like, "An encrypted USB drive."

But if you ask the question about Tanya bringing home the salary data, you'll get more discussion. If someone suggests using an encrypted USB drive, someone else might say, "I'm not sure that's the best idea. If she puts the drive in her purse, it could fall out when she's checking out at the grocery store. And what if she leaves her purse in her car when she picks up her kids, and someone grabs it?" This could also lead to a discussion about what type of encryption to use and how effective it is.

These are the types of issues that we want people to consider when they make decisions in the real world.

They help people remember

Like a test question, a practice activity asks you to recall bits of information, such as "encrypted USB drive = pretty safe." But it also has you apply that information in a specific context, and that context can help you remember it.

Let's say that you've taken a conventional data privacy workshop in which the trainer told you that an encrypted USB drive is pretty safe. Then an assessment question asked you, "Which of the following is a pretty safe way to carry data?" and you correctly chose "encrypted USB drive."

During the training, you needed to file the concept "encrypted USB drive = pretty safe" in your already crowded brain. You probably tossed it in the grey bin labeled "Miscellaneous stuff from compliance training." After the assessment, you didn't need that bit of information anymore, and it eventually disappeared under all the other stuff you toss in that bin.

But if you have to choose how Tanya should bring the data home, the context gives you a more memorable way to file the concept. And when you see the best choice, an encrypted USB drive, it's accompanied by several realistic risks. When you find yourself in the same context, needing to get data home, you'll remember the story, the USB drive, and the possible perils of the drive as it accompanied Tanya home.

If you carry a purse, you might also remember the story of the USB drive when you check to make sure your keys are in your purse. Or if you pick up your kids on the way home, you might remember the risks of leaving data in the car even if you think you'll just be gone for a minute.

That's why practice activities as I define them take place in realistic contexts and not, for example, during battles with space aliens.

> When facing a new problem on the job, most experts search their memory banks for a similar situation they faced in the past. Problem-based lessons give learners an opportunity to build those memory repositories for later use.
>
> — Ruth Colvin Clark in Evidence-Based Training Methods (2015)

They help people change what they do

Practice activities can also improve our chances of changing what people do. If we have learners apply their knowledge to solve a realistic problem, we're helping them practice what they need to do on the job. The more practice we can provide, the better.

They help people see if they're ready for their job

Practice activities help people gauge their progress toward mastery. A knowledge check just tells me if I can remember something. A practice activity shows me whether I can apply it to situations like the ones I face on my job, helping me decide if I'm ready for the real world or need to practice more.

They're efficient

Practice activities do two things at once: they test whether people can recall something, and they help them practice applying it. When you provide rich feedback and link to additional information, they can also replace information presentations, as we'll see in detail later.

As a result, a "course" of practice activities can require far less development time than the traditional presentation occasionally interrupted by a fact check.

They treat people like the adults they are

Finally, practice activities show our respect for people. We're not wasting their time or talking down to them. Instead, we're giving them challenges they care about and letting them draw conclusions on their own.

Who's going to be more motivated? Someone who's quizzed like a child and immediately corrected, or someone who's challenged to make decisions and allowed to draw conclusions?

Let's practice: Are these practice activities?

At this step, you're just writing notes for possible activities. One way to record your idea is to write a brief version of the question. But because the school model has such a powerful grip on our brains, you might write a test question when you meant to write a practice activity.

First, you need to recognize whether you have a test question or a practice activity. One way to distinguish them is to ask, "Does this actually happen on the person's job?" If the answer is no, you've got a test item.

Here are some examples. What do you think? Is each one a test item or a practice activity?

a) Drag the steps of the process to put them in the correct order. (Ask yourself, "Does this actually happen on the person's job?")

b) Sarah has completed the purchase order and saved it in the PO folder. What should she do next?

c) Brenda plans to retire in 15 years and has nearly reached her savings target. Which investment product would be best for her now?

d) Which of the following investment products provides the safest return?

e) Barry needs just a microwidget, but Julia convinces him to buy a megawidget. Which term best describes Julia's error: undeserved upselling, or customer misvetting?

f) What are some examples of open-ended questions?

g) You're interviewing Jason for a customer support position. His resume shows that he changes jobs every year. What could you ask him to learn more about this?

Here's how I'd judge the example activities above.

a) Drag the steps of the process to put them in the correct order. — Have you ever arrived at work to discover that colored blocks are scrambled on your desk, with each block representing a step in a process, and you have to put them in order so you can do your job? This is a test activity, because it's asking you to manipulate abstract information in an unrealistic way. It's testing your knowledge, not your ability to use that knowledge.

b) Sarah has completed the purchase order and saved it in the PO folder. What should she do next? — This helps people not only recall the steps of a process but also apply that knowledge to the situation they face on their jobs. It's a practice activity. It simulates the action that it's linked to on the map, which is probably something like, "After saving the PO, send a copy to the requestor."

c) Brenda plans to retire in 15 years and has nearly reached her savings target. Which investment product would be best for her now? — This helps the learner practice not only recalling features but also matching those features to the needs of specific customers. It's a practice activity and is probably one of several linked to an action like "Identify the best investment product for the customer."

d) Which of the following investment products provides the safest return? — This just tests learners' recall of product features, not their ability to choose the best product for a particular customer. However, if it's part of a longer activity, such as finding the best product for Brenda, it could qualify as a practice item. For example, the list of products could be a list the learner created during their discussion with Brenda, and now it's time to identify the safest one, making it part of a realistic practice activity.

e) Barry needs just a microwidget, but Julia convinces him to buy a megawidget. Which term best describes Julia's error: undeserved up-selling, or customer misvetting? — This looks like a practice activity at first because it has people with names. However, what kind of thinking does the question require? It wants us to recall the correct label for Julia's action. We're not making any real-world decisions; we're just remembering a definition. This is a test question, unless your job as Julia's coworker is to spy on her and label everything she does.

f) What are some examples of open-ended questions? — No one sits around on their job coming up with examples of open-ended questions without a specific need for them in a specific context. This happens only in Testland.

g) You're interviewing Jason for a customer support position. His resume shows that he changes jobs every year. What could you ask to learn more about this? —This not only tests the learner's ability to generate good questions but also lets them practice choosing the best ones for a specific situation. On the action map, it's probably one of several activities linked to the action "Use open-ended questions to learn about applicants' job history."

"But they have to KNOW stuff!"

"Why are you ruling out activities that manipulate information, like putting steps in order?" you might ask. "You can't expect people to make decisions in practice activities without any knowledge."

I agree. We can't expect people to make decisions without the necessary knowledge. But first we're focusing on simulating what they need to **do**, not what they need to know. Once we have activities that help them practice **doing the thing,** we'll decide how to provide what they need to know to do that thing. For example, we might provide optional information that the learner can look at if they can't make the decision on their own.

This reverses the usual information-first focus. It's designed to keep us from drifting into information-obsessed Testland, which thanks to our long experience in school, constantly calls to us, saying, "I'm so familiar! I'm so easy! Come back to me!"

What happens if you open the door to all activity types?

Imagine what would happen if you removed the requirement that all activities at this step have to be realistic, contextual practice activities.

"Let's brainstorm some activities!" you tell your SME, or just yourself.

Which activities immediately come to mind? Thanks to the siren call of Testland, many of them will be knowledge checks, abstract manipulations of information, click-to-reveals, knowledge games, research-and-present, or other tasks that just move information into and out of brains.

Because they're so easy to write, soon most of your activities are test activities. You've lost the advantage of using action mapping.

That's why, **at this step,** I recommend you rule out any information-focused activities. In a later step, you'll ask, "What do they need to know to complete this practice activity?" Then, you might decide that drills or other information-based activities have a role.

Focus on the idea, not the format

Your client probably came to you with a certain format in mind. "We want a workshop for the annual meeting," they might have said. Or, "We need an online course."

I hope you avoided agreeing or disagreeing with that format when you talked with the client. You kept your options open. Now you'll brainstorm the most effective activities **regardless of format,** and only then (in the next chapter) choose the best format for each activity.

Activities aren't just for elearning

When you saw the activity ideas I listed above, you might have thought, "Those are for elearning." This probably happens because few presenters in live training ask these kinds of questions — they're too busy telling people what they supposedly need to know or having them identify which color represents their personality.

However, practice activities can be used in any format. I use them in my webinars and workshops, not just in elearning. They're not specific to any technology. They're just a technique.

Some of the examples I'm about to describe are from elearning because it's easier to show an elearning activity, while it can take several paragraphs to describe a different format of the same activity. However, **the same challenge can be provided in any format.**

For example, a scenario like the needlestick activity we saw earlier can be included in self-paced elearning, projected for group discussion, or distributed on paper for small groups to debate.

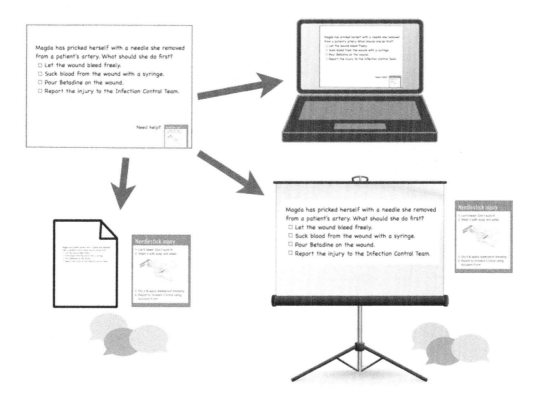

Example: Elearning to live training

Here's the question we saw earlier:

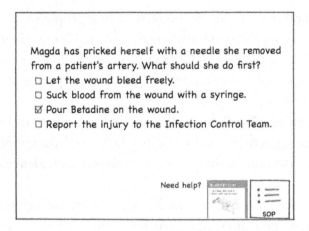

The feedback showed the result of the decision and highlighted the relevant portion of the job aid.

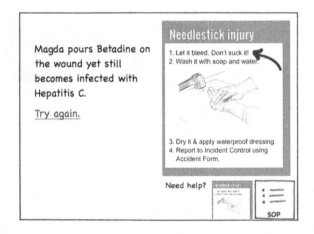

How could you use this in live training?

Project it

The simplest solution is to display the activity and have people debate each decision, whether you're in a webinar or face to face. Branching scenarios in particular are great for provoking discussion.

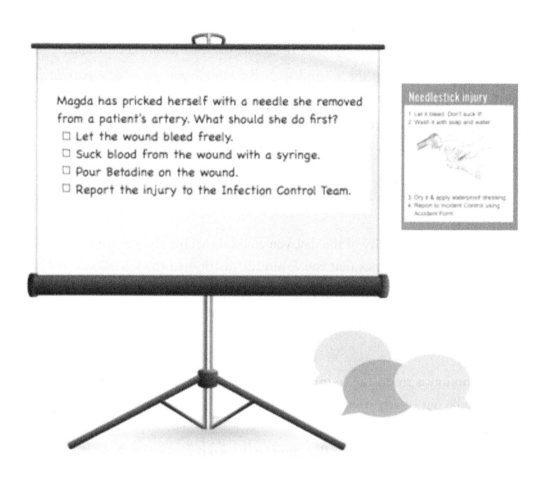

Talk it through

Don't want to have people stare at a screen? You can present the same challenge without any slides in a face-to-face session or webinar.

The simplest option is to just say something like, "Let's say that a clinician named Magda has just jabbed herself with a needle that she took out of a patient's artery. What should she do first?"

Let people call out or type their recommendations, and choose one. You might selectively hear a recommendation of Betadine, the most common mistake.

"Okay, Magda washes the wound with Betadine," you say. "The patient has hepatitis C. What are the chances that Magda has it now?"

If the participants don't mention the consequence on their own with discussion, report the consequences of the choice: "Magda doesn't know it yet, but she just caught hepatitis C."

Finally, remind them of the job aid: "What should she have looked at before she made her decision?"

If this is the first activity of the day, you could distribute the job aid now. If this is a later activity, it assumes that you've already distributed the job aid or have had participants describe what's on the wall of a typical examination room.

Act it out

Another option is to do the training in an actual examination room. Pretend to take a needle out of a participant's arm, pretend to jab yourself with it, and then ask, "What should I do first?"

If someone suggests you pour Betadine on the wound, obediently pour Betadine on it, and then ask the participants, "The patient has hepatitis C. Could I have it now?"

During the discussion, reveal that you've "caught" hepatitis C and ask, "What information in this room should Magda have looked at?"

> **It's the decision, not the technology**
>
> *Your activity ideas can be developed in any format because they're focused on the decisions that people make on the job. They're not, for example, arcade games that depend on technology.*
>
> *During the heyday of elearning, every performance problem was a nail, and elearning was the only hammer. Luckily, perspectives are broadening, and you can help broaden them further as you **design for the problem, not the tool**.*

Again, don't obsess about the format

We've looked at some formats just to keep you from assuming everything is elearning. In this chapter, don't decide on any format in particular. Instead, focus on the activity idea. You'll decide on the best format for each activity in the next chapter.

A scenario is a type of practice activity

I use "practice activity" as an umbrella term to describe any type of activity in which a person practices doing something or making decisions. Defined this way, it's easy to see that a practice activity could take place in any format. For example, if my dance instructor has me do the same three tango steps over and over, that's a practice activity.

A scenario is a type of practice activity. It's designed as a multiple-choice question, though it might not look like one in its final format.

Lots of people think scenarios are for elearning only. That's not correct. We just saw an example of a scenario that started as a multiple-choice question and became an open-ended discussion in a live session. There are many ways to use scenarios in all types of performance support, and it's a serious mistake to limit them to elearning.

Some people use "scenario" to refer to a case study or story that doesn't require learners to make decisions. That's not a practice activity, so it's also not a scenario as I define it. Players have to make realistic decisions and see the consequences for the activity to qualify as a scenario.

An activity in which learners interact with tools or software rather than other people is still a scenario in my book, as long as the players are making realistic decisions and seeing the consequences. For that reason, "simulation" and "scenario" are the same for me.

I like to divide scenarios into three categories.

Mini-scenario

A mini-scenario is short, usually just one question. It gives you a realistic challenge, you make your choice, you see the consequence, the end.

The following is a bare-bones mini-scenario. It just squeaks into "practice activity" territory because we have people with names in a specific context and we see the consequence of our decision.

> Bill needs to pass a scalpel to Sara during surgery. What should he do?
>
> a) Put the scalpel in a sterile kidney dish and hold the dish out to Sara.
>
> b) Hold it by the neck and place the handle in Sara's palm.
>
> c) Put it on the surgical drape for her to pick up herself.
>
> d) Toss it gently in her direction, handle first.

The feedback shows the consequences. For example, if we choose option B, we see this: "Sara is distracted by a loose clamp and moves her hand just as Bill places the handle in her palm. The scalpel cuts Bill's thumb." We don't say, "Incorrect. You should never..."

The Testland version would be, "What's the safest way to pass a scalpel?" This lacks people and context and can only end with telling feedback like "incorrect."

Other people use "mini-scenario" differently. In this book, "mini-scenario" means "short scenario, probably just one question." It doesn't mean an activity that forces people to go back and do it right, an "easy" activity, or something that happens only within a limited timeframe.

When to use a mini-scenario

Mini-scenarios are useful when...

- The real-world decision is self-contained. You might make the choice as part of a longer conversation or process, but its consequences don't seriously affect anything later in the process. An example:

  Andreas, a 33-year-old single man with no health issues, wants a health plan with international coverage and no copay. Which plan should you offer?

- You want to help people practice the same task with many different variables. The health insurance example could be repeated with several other customers, including a 55-year-old woman, a couple planning to have a baby, etc. You don't need to practice the entire conversation; you just have people practice recommending the right product.

The consequence can be immediate or in the future

The consequence of your choice could happen immediately or in the future. In the above example, if you chose the right plan, the feedback could say that five months later, Andreas gets hit by a bus in Zambia but is treated at no cost thanks to you having sold him the correct plan. If you chose the wrong one, poor Andreas has to limp to an ATM and withdraw large amounts of cash. So even though the consequence happens in the future, structurally this is a mini-scenario because just one decision was required.

Mini-scenarios can be strung together to make a pseudo-story

A series of mini-scenarios can be strung together to create what feels like a story, but the consequence of one decision doesn't determine how the next decision is made.

A typical example is a "day in the life" story of disconnected decisions. For example, we play the role of a security guard who has to recognize and resolve unrelated issues during the day. Our decision about the tripping hazard at 10 AM doesn't affect what we do about the unlocked door at 1 PM.

No special tools are required

You might be able to create a mini-scenario with the same tool you use for multiple-choice questions. Just make sure your question tool lets you provide **contextual feedback,** meaning you can write entirely different feedback for each option. You're not restricted to just two types of feedback, one blurb for "correct" and another for "incorrect." It's helpful if you can also include other media in the feedback, such as images or video.

A surprisingly large percentage of elearning tools and quiz plugins don't support contextual feedback, including some of the spiffy new tools that claim to be cutting-edge. The tools' creators are apparently infected by the school mindset. They seem to assume that the only time we'd want to ask a question is to see if the "learner" can correctly regurgitate a fact.

Branching scenario

A branching scenario contains multiple questions ("decision points"). The consequence of one decision affects the next decision. Two people going through the same branching scenario could see different questions and story lines.

Below is part of a larger branching scenario. It shows the plot at a high level. Each diamond represents a decision point. Each decision point includes the consequence of the previous decision and several options to choose from.

In decision point 1, one player might choose the option that takes them directly to decision point 4. Another might end up going through points 2 and 3 to get to 4. And others might never see 4 – they could fail at point 3, for example.

This is true branching: different players have different experiences, based entirely on their choices.

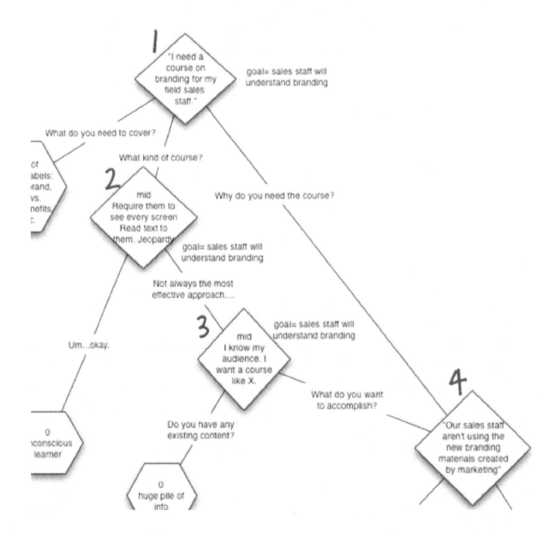

When to use a branching scenario

Branching scenarios are useful when...

- A decision made at one point determines the input for a decision made later. A classic example is a tricky conversation in which you ask the wrong question, limiting the information you have to work with in a later part of the discussion.

- You want to help people practice recovering from mistakes. In a strong branching scenario, players can realize that they're heading down a bad path and make a decision that will get them onto a better path. For example, let's say you're trying to establish rapport with someone from a culture that values lots of small talk, and you bring up business too soon. The person you're talking to appears to grow cool. Now you're supposed to decide the next thing to say, and the scenario designers have included an option that pulls the conversation back into small-talk territory. This lets you practice recognizing and recovering from your mistakes.

A common mistake is to assume you need a branching scenario if you want people to practice a multi-step process. However, you need branching only if:

- There are multiple grey areas – multiple decision points where people make a judgment call that can pull them on or off track.

- Decisions made at one point limit or expand the options available at another point.

- People commonly make a mistake in the process and need to recognize and recover from it later.

If you decide that you don't really need branching, you might consider offering several mini-scenarios that focus just on the tricky steps of the process. If you feel it's important for people to practice the entire process, you could string several mini-scenarios together.

Teaching scenario, aka "control-freak scenario"

A third type of scenario might look at first like a branching scenario, but there's just one path. Two people going through the activity will see the same questions because there's only one way through the story.

To progress in the story, you have to answer "correctly." If you choose a "wrong" answer, you're forced to go back and try again until you get it right. Then the story continues.

My favorite term for this structure is "control-freak scenario," because that's how it feels to the player. You're not allowed to experiment and recover from mistakes. You're punished for bad choices by being made to go back and try again until you get it right.

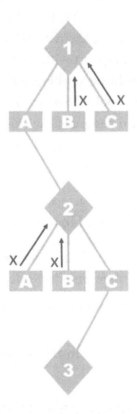

It's possible that the control-freak approach could be useful when you're helping novices learn to do something completely new. The immediate correction can help them get the basics down before you give them a real branching scenario, where the consequences are messier.

However, since we're helping adults learn stuff, I doubt there's anything so new that they could never figure it out without this constant correction.

We'll look more closely at this approach when we consider feedback in a later chapter.

Examples of practice activities

Below, I describe several types of activities to help you get ideas for your own. To see actual examples, go to map-it-book.com.

See examples at map-it-book.com.

Simulated job task

Many activities have people practice making the decisions they need to complete a task on the job.

Here's a simple example. It's a mini-scenario. In addition to making a realistic decision, you can access optional information. In this case, it's the chart of plans and features that you'd also be able to refer to on the job.

> Paul is single and has no children. He has diabetes, is overweight, and enjoys skydiving while blindfolded. Which insurance plan would you recommend for him?
>
> a) Basic
>
> b) Mega
>
> c) Monster
>
> <u>See the chart</u>

If this is self-paced elearning, people click the link to see the chart. If this is live training, you could make the chart available in the format it's used on the job, and project, distribute, or simply ask the question.

Again, **you could present these activities in any format** — as self-paced elearning, projected for discussion in a live session or webinar, distributed on paper for discussion in small groups, simply described in an informal stand-up session...

Simulated conversations

Many job tasks require people to talk to others. If the conversation is tricky, it might deserve its own practice activity.

The strongest simulations show the consequence of what you say – the prospective buyer loses interest; the patient confesses to a drug habit. No Omniscient One interrupts to say, "Incorrect" or give you advice. You might also be able to ask for optional help – in elearning, I like to use a "Why did this happen?" button – but the immediate feedback is simply what happens next in the story.

While many designers choose to create a branching scenario, you can also help people practice the tricky part of a conversation with mini-scenarios. For example, if we want to help sales people practice overcoming common objections, we can write several short scenarios that drop the player into a sales conversation that's already under way. The prospect raises an objection, the player chooses a response, and we fast-forward to the end. This lets us cover a wide range of objections without dragging people through multiple branching scenarios or writing a contrived scenario in which one prospect raises 17 objections.

As you try the sample activities at map-it-book.com, you might consider these questions:

- How realistic is the conversation? Does the situation seem like it would really happen? Does the dialog sound efficient but natural?

- Are the decisions challenging? Could the options be made more subtle?

- Do the designers interrupt with "telling" feedback, or do they let you learn from experience?

- What type of help, if any, is provided? When can you access it – only before you make a decision, only after, or at all times?

- Did the designers use stock photos or other images of the characters? Do the images help, or could they hurt?

- Did the developers use expensive media, such as video? Do you think it was necessary, or could the budget have been better spent on making the scenario more challenging?

Again, you could use this type of activity in many types of training. For example, you could project it and have a group debate each choice. You could print it on paper and use it in live training, as described in the next chapter.

Simulated job decisions with multiple characters

Often, the decisions required for a job go well beyond what to say to people. You can use practice activities to help people make any type of decision as well as interact with a variety of people.

Again, the decisions could be standalone mini-scenarios that might be connected by one story, such as in a "day in the life" series of questions. In this case, an earlier decision doesn't affect a later one, so you don't need a branching scenario.

For more complex situations, branching will help players practice recovering from mistakes or learn from the consequences of common mis-steps.

As you try the examples on map-it-book.com, you might consider these questions in addition to the questions for simulated conversations:

- Is the activity a branching scenario, or is it a series of mini-scenarios tied together by a story line? It's a branching scenario if a decision you made earlier affects what you can do later in the story. Many activities that appear at first to be branching scenarios are actually linked mini-scenarios.

- If you make a bad choice, can you try to recover by making a good choice later on? If the activity is a series of mini-scenarios, you won't be able to do this.

- Does the activity link to the information you need to make a good decision, such as the references you'd have on the job? A strong activity will simulate the job by linking to real-world references, so you practice using the real-world job aids.

- Do the designers interrupt the story with a presentation or advice? How does that affect your motivation to continue?

Roleplay

If you're meeting face to face, a **well-designed** roleplay will help people practice skills that have an interpersonal component.

By "well designed" I mean that at least one person in the roleplay has clear guidance on their role, the other person is practicing clearly specified skills, some choices are identified as being better than others, and the facilitator elicits the overall concepts and goal behaviors during the resulting discussion. Otherwise a roleplay risks becoming a vague discussion that doesn't practice anything in particular.

173

Simulated software task

This type of activity lets you use the same software you use on the job to practice completing tasks. However, unlike in your real-world software, you can't break anything, and you receive more hand-holding – ideally, only if you ask for it.

As the fictional tasks increase in complexity, your skills and confidence increase until you're ready to use the live program.

And not to beat you over the head with this, but **you're not restricted to self-paced elearning**. In a live class, you could sit people in front of the actual software and give them the same assignment, helping them as they need it. If you're the only one with a computer (definitely not recommended, but it happens), you could project this or share your screen and have people in the session tell you what to click.

Real task on the job

Often the best way for someone to learn how to do their job is right there on the job: they learn as they work. This often gets overlooked in the assumption that "a course" is the best solution.

Your options for providing realistic on-the-job training are infinite. You might have discovered some solutions already in the analysis of your client's problem. For example, if you found that you could fix one problematic behavior with a new job aid, you're providing a light form of on-the-job training. People will use the job aid as they perform the task, learning as they work.

Most people picture a mentor or coach when they think of on-the-job training. While that's often a good idea, it takes one person away from their job in order to train the other, which could be difficult if you have a lot of people to train.

One answer to this concern is to point again to the project goal. It should show a significant benefit to the organization. Your client should understand that to get the benefit, they'll first incur some sort of cost, whether it's paying for training and job aids or paying for reduced productivity as experienced employees help newbies.

Other options include having the new person shadow or work next to a more experienced one whose work isn't seriously affected by having an observer. That takes only one person away from productive work during the training.

Your client might resist mentoring or shadowing out of concern that bad habits could spread. One of the appeals of having everyone take the same course is that it standardizes how the tasks are done. However, a course isn't the only way to standardize things. Job aids are great at that. If you give people self-explanatory job aids and, at first, simple tasks, they'll learn while working, and they'll all learn to do it the same way.

Real task in the classroom

If on-the-job training is problematic, you can still reap some of its benefits in classroom training that replicates the workplace as much as possible. Of course, it's best to do this by having everyone use the real-world tools, but you can still provide realistic activities even if you can't give everyone the right tools.

For example, one approach is to attempt to complete the task yourself with the participants' coaching. I used to do this when I was a technical trainer in the early 1980s. I'd use a projector to display the screen of the one IBM PC we were allowed to have in our group of 30 people. Then I'd describe a task, like, "We have to write a memo that lists what everyone is bringing to the staff party. Which program should I open?"

I'd pause at each step, asking people what they thought I should do next, offering hints as needed, pointing out patterns, and reminding them of the job aid.

You could take a similar approach with volunteers from the audience, such as having the group tell the volunteers what to do, or having the volunteers complete part of the task and then ask the group to evaluate what they did.

Would you steal this activity?

The above examples are only a small sampling of what's possible. I'm sure you've seen other activity types. Your job is to sort through the ideas, keeping the good ones and abandoning the not-so-good, and keeping your focus on the problem, not the development tool.

Let's practice sorting through ideas. Imagine you're at a training conference. In one session, attendees described activities that they recently used. You've also wandered the exhibit hall and seen activities that vendors created to demonstrate their products or services.

Below are some activity ideas you've heard and seen. Which would you steal and adapt to make a practice activity, and which would you leave behind?

a) A vendor is selling an online fraud-prevention course for bank tellers. They show you an activity in which a series of customers appears at your teller window. Each customer wants to deposit a check, which you need to examine and then accept or reject. If you reject the check, you choose how to explain the rejection to the customer.

b) "We did some elearning on change management," one conference attendee says. "The course had a fictional team of people who worked for a company that was being bought. They had to decide how to manage the change. In one activity, learners dragged cartoon dialog bubbles to a person's face to make them say the phrase."

c) "We have a two-day workshop on some pretty boring financial regulations," another attendee says. "Instead of just talking about the rules, we have the participants form small groups and research the rules about a specific topic. Then they present what they learned to the rest of the group."

d) "For one of our online safety courses," another attendee says, "we created a clickable warehouse that people could explore. For example, they'd click on the overflowing wastebasket to learn about the risks of letting slippery wrapping materials overflow onto the floor."

e) At one elearning vendor's booth, you see a colorful map of an island where treasure is hidden. Learners click on items on the island, such as a hut or palm tree, to reveal questions. When they answer the question correctly, they get a gold coin. When they get enough coins, the location of the treasure is revealed and cartoon pirates present it to them. "The questions could be about anything," the vendor says. "It's up to you."

f) "We like to use stories," one participant says. "For example, we start our anti-harassment training with true stories about harassment cases. This shows people how the content applies to them and motivates them."

g) "We use a story in a webinar," another participant says. "We're training social workers who work with families. We use a true story about two struggling parents and their treatment of their little girl. It's actually a story of a failure by our agency, but we don't tell people that at the beginning. Instead, we tell a bit of the story, and then we ask what, if anything, the agency should do at that point. People type their opinions in the chat, and the discussion can get pretty heated. Then we tell the next bit of the story, what really happened, and we discuss it, and so on."

Which would you steal, and why? Below are my thoughts about each one.

a) Bank teller accepting or rejecting checks: I'd steal this. It helps people practice making the same types of decisions that they have to make on the job.

b) Change management training where you drag dialog bubbles to characters: I'd halfheartedly steal this if the learner is determining what the character should say as they decide how to manage the change. If the bubble-dragging is just a way to make characters present information or answer quiz questions and doesn't require a realistic decision, it's only a gimmick, and one that might not work on all platforms or for all people.

c) Workshop participants research and present rules: I'd leave this common activity behind, because it's just a different way to get information into brains. The activity doesn't require people to practice something they do on the job, unless their job is to research and present information. In its place, I'd have people decide how to apply the rules in realistic scenarios.

d) Clickable warehouse for a safety course: This is a typical click-to-reveal activity that I'd leave behind. There's no realistic decision involved; the only decision is "What shall I click next?" However, this activity could be tweaked to be more useful. For example, we could ask the learner to identify a (subtle! realistic!) safety hazard in a (realistic!) warehouse, and then ask them to not only fix the hazard but also find a way to keep it from happening again.

e) Answer questions to reveal the treasure: I'd leave this one behind. Some people would argue for stealing it, because the activity lets us use any type of question. "We could write challenging mini-scenarios that have people make the decisions they make on their jobs," they'd say. "The treasure would just be a fun way to motivate them."

My concern is that the learners' jobs don't happen on an island with pirates. Even if we ask challenging, realistic questions, we're flinging people back and forth between worlds. First, they're in a place like their job, making a decision, and then they're on the island. Seconds later, they're back in their job, and then they're back on the island. It seems like an unnecessary distraction.

I'd rather motivate adults by giving them interesting challenges that will make their jobs more satisfying, and rather than cartoon pirates, I'd prefer smart humor for grownups.

f) **Tell stories at the beginning of anti-harassment training:** I'd leave behind this common approach to "motivating" people. The learners aren't making any decisions; they're just supposed to passively listen to the story and feel something, often fear (the moral of the story is guaranteed to be, "If you act like the person in the story, bad things will happen!"). Also, the story is inevitably followed by an information dump, making people leery of any future stories in training. If you want to motivate them, you could start with a controversial decision-making activity that has realistic, motivating consequences, and then keep going with more activities and discussion.

g) **Use a real-life story to inspire discussion in a webinar:** I'd steal this in a heartbeat. However, some people would argue against it. "The participants aren't really making decisions and seeing consequences," they'd say. "They're just debating something that happened, one chapter at a time."

I'd respond that the focus of the debate is, "What should we have done at this point?" This helps participants repeatedly practice an important decision: "What should we do?" It's true that the story shows the consequence of only one choice, the one made by the agency in real life, but the discussion models the thinking that's required, and a good facilitator will help participants identify other potential consequences.

I think the designers were right to choose a story of a failure. As the story unfolds, people see the deterioration in the family — they see the consequences of real-life mistakes — and the urgency of the debate increases.

If managed well, the discussion will unearth issues within the agency and possibly find ways to deal with those issues. Also, discussing mistakes helps identify ways to **recover** from mistakes, an important skill that's often ignored in training.

Finally, which employer would you respect more: one that says, "We screwed up. Let's look at what we did wrong," or one that says, "We always make great decisions! Let's hear a story that shows how great we are?"

What's "realistic?"

You've probably seen elearning activities that try to be realistic by situating the challenge in, for example, an office like the one the learner works in. You're required to click the door to enter, click the phone to check for messages, click the paper on the desk to read it, and so forth.

While these look "realistic," don't just look at the setting. Look at the type of decision that's being made. For example, what's the difference between these two variations of the same activity?

> a) You click the paper on the desk, and a message appears saying, "Make sure you don't leave confidential client information on your desk."

> b) You click the paper on the desk, and you see what's on it. The paper shows a client's name and a list of the services they've bought, but not their address or other identifying information. The program asks you whether this paper should be shredded, filed, or left on the desk.

It's the decision that matters. Activity **a** is just a click-to-reveal requiring no decision; activity **b** asks you to make a realistic decision.

Finally, "click to explore the realistic scene for no reason" activities can quickly feel like busywork for the learner. If your budget is limited, it's probably better to engage adults with challenges that require them to use more brain.

"This is problem-based learning, right?"

Here we enter a fog of fuzzy definitions. I've seen "problem-based learning" interpreted as, "Throw people who know nothing about the topic into a situation in which they have to search for all the necessary information without even knowing where to find it, and then require them to figure out how to apply the information that they managed to find, and finally maybe they'll stumble on a halfway decent solution."

That's not what I'm describing in this book. I respect learners' time too much. Research also shows that (in education-land, at least) this approach fails, because it puts too much cognitive load on people as they scramble to figure out what they need, where to find it, and how to use it.

What I'm suggesting is that we give adults relevant problems that call on their pre-existing knowledge, which is often substantial, **while providing generous but optional help** (which we'll look at later in the book). We also arrange the activities so the earlier ones build the knowledge and experience required by later activities. Our recipe will mix scaffolding (help plus a slow escalation of difficulty) with productive failure (encouraging people jump in and try it if they want). We'll look at this in more depth in the chapter about providing information.

> *Our goal is to help people learn through experience by practicing in a safe place with optional help that we provide in its most efficient form.*

Your project: Write your activity ideas

In your action map, add your ideas for practice activities. Connect each activity to the behavior it supports. You might decide to have several activities for one behavior, or you might decide that multiple behaviors could be covered by one activity.

Write each activity as a question or a very short problem. Don't write the options or provide lots of details. Some examples:

- Customer calls to complain that widget is wobbling. Diagnose it over the phone as efficiently as possible.

- In Zekostan, local politician offers to buy you lunch as you discuss possible contract. Respond applying ethics rules in Zeko-appropriate way.

- Patient who makes many non-emergency requests of nurses complains of cramped muscle during busy shift. Prioritize and respond appropriately.

Here's an illegibly small snippet of my "how to use action mapping" map with activities added. The green (first and third) nodes are actions and sub-actions, the normal text represents notes answering, "What makes this hard?" and the yellow (final) blurbs are activity ideas.

Let's take a closer look at the activities. Notice how they're just ideas; they're not fully developed activities.

Ignore, for now, what the client wants

Focus on the idea, not the format ⊖   How could you develop this activity idea in formats X, Y, and Z? ⊕

Brainstorm realistic activities that help   Are these examples practice activities, or knowledge checks? Why? ⊕
people practice, not knowledge checks   How would you design a practice activity for this task? ⊕

Don't get distracted by trends from education ⊕

Right now, you're just recording ideas. **You're also not identifying the format for the activity,** such as elearning or a webinar. That comes later.

Do you need an activity for every action?

A common mistake is to design a practice activity for every behavior on the map. However, simple actions that don't require any thought probably don't need practice activities.

For example, let's say that we're training receptionists who answer the phones. One of the behaviors on our map is, "When a caller asks for Nigel, connect them to line 3." How much thought is involved? Do people really need to practice pressing the line 3 button when they hear, "Nigel, please?"

The receptionists would benefit from practice if, for some reason, they're required to memorize "Nigel = line 3" and perform the task as quickly as possible. In that case, the activity is more like a drill, since no decision is involved. If they don't need to memorize staff and line numbers, we can just give them a job aid listing names and lines and move on to more challenging tasks, such as detecting sales calls or handling angry clients.

If your map has simplistic behaviors that don't require thought, they probably don't require practice activities. However, if people need to memorize information and respond to it quickly and accurately, they'll benefit from realistic drills. Just make sure the information really does need to be memorized and can't be provided with a job aid.

Don't get stuck in courseland

Could you recommend on-the-job learning, such as shadowing a more experienced person, or giving the learner more time to perform the task, along with access to a helpful colleague?

You might be expected to create formal training, but don't let that expectation limit your ideas. If you find yourself just listing activities like scenarios, look through that list of ideas and ask for each one, "Is there no way for them to do this on the job? Do they really have to practice in a fictional scenario?" Scenarios are great if mistakes have dire consequences, but many tasks can be learned on the job without bringing on disaster.

Common challenges

Your team (or your own brain) keeps proposing fact checks and trivia games.
   If someone is pushing for knowledge checks, ask:

- "What real-world behavior requires knowledge of this fact?"

- "How could we tell by watching a worker that they know this fact?"

- Use that behavior as inspiration for a mini-scenario that requires the learner to make realistic decisions using the fact.

- Also, make sure your team isn't assuming any particular activity format. Remind them that you're brainstorming activity ideas, not an online course, and maybe not even "training" as they picture it.

You're concerned that writing specific scenarios means the material won't apply to everyone.

- Make sure you've limited your audience to a specific job role or group of related roles; if necessary, create a separate track for each role.
- Use multiple mini-scenarios to cover several typical situations and trust people to extrapolate. (Think of the story of the tortoise and the hare. You're not a tortoise or a hare but you got the point.)

You can't think of activities that will work in the format that the client requires.

- Ignore what the client wants, just for now. Think of the best activities for the learners and their work context. You'll consider the format in the next chapter.
- You might review the section above called "Focus on the idea, not the format," for an example showing how the same activity could be delivered in multiple ways.

The client has specified the type of activities they want, such as "I want a Jeopardy game" or "I think a research-and-present activity would be good."

- Ignore what the client wants, just for now. Think of the best activities for the learners and their work context. Soon, you'll show the client a prototype of the type of activity you recommend and they could easily abandon their idea and choose yours.

Everyone expects a certain type of training ("what we've always done").

- Ignore what everyone expects you to do, just for now. Think of the best activities for the learners and their work context.
- Soon, you'll show your stakeholders and learners a prototype of the type of activity you recommend and they could easily abandon "what we've always done." The learners are especially likely to help you break free of the standard approach.

Notice the pattern?

There's a pattern in my suggestions above. It's "ignore what everyone else wants." You should be working mostly or entirely on your own on this step, brainstorming freely. You shouldn't have anyone looking over your shoulder, including the client or SME, unless they're already 100% committed to creating opportunities for practice and understand what that means. Your focus in this step and the next is on the learners, their context, the problems they need to overcome, and the activities that would be most helpful for them.

Chapter 8. Consider the format

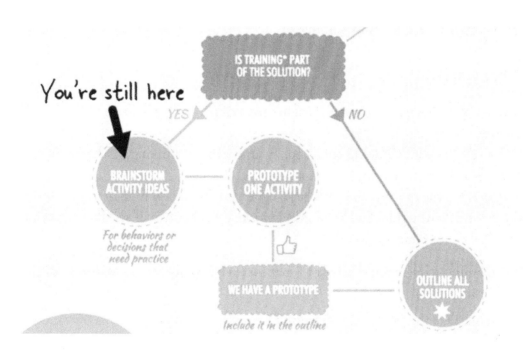

Task	Who does it	How long it might take
For each activity idea, identify the best format (face-to-face, live online, self-paced, etc.). Consider what would be best for the audience and each activity. Don't think in terms of a course or other training event, even if that's what the client requested. Note your ideas in your action map. You won't present them to the client yet.	Do this on your own.	A few minutes per activity

Result: A clear idea of which formats you'll propose to the client and the arguments you'll make for your recommendations. You're doing this thinking now because you'll develop a prototype activity in the next step. You'll want to develop that activity in the best format, and if the format is different from what the client is picturing, you'll have good arguments for your choice.

What you've done

In the last chapter, you noted your ideas for practice activities, connecting each activity to an action (or actions) on the map. You haven't actually written any activities yet. You're still brainstorming.

What you'll do

Now you'll decide which format (face to face, online, etc.) would be best for each activity.

"There's no point in doing this step," you might be thinking. "The client has already said what they want."

Ignore that thought for now. You're just going to take possibly an hour to identify which formats would be best in an ideal world, and then you'll see about making that ideal world happen. You'll:

1. Commit to choosing the best format **for each activity**, not one format for the entire project

2. Challenge the assumptions that influence format choice

3. Consider the culture of the audience

4. Identify the best format for each activity, especially considering the job context

5. Determine when people should use the activity. Should they use it right before they need it? Could you space the activities so people practice over time?

6. Decide: Should all the activities be packaged as one course or event? (Probably not!)

7. Determine the best mix of formats

You're still in the "activities" ring of the map, represented below by the hand icons.

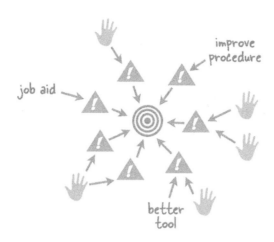

Who's involved?

Assuming you got to know the learners and their workplace in the "Why aren't they doing it?" chapter, you'll do this mostly on your own, checking with the client or SME if you have questions. If you haven't had a chance to talk with future learners, consider doing it in this chapter.

1. Commit to choosing the best format for each activity, not the entire project

First, put aside both the school mindset and whatever the client has said that they want. You need to clear your head so you can find the best solution, which might not be what everyone around you expects.

Thanks to the school mindset, we're expected to do the following when we "train."

1. Take people out of their jobs and put them in a training event
2. Fill their heads with information, including stuff that they'll need to know "someday"
3. Send them back to their jobs and expect them to rely on their memories

Action mapping has us focus on **designing activities, not events,** so we can stay flexible. A designer following this model might do any or all of the following.

- Create quick references for use on the job
- Design activities that are best done live at scheduled events and others that can be accessed online at any time
- Provide practice activities to be used right before a task (for example, let people practice on a fictional client right before meeting with a real one)
- Give people a platform through which they can ask colleagues questions and share knowledge
- Distribute ongoing reinforcement activities, such as scenario questions sent every week through email
- Create regularly scheduled mini-events for discussion, such as informal lunchtime gatherings

> *Training doesn't have to be one big event or even a small event. There might be no event at all.*

2. Challenge the assumptions that influence format choice

The training world is full of assumptions that lead to weak decisions. The brief bit of thinking that you'll do in this chapter will show you if your client's decision is the best one. If it isn't, you'll be prepared to offer alternatives, which you'll do later.

> *Your client isn't an expert on how people learn. You are. It's your job to determine what will work best.*

What drove your client's decision?

If the client originally asked for one format, recognize their reasons now, before they influence your own brainstorming. Some possibilities to consider:

- **It's what they always do**: If the client chose the format because it's what the organization always does, ask yourself why the organization always does that. For example, is there a tracking requirement that makes a one-time event or online course appealing? Does someone insist on being given a list of everyone who was "trained" and when they were trained? If so, why? Is someone covering a legitimate legal requirement, or are they tracking for the sake of tracking?

- **It looks like a quick fix:** A busy, distracted client might want a one-shot fix that looks quick. However, a shot in the arm rarely fixes a real performance problem. It isn't a quick fix; it's a waste of everyone's time. Ideally, your client has already begun to see this during the "Why aren't they doing it?" analysis.

- **The client saw something they liked and wants one of their own.** Sometimes the client will see an impressive course or experience a type of event and decide that they want that same format for their project. They might want this because they think everyone else will like it as much as they did, they need to impress someone, or a combination of these.

- **They were misled by pseudoscience or trends:** Your client might believe in learning styles, or they might have read that brain-based-mega-micro-learning is the new thing and therefore the best thing. The client means well, but it's your job to know the research and to recognize when a format is useful and when it is not.

- **They invested a lot in one tool, so they think they have to use it.** Got an expensive LMS? Better use it to recoup all that money! However, creating an unnecessary online course to justify the purchase of an LMS does nothing but throw more money into a bottomless pit.

- **The client wants to fill a hole in a schedule:** A classic example is, "We're having our quarterly meeting on the 10th and need a two-hour session in the afternoon. Do you have something on leadership skills?" This views training as a time-filler that's intended to look useful and get positive feedback. Creating real change is a secondary goal and is unlikely to be the result. If you're required to fill that particular hole, consider designing the live event as a kickoff for an ongoing series of practice activities or smaller events.

Is the client's preferred format also the best format for the learners? ***Should the desires of one person outweigh the needs of thousands of others?***

What's influencing your own thinking?

The client isn't the only one who's influenced by unexamined assumptions. You might have beliefs that keep you from seeing the situation clearly. Some possibilities to consider:

- **"I have to do what the client wants."** Is this really, objectively true? If the client told you to hook all workers to a shock generator and zap them every time they made a mistake, would you do it? As long as you're reading this book, your job is to give the client what they're really looking for: the best solution to their problem. You're the expert in how people learn and change. You provide the best service when you use your expertise, not when you blindly obey every request. (If your organization or department literally says, "Your job is to obey orders and never think," you might check Appendix 2 for some ideas on how to change how you're viewed.)

- **"I do my best work in Tool X, so I should use that tool."** I once had a chainsaw I loved. I wanted to solve every problem with it. Is your bedroom too dark? Let me cut you a skylight with my chainsaw.

  Your favorite tool is good only for specific problems, not every problem. It makes sense that you'd want to use the tool that makes you look good, but consider what could make you look even better: actually helping people do their jobs with less frustration and more confidence, while delivering measurable results that will make your client sing your praises.

  Some of the most public and enthusiastic feedback I received came after I helped a client see that they shouldn't create the online course they were planning. Instead, they refocused the project and used a mix of branching scenarios, small-group discussions, and new messages from leadership.

- **"I can't picture a tool that will create what I want."** You might decide that a particular format would be effective, but you can't imagine how to create it.

  A common example is spaced practice. At this writing, there are a few tools that help you deliver activities over time, but the vendors appear to assume that you're delivering information and quizzes, not practice activities. For example, tools I've looked at don't let you provide contextual feedback, just one "correct" and one "incorrect" message.

  Since most of our industry is still stuck in the school mindset, so are our vendors. They tend to view their tools as ways to make information more engaging.

Instead, look outside our industry. For example, if you want to provide spaced practice, ask, "Who else wants to send interactive messages to people, spaced over time?" Marketing. Online marketers use slick tools that not only let you deliver a clickable email but that will track who has clicked what, send follow-up emails based on what they clicked, and even track their behavior on your website and send emails based on what they do there – and then give you a bajillion reports letting you know how people are responding. Active Campaign is one such tool, but there are many others.

So rather than wait for the L&D vendors to change their mindset, look outside their world. Describe what you want to do to your IT or marketing staff, or research it online. I'd bet thousands of people are already using a tool that does what you want.

- **"All my teachers told me to do it this way."** If you have a degree in instructional design or education, you spent a long time in the school mindset. You paid a lot of money to be taught that a request for training should be answered with a course or other event that transfers knowledge.

  "The type of organization is irrelevant," your program might have told you. "If someone says that people need to learn a thing, then people need to learn that thing. Your only job is to help the people learn that thing. You'll do it by applying adult learning theory and using other techniques that good 'educators' use. The knowledge test tells you if you succeeded."

  If that's what you were taught, you need to unlearn it. In addition to applying the deprogramming in this book, you might look again at your instructors, if they still seem to be influencing your choices.

  Did any of them actually work in a business setting? Did any of them provide examples of times when a client asked for training and training wasn't the best solution? Did they teach you the metrics that businesses use and want to improve with training? Should they really be influencing what you do on your job, especially if they never held such a job?

Learning styles: The myth that won't die

The idea of learning styles has been propagated by well-intentioned people, including possibly your professor of instructional design. However, the claim that we have to accommodate different learning styles has been repeatedly debunked by research.

If somehow you've missed hearing about learning styles, here's the claim: We all have different ways in which we learn best. In the currently popular "visual - auditory - kinesthetic" (VAK) variation, some people need to see the information, some need to hear the information, and some need to physically manipulate things.

As "teachers," we supposedly should design our instruction so the knowledge is delivered in the format that suits each learner's style. That will help them learn better. If this claim is true, we should describe a map in spoken words for the auditory learners and not expect them to understand it by looking at it.

Other people have proposed different types of styles. Many learning-style proponents sell style inventories, training on how to change instruction to match the styles, and lesson plans for use in the classroom. No matter which styles are being sold, the claim remains the same: We have to adapt our designs to suit the styles, or people will struggle to learn.

That claim has been repeatedly debunked by scientists. While learning-style sellers claim they have research support, their studies are weak. One meta-analysis of learning-style studies concluded, "Research into learning styles can, in the main, be characterized as small-scale, non-cumulative, uncritical and inward-looking."[2]

Many strong, respected studies debunking learning styles have been published over the last 10 years, yet reports I've seen say that the vast majority of teachers in the UK and US still believe that they must test children to determine their learning styles (usually they're thinking VAK) and then tailor their instruction to that style. Like many myths from education, this one has spread into the training world. And like many myths from education, this one is so loaded with emotion that critical thought takes distant second place.

Obviously, people have preferences for how they learn. No one denies that. No one is saying that you and I aren't special snowflakes. But research doesn't support the claim that we should tailor our materials to specific "learning styles." Our limited resources would be better used on more effective techniques.

Most importantly, the entire premise of learning styles is based on the assumption that teaching means presenting information. The recommendations focus on what media we should use in these information presentations. As I hope I've made clear, information presentations should be a minor part of our job, not its focus.

---

[2] Learning styles: Concepts and evidence by Harold Pashler, Mark McDaniel, Doug Rohrer, and Robert Bjork. Psychological Science in the Public Interest vol. 9 number 3, December 2008, pp. 105-119.

We're here to solve performance problems. An information presentation is rarely the best solution and could easily not be part of the solution at all.

If we stopped defining learning as content absorption, we could stop obsessing about the format of that content.

If we end up putting anything on a screen, including an activity, the learning style fans will have lots of recommendations. "You should have a narrator read the text for the auditory learners," they might say. "And add some images for the visual learners."

Instead, we should apply techniques that **research shows actually work,** such as helping people see where they need to improve and helping them practice their new skills over time.

The following challenge highlights the fallacy at the heart of learning-style claims.[3]

If I were to tell you "I want to teach you something. Would you rather learn it by seeing a slideshow, reading it as text, hearing it as a podcast, or enacting it in a series of movements," do you think you could answer without first asking what you were to learn—a dance, a piece of music, or an equation? While it may seem like a silly example, the claim of the learning styles approach is that one could make such a choice and improve one's learning through that choice, independent of content.

— Cedar Riener and Daniel Willingham, "The Myth of Learning Styles"

Obviously, some content is best presented in specific formats. For example, a map is best shown visually, not described in narrated words, and research backs this up.

When instructional style matches the nature of the content, all learners learn better, regardless of their differing preferences for how the material is taught.

---

[3] From the September-October 2010 issue of Change Magazine, available here: www.changemag.org/archives/back%20issues/september-october%202010/the-myth-of-learning-full.html.

— Peter Brown et al. in Make It Stick (2014), a very useful summary of research

I also recommend that you ignore the following popular myths:

- "Digital natives learn differently."
- "We remember 10% of what we hear..."
- "We use only 10% of our brains."
- "Some people are left brained, and others are right brained."
- "Young people won't read."

The following books contain readable debunkings of many myths, and *Make It Stick* goes a step further to recommend alternative approaches that research shows actually work.

- *Urban Myths about Learning and Education* by Pedro De Bruyckere et al., 2015
- *Make It Stick: The Science of Successful Learning* by Peter C. Brown et al., 2014

For tips on how to persuade stakeholders to let go of their belief in learning styles, see the following post in my blog: blog.cathy-moore.com/2015/06/how-to-respond-to-learning-style-believers/.

3. Consider the culture of the audience

Your learners are members of at least two cultures: their society's culture, and the culture of their organization. Those cultures can affect how well a format works.

For example, you might have heard that self-paced elearning, even when it's well designed, isn't popular in cultures that value social connection. In my limited experience, that appears to be true. I've heard from designers in Latin America that their audiences prefer learning together in person rather than using self-paced materials. And when I participated in projects for the US Army, we learned that the soldiers strongly preferred to learn in groups, with discussion, and from peers.

Even when you choose a format that will likely work for a particular culture, you might need to adjust the activity itself. For example, one of my favorite techniques when I facilitate an online session is to display a controversial statement or problem and ask people for their opinions before I share mine. This usually generates lively discussion in the chat.

However, when I ran sessions in a culture where collective agreement is more important than individual opinion, the technique bombed. I found myself filling awkward silences because no one would give their opinion. Now when I run a session for a collective culture, I phrase the question as a survey with multiple-choice options so participants can answer anonymously and I can position the exercise as seeing what the group thinks.

Finally, action mapping is all about creating challenging activities, partly because challenge is motivating. However, in *Changing Employee Behavior* (2015), Nik Kinley and Shlomo Ben-Hur point out that people in individualistic cultures find challenge more motivating than people in collectivist cultures, and, as I learned in that painful webinar, in collectivist cultures it might be better to frame the challenge as a group effort.

> *For example, one study found that in Singapore people tend to set moderate rather than difficult goals — possibly because being part of a group rather than distinguishing oneself is more central to people's wellbeing. This does not mean that challenge cannot be motivating in collectivist cultures, but rather that, for many people in them, tasks that are positioned as team or group challenges are more likely to be intrinsically motivating than challenges specific to individuals.*
>
> *— Nik Kinsley and Shlomo Ben-Hur, Changing Employee Behavior: A Practical Guide for Managers (2015)*

4. Identify the best format for each activity, especially considering the job context

For each important activity, identify a format that, ideally, makes the practice context match or simulate the real-life context. Research (and common sense) suggests that people are better at remembering and applying what they've learned when the learning and application contexts are similar.

Often, the client pushes for a particular format because it's useful for them, not the learners. Instead, you're considering what's best for the **learners** and then adjusting that to account for logistics and budget.

What would you do?

Below are some behaviors that learners need to practice. Which activity format do you think would be best to replicate the real-life context? If you're not able to use that format for some reason, what would you propose as an alternative? **Remember, self-paced elearning isn't our only option, and it could be the worst option.**

Here's what people need to practice doing. How would you replicate the real world in your activity?

a) Managers need to practice managing a cross-cultural team that meets only online using voice and chat, keeping everyone on schedule. The managers are confident people who value efficiency.

b) Managers need to practice having difficult conversations that take place in person and in situations where emotions are likely to run high. Everyone is located in one small region.

c) Database users need to practice adding new products to the inventory control system, choosing the correct categories and labels. They're located all over the world and prefer to work alone.

d) Liquor sales people need to practice checking IDs to prevent underage people from buying liquor. They're located in one small region and like to socialize.

e) Salespeople need to practice selling a new pharmaceutical to doctors without violating regulations. The salespeople are located around the country and the product will be released in two weeks.

f) Analysts need to practice examining the financial records of a business and deciding if it would be a good acquisition. The analysts are located in time zones that differ by as much as three hours.

Here's my take on some formats to consider for the above examples.

a) Practice managing a cross-cultural team that meets only online using voice and chat

Consider: A live, virtual classroom that simulates the virtual team's face-less environment, with scenarios that simulate the decisions that the managers have to make. One option is to display each decision point of a scenario on the screen and ask people to type in the chat what they think is the best option and why. Once people understand the model they're supposed to apply, you can send them as pairs or small groups into private "rooms" to role-play tricky conversations for which you provide background and partial scripts. Also offer a forum and populate it with additional scenarios as practice over the following weeks.

Alternatives: Self-paced branching scenarios with asynchronous online discussion, though this would be a distant second best

b) Practice having difficult conversations

Consider: Live, in-person roleplaying with scripts or models to structure the conversation, plus a good facilitator; also provide online scenarios so people can practice again right before a conversation. Before the live session, you could have people complete a self-paced branching scenario of a conversation to provide a common example and fodder for discussion.

Alternative: Branching scenarios in which the learner chooses things to say to a person shown in video; these could be self-paced or used in a virtual classroom. One advantage of using scenarios is that you as the designer control what happens and choose which points to make.

c) Practice adding new products to the inventory control system

Consider: Self-paced online simulations in which people add fictional products using real-world job aids and help screens, plus additional help from the course or a fictional expert.

Alternative: Virtual training with a shared computer screen, using scenarios that require participants to enter or tell the facilitator how to enter realistic products into the system. This might not be popular, since the learners prefer to work alone.

d) Practice checking IDs of liquor store customers

Consider: Face-to-face training with several youngish people who have real and fake IDs, plus a job aid on how to spot a fake ID. People could also practice responding to people who become angry when their ID is rejected. It would be ideal to base this in an actual liquor store and have refresher sessions at periodic gatherings.

Alternative: Live training (online or face to face) with photos of the youngish people and photos of their IDs, plus the job aid, or an online, self-paced version of the same activity. Self-paced elearning would be my least favorite because live discussion is valuable in situations that have grey areas or upset people.

e) Practice selling a new pharmaceutical to doctors without violating regulations; timeline is short

Consider: Virtual or in-person roleplaying, with other participants listening for any statements that violate regulations and offering alternative wording. This would be the most realistic and easiest to develop quickly.

Alternative: Self-paced branching scenarios in which the learner has to choose what to say next in the sales conversation, plus videos or transcripts of sales conversations to evaluate. It would be hard to produce this in our very short timeframe.

f) Practice analyzing the financial records of a business to determine if it should be bought; time zones can vary by three hours

Consider: Live virtual workshop in which the participants analyze data from fictional or real businesses and discuss or defend their decisions, plus a job aid that summarizes the good and bad signs to look for or the decision-making model they should use. I'd also recommend an online discussion forum so people can ask colleagues for advice about acquisitions they're considering. You can periodically post links in the forum to scenarios in which people have to decide whether to buy a business, or at least post case studies.

Alternative: Self-paced scenarios in which learners decide whether to acquire fictional businesses and see the results of their decisions, with feedback comparing their decisions to the decisions of an expert, plus a job aid or decision-making model, plus the forum mentioned above.

Give learners control

Your audience members have a mix of pre-existing knowledge and skills. Even if what they're about to learn is brand new, they learn at different speeds and in different ways. The more control you give them over how they learn, the less they'll be bored or frustrated.

A major design decision that will affect learners' control is the choice between live and self-paced activities.

Live sessions

The typical live session moves at the pace determined by the facilitator. Participants can't make the facilitator speed up or skip what they already know, and they might hesitate to ask questions when things are going too quickly.

However, live sessions offer a major benefit: they allow discussion, both among participants and between participants and the facilitator. When that discussion is managed well, a live session can inspire deeper learning than self-paced solutions. Participants consider all sorts of shades of grey that they could miss in solo learning, and they hear a mind-broadening variety of perspectives.

Make sure you're making a point

While shades of grey are important, it's vital to also make clear what's black and white. This clarity can be lost in some types of live training.

Maybe you've been in this type of session: The friendly facilitator makes sure that every question they ask is easy and every answer from participants is labeled "great!" There's no one best way to do the thing, apparently because if there's a best way, then other ways would be less than best, and that might make someone feel bad. At the end I'm left thinking, "Why did I just spend an hour in this supposedly skill-building session if every question asked for feelings or vague ideas, every answer was great, and there was no clearly better way to do it? How did that improve my skills?"

Instead, our job is to help people see through guided experience what is the best way to do the thing, why it's the best way, how they'll benefit from it, and how they can apply it on their job.

Democracy has its drawbacks

If you use a multiple-choice activity in a live session, it can be tempting to display the options, have people vote, and then show the consequence of the most popular option. For example, if a majority of participants say the hero of the scenario should choose A, you choose A, even though you think the audience really needs to see the consequence of B.

Instead, culture permitting, it might be better to have people call out their opinions (or in a webinar, type them in the chat) and **selectively hear** the one that makes the point that you think needs to be made.

For example, let's say that you've displayed a scenario question, and option B will give you the consequence that you think people need to see. If you did a conventional poll and A won, with B in close second place, you'd have to choose A and continue the scenario. Then you'd have to go back and show B separately to make your point. But if instead you have people type or call out options, soon the chat or room fills with opinions. You can say something like, "I'm hearing lots of As, lots of Bs... B seems pretty popular, so let's choose that."

Also, a poll limits thinking. People just click a letter or raise their hands. If you use discussion instead, you can have people not only identify which option they'd choose but also briefly explain why. This gives you an idea of how people are thinking and can expose misconceptions that you need to address.

Printed branching scenario in live sessions

Scenarios can work well as printed choose-your-own-adventure packets that people complete in small groups. The packet might include the scenario and the real-world job aid that will help people make decisions in the scenario.

Below is one scene from a branching scenario that was distributed to small groups. Each group ran the scenario separately, debating their options. Then the larger group discussed the issues raised by the scenario. During the discussion, the facilitator helped participants identify the main takeaways.

In this case, future officers played the role of an American officer in Iraq. In the story, someone has started a small bombing campaign to scare civilians in the village, apparently as part of long-standing friction between two groups. The American's role is to advise the Iraqi army, and he needs to manage his sense of urgency in the face of slower, more collective decision-making.

In this scene, he has told his translator, Omar, that he's going to tell the Iraqi commander to act immediately to identify and punish the bombers, who appear to be a group called the Brothers in Blood. Omar responds as shown.

5

Omar looks uncomfortable.

"It might be best to let Commander Sadiq handle it," Omar says. "He understands the situation, and he'll probably say something at this afternoon's meeting."

The leader of the Brothers in Blood will be at the meeting, but it isn't going to happen for five hours. Omar agrees to visit Commander Sadiq with you now.

What do you say to the commander?

Choice		Go To
1	"I'm concerned about the IEDs and would like to know what you're planning to do about them."	11
2	"Five hours is too long to wait. We should bring the leader of the Brothers in Blood in for questioning now, or you could be seen as approving of the IEDs."	12
3	"As your advisor, I have to say that the people who set the IEDs need to be identified and arrested as soon as possible. What are you doing to accomplish that?"	13

Each decision point had three options. Each group contained four participants. Before they started the scenario, we had each participant choose a role: they could be the reader, or they could defend one specific option. For example, one member of the group had to defend option 2 whether or not he or she agreed with it. Then the group would make a decision and go to the next scene.

Groups who finished with time to spare were encouraged to go through the scenario again to see what happened as a result of other options. There was no going back; once a decision was made, players had to live with it and, if possible, choose an option that repaired the damage.

This was a popular format with young people who originally said they only liked video games. Don't be afraid to try it with your audience.

> **Elearning isn't the only option.** In fact, it's often the worst option. Your activities require people to make important, challenging decisions — the kind of decisions that often need discussion.

Self-paced methods

While "self-paced" is often followed by "elearning," there are roughly a bajillion more ways for people to learn at their own pace. This book is one of them. The list of other options would fill another book, but here are a few:

- Job aids and other references created by others
- YouTube videos
- Asking a colleague in person, on Twitter, through email...
- Searching the internet
- Building your own reference

- Trying it and seeing what happens

Self-paced methods let people go at their best pace, skip things they already know, and slow down when they reach a tricky spot.

However, some self-paced methods can alarm the client's inner control freak. "They all have to do the procedure the same way," the client says. "We can't let them learn it from random teenagers on YouTube."

You can standardize the method but still let people control how they learn it. For example, good job aids made available at the point of need could easily standardize practice. Even if you end up doing more conventional elearning, you can at least let people place out of what they know, go back and try things again, and seek out additional practice.

Elearning isn't just slides!

Elearning gets a lot of disrespect because at some point it was defined as "slides displayed on a little screen that people click occasionally." This probably happened because trainers wanted a simple solution they could grab without thinking, and they had a pile of slides at their elbow. It's the "quick, don't think!" approach to design.

Myths also appeared thanks to the "quick, don't think!" approach. I've heard claims that people won't read more than X bullet points at a time, elearning must be narrated or "audio learners" won't understand it, and everything must be on a little screen because "no one will scroll."

Here's the irony: The minute the "learner" closes the little elearning screen, they probably hop onto a web site and scroll happily away as they read (silently, without even moving their lips) some interesting article that teaches them in one minute far more than they learned from the ponderous narrator and flying bullet points.

Worse, "chunking" information into little unrelated crumbs and sprinkling them across 20 slides can make it hard to see how the crumbs relate. When we learn, we have to do far more than receive and store bits of information. We have to build connections and see overarching concepts.

At the very least, we need to expand our definition of elearning to include a mix of online formats that let us combine information and activities in ways that show the larger picture. For example, the materials I provide to supplement this book use a mix of conventional web text, embedded video, branching scenarios, and HTML5 interactions. Each proudly scrolling page focuses on one concept or step, so all the activities on that page support that concept or step.

When you break out of the slide mindset, you're free to **choose the format that works best for the activity** and show how everything relates.

Consider asking the learners

Your audience has preferences for how they'd like to learn. If you're not already familiar with them, ask them how they'd like to learn to do what you're supposed to help them learn.

My favorite way is to use a small focus group in which you provide real-life examples of what you're talking about. For example, if you're considering elearning for some aspect of the solution, show the type of activity you're thinking about, so people don't immediately assume you're describing the stultifying click-next "elearning" they suffered through last month.

Doing this in a group useful because you can learn a lot from the discussion among participants, and they'll remind each other of learning materials they liked or didn't like. For example, the word "elearning" was barely out of my mouth when the members of one focus group said, "We hate elearning! Hate hate hate!" But then one person said, "Wait, remember that activity where you had to keep the person from killing themselves? That was online, and everyone got into that." Then the consensus became, "We hate that click-next stuff, but if you do something like that simulation, we'll be all over it."

However, keep in mind the lessons that market researchers repeatedly learn: People don't necessarily do what they say they'll do. They might tell the researchers, "Yeah, I'd buy this product if you made it," but once the product is on the market, they buy something completely different. What counts is what people actually do when given the option in real life. This is one reason that you'll create at least one prototype of a typical activity and test it on learners.

5. Determine when people should use the activity

Your client is probably picturing a course or training event. Both of these happen apart from the job, and often people are expected to be "trained" long before they'll actually perform the task.

For now, ignore what the client is picturing. Consider when would be the best time **for the learners** to complete each practice activity.

Again, you're focusing on one activity at a time, not the project as a whole. The most useful timing for one activity could be very different from the timing for another.

Can you deliver the activity at the point of need?

Could you have people on the job learn through a practice activity shortly before they perform the task, or even during it? This depends on the type of job and task.

Practice before the task

If someone is about to perform an important task that they don't do every day, they'd probably benefit by doing some practice activities right before the task.

For example, let's say that Roger is about to interview a job candidate. He doesn't do a lot of interviews and isn't sure what questions he can legally ask and which questions would be the most useful.

Half an hour before the interview, he goes through some practice activities in which he has to interview fictional candidates. The activities help him practice asking questions that elicit useful information without breaking the law. He also looks at a one-page PDF of tips. Now he feels more prepared for the interview.

A good format for Roger's activities would probably be self-paced elearning, because it's easy to make it available on demand. However, when I say "elearning," I don't mean an online course. Roger isn't trudging through a conventional course about how to interview. He's just running through some highly targeted activities to help him practice. The information is supplied as a page of tips.

> *Often a course isn't necessary at all. The best solution might be activities that help people practice specific skills right before they need them.*

Practice during the task?

We had Roger run through some activities right before an interview. It's easy to think of other situations in which practice beforehand would be useful. However, it's harder to imagine a situation in which someone could pause the task to do some practice activities.

Roger can't stop in the interview to practice asking questions. He could hide the information — the PDF of tips — in the folder on his lap and glance at it as if he's looking at his notes. But he can't stop and complete activities.

For other types of tasks, such as data entry, it's possible to stop. But would it be **useful** to stop mid-task and practice something, or is the person more likely to need information at that point? It depends on the task and the person's prior knowledge.

Remember a procedure: information

Remember Grace and the problem with entering Hispanic names on TPS reports? Let's say that Bonnie, one of Grace's employees, learned how to enter Hispanic names a month ago. Now it's Monday morning after a weekend in which Bonnie had a lot of fun and very little sleep. She's completing a TPS report, and she realizes she's forgotten how to enter Hispanic names.

Does she need a practice activity, or just a reminder of the pattern? I'd say she just needs the reminder. She needs information, not practice. She looks at a small job aid, and once she sees the pattern again, it all comes back, and she's fine.

Learn it for the first time: activity, maybe

Let's say that Bonnie has a new coworker, Sean. He's had no official training. With Bonnie's help and the on-screen tips, he's doing a good job of entering TPS reports. But now he's faced with a Hispanic client who appears to have two last names. Which is the last name for the database?

He asks Bonnie what to do. She sends him a link to the names activity so he can learn the pattern and practice it on several different names. He needs the practice because it's new to him, and because he'll be using the skill repeatedly, both in TPS reports and in conversations with clients. Then he goes back to his work and completes the report.

Would your activity be most useful at the point of need?

If you have some activities that help people practice new or infrequent tasks, consider ways to make them available on demand. The on-demand approach is especially useful for activities that don't have major grey areas and that have consequences that aren't dire.

If instead the task requires a lot of complex decision-making and the fluency that can only come from practice over time, it's a good candidate for spacing.

How could you space the learning?

"Spacing" refers to helping people practice performing a skill or retrieving information in sessions that are spaced days or weeks apart. It's an under-utilized technique that can seriously boost the effectiveness of your activities.

Most corporate training is a one-time event, using the "shot in the arm" approach. We're supposed to attend a one-day course, learn everything right then and there, and return to our jobs as changed people.

However, we learn best when we practice a new skill repeatedly, with some time passing between practice sessions. We also remember new information better if we're asked to recall it several times over a period of time.

Just as we start to forget something, a new challenge appears that makes us retrieve it again, clearing the mental brush from the path to that information or skill. When we do this repeatedly, the path finally stays clear.

Marketing professionals are very familiar with the power of spacing. Their goal is the same as ours: to change what people do. But unlike us, they don't broadcast a commercial once and then say, "Okay, we've told them to buy our product. We're done." They make sure that commercial and all their other messages reach us over and over again, and all that time they're tracking how well the message works.

I'm not saying we need to reach the levels of obnoxiousness that advertising can achieve. But our belief that one training session will "fix" a problem is a big reason why so much training falls short of its goal. As several learning leaders have been arguing, we need to think in terms of campaigns, not courses.

What would it look like?

Spaced activities could be mini-scenarios delivered every few days and then every few weeks until the new skills are well embedded. They could be informal lunchtime sessions that include discussion-provoking questions. They could be frequent thought-provoking posts to a communal blog or forum. What they don't include are emails that simply remind people of what they learned, because we need to practice **retrieving**.

For example, it could be best for your audience to learn through just-in-time activities on the job, like we saw with Sean above. These activities aren't all bunched together in one "learn it all now!" session. They're called up when necessary and are immediately useful, probably making them more memorable.

Another option is to deliver practice activities as periodic challenges. The email software used by marketers has the features you need to send people a series of messages on certain dates and track what they do with those messages. A good LMS should have this function as well.

You could deliver activities spaced over an entire month and then have a live discussion session to help people process what they've learned. This would work especially well if your activities are controversial or surprising.

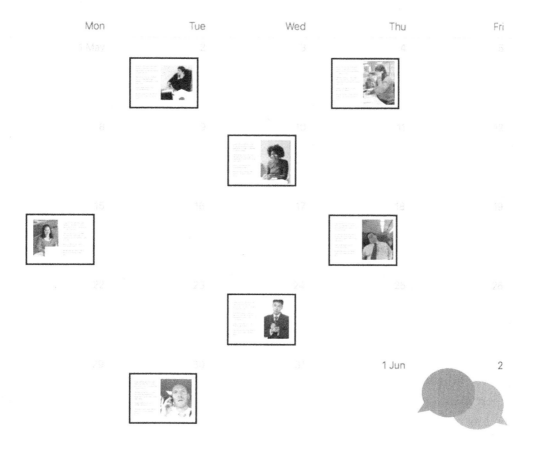

Is spacing a good idea for your project?

Since spaced practice helps us learn, it's a good idea for many projects. It's especially useful for tasks that require people to think on their feet and act without hesitation, such as having difficult conversations or responding to complex emergencies that can't accommodate job aids.

Spacing is also useful for anything that benefits from periodic practice, such as changing a habit, building a complex skill, or memorizing information (if you're convinced that people really need to memorize it).

6. Decide: Should all the activities be packaged as one course or event? (Probably not!)

You've considered multiple formats for each activity as well as the timing for each activity. If you've successfully put aside "the way we've always done it," you should have a mix of formats and times. Your answer to "Should it all be packaged as one event?" is probably "No."

For example, you could easily end up with some job aids on the intranet that people use while completing a task, several self-paced activities available on demand for use right before some tasks, a series of mini-scenarios spaced over a month to help people practice tasks that have grey areas and judgment calls, and a webinar at the end of the month to discuss the scenarios.

You might have decided to have no event at all. Maybe the best solution is a mix of on-the-job practice, job aids, and on-demand activities, with nothing to schedule.

In other words, you might not have "a course" or "a full-day workshop" or any one-time, shot-in-the-arm solution that the client might be expecting. You have a collection of activities and other solutions in multiple physical formats to be used at different times.

"But the client wants a one-time event!"

You've thought about this more than the client did. You, not the client, are the expert in how people learn. You have the responsibility and the right to recommend the most effective formats.

To practice responding to the client's possible concerns, consider these questions:

- Is there any **cognitive advantage** to making people complete all activities in one sitting? For example, must people learn A, B, and C all in one sitting? If someone learns to do A on one day and B on another day, will they be hopelessly lost? Or will learning B on that later day help them practice retrieving A, making them remember it better?

- Are there **cognitive drawbacks** to expecting everyone to learn everything in one sitting? (Yes, most likely. We don't learn well when everything new is crammed into our brains at once. The traditional one-time event was created for the convenience of trainers and people-trackers, not learners.)

- Are there **cost advantages** to making everyone learn it all in one sitting? For example, would it be cheaper to force all the activities into an online format and package them as a course? Would that really be cheaper than, say, providing a PDF job aid that people can learn from on the job, publishing a list of colleagues who are willing to answer questions, and putting a few activities online to be used on demand?

7. Determine the best mix of formats

You should now have several ideas for activities and solutions in different formats. You can probably see how some items could be delivered in multiple ways, giving you some flexibility as you determine how best to tie it all together.

Looking at your map as a whole, consider the following questions.

- **Which items fit best in the learners' workflow?** You probably have ideas for job aids or help screens, and you might have ideas for stand-alone practice activities that people can use right before they do the task in the real world. These can be produced in whichever format fits best into the workflow and best simulate the real-world context.

- **Which activities should be delivered over time?** If you're trying to change entrenched habits or help people learn complex processes, consider delivering practice activities over time. Rather than letting people blast through all activities in one sitting, you could drip-feed the activities, along with reinforcing information, so people practice a bit each week. Have each week's activity require people to draw on what they learned from a previous activity, so they practice retrieving skills and information while they learn new skills.

- **Which activities really require an event, such as a live session?** A live session done right supports lots of discussion. Consider a live, discussion-rich event if people are learning something that requires judgment calls, a new process is controversial, people will benefit from watching and evaluating how others do the new thing in real time, or when any other type of (challenging, deep!)

discussion will help embed the new habits.

If you think a live event will be useful, don't let yourself become convinced that it has to include everything. The live session that you're picturing should probably be mostly discussion, not presentation. For example, you might have people do several activities on their own, spaced over time and completed by each person at their own pace, and then meet to discuss the issues raised by the activities.

- **How can I meet the client's need to impress?** This might seem cynical, but it can actually serve the interests of both client and learner. Most clients need to look good to someone, whether it's their boss or their colleagues. Of the activities and materials on your map, which can **legitimately** be made more effective with high-end development and meet the need to impress?

  I'm not talking about adding pointless bling to an online activity. I mean if you have some ideas for scenarios, can those scenarios be developed in a way that looks professional **and** that supports the goal of the scenario? An example would be using custom photography or branching video for scenarios that involve conversation and emotion, rather than text alone or cheesy stock photos. Or, if you think an online reference will be helpful, can it be created using an attractive template that makes it more appealing as well as more useful?

  The idea is to meet the need to impress with just a few high-profile, **useful** items, not to crank out an entire bling-filled experience. Some items on your map undoubtedly deserve a bigger share of the development budget than others. There's rarely a reason to develop everything to the same high level.

Add your format ideas to the map. Don't present them to the client yet; it's probably best to wait until they're trying the prototype activity so they can see at least one example of what you're talking about.

"This is blended learning, right?"

Maybe. I avoid the term "blended learning" because it's commonly interpreted as pushing information through elearning and a face-to-face session.

"You should have people take an online module before the workshop, to get them all to the same level of knowledge," a colleague might say. "Then use the workshop to cover the more advanced stuff."

This views training as information presentation and just divides the presentation into two parts. It also assumes that an event is necessary. Instead, what I'm suggesting is to remember that you're mostly designing practice activities, not information, and then **let the audience, task, and job influence your choice of format**.

Base your recommendations on your analysis of the problem. Since most problems require several different solutions, your recommendations will probably include several different formats and different "delivery" times.

As I've said repeatedly, a course is often not the best solution. Training might not even be part of the solution.

> *Rather than asking which technology is best for learning, you will find more fertile ground by using a blend of media that allows you to space out learning events, provide post-training performance support, and foster synchronous and asynchronous forms of collaboration.*
>
> *— Ruth Colvin Clark in Evidence-Based Training Methods (2015)*

"Are you saying courses are bad?"

Courses are bad when they're not the right solution. To find the right solution, we have to (1) analyze the problem, even when nobody seems willing to do it, and (2) consider the many ways we can help people change what they do in the conditions that we learned about in the analysis. A formal event like a course is just one way to help people change, and it could easily be the worst way.

This isn't an original idea. The proponents of several workplace development models have been saying for years that we should stop throwing courses at people and look at more varied, in-the-workflow, self-driven solutions.

If your organization is implementing one of these workplace learning models, action mapping should help, for several reasons.

- **You don't let clients assume that formal training is the solution.** Rather than obediently producing training on demand, you analyze the problem and look for the best solution. If you do a careful analysis, you'll probably find that formal training is only part of the solution, if it has a role at all.

- **Your activities focus on what people need to do on the job and not what they supposedly need to know.** If you develop training, your material simulates what people do on the job. You create practice activities, not knowledge checks.

- **Your solution could fit in the workflow.** Because your analysis focuses on actual behaviors in the workplace, you're in a good position to find solutions that fit in the job. For example, instead of pulling people off work for a course, you might decide that job aids would help them learn while working. Or if you develop practice activities, you could decide to make them available on demand, on the job, and not in a separate training event.

- **Your solution could include social methods.** Your analysis looks for barriers to performance, and when you consider the environment, you could easily find issues that keep people from sharing information. Instead of shoving that information at people through training, you might set up a social platform or knowledgebase for people to contribute to, organize gatherings to make it easier for people to share knowledge, or encourage managers to be more accessible.

Be careful: Models can be misused

If your organization has adopted a specific model of workplace learning, make sure that the people interpreting it don't assume that "learning" is always the solution.

For example, many L&D industry leaders say that we should support all types of learning, not just formally designed events. We should recognize and support the fact that people also learn from informal conversations, job aids, social networks, peer-produced videos, and a zillion other methods. I completely agree.

However, the statement that our job is to support all types of learning can unfortunately encourage L&D staff to continue assuming that our job is knowledge transfer alone. We just need to do it better with this new model.

For example, people can assume that the self-motivated, social learning that we'll support with New L&D Model X will automatically improve performance as silos collapse and information finally runs free. They make the familiar assumption that knowledge transfer must be the solution, so we don't need to look closely at any problem.

Sharing knowledge is the solution only if a lack of knowledge has caused the problem. Models that focus on how knowledge is shared can tempt L&D staff to stay in the traditional training mindset: "They need to know this and understand that." But instead of throwing a course at the "learners," they set up an online forum.

I'm not saying that the people advocating for new models are claiming that we don't need to analyze performance problems. I'm not saying that they claim we should just set up hashtags and sprinkle "microlearning" through the organization. However, it's very tempting for people to **interpret** the models as saying that, because no one wants to do the work of analyzing the problem.

Yes, we should support all ways that people learn. However, our first responsibility to our clients is to question the assumption that knowledge transfer will solve the problem.

The issue might be unrelated to whether people "understand" something. It could be completely unaffected by the fact that hundreds of people are helpfully sharing everything they know in an endless Slack stream. We have to examine the problem before we can identify what role, if any, knowledge has in its solution.

If we don't bother to define a problem beyond "our managers need to be better leaders" or "we're not innovative enough," then we have no hope of solving it, no matter what learning model we use. And if no one else in our organization is asking the hard questions, then we have to do it. We're the last line of defense.

Common challenges

The client has already identified the format they want.

- Ignore what the client wants, just for now. Soon you'll show them a prototype of an activity in the format that you recommend, and when they see that, they could easily change their mind and choose your format.

You can't imagine a format that isn't elearning.

- This is a common problem, thanks to the dominance of elearning and the tendency to treat all other training as information presentation. Maybe everyone expects you to develop elearning, and you've never seen practice activities used in any other format. You might revisit chapter 7 to see how the same activity can be delivered in multiple formats.

You have limited development time.

- Your analysis should have identified some low-tech solutions, such as PDF job aids or tweaks to a process, which will take much less development time than the usual online course. If online activities are part of your solution, you might try using text, such as a text-based mini-scenario. Novels have used text for centuries.

Everyone expects high production values or bling, but you'd rather spend the budget on designing challenging activities.

- Plan to create a working prototype of a challenging but bling-free interaction to get your stakeholders to see that cognitive challenge is more interesting than bling.

- When you present the prototype, plan to point out that the materials will consist almost entirely of challenges, with less information presentation than usual. Discourage stakeholders from comparing what you're doing with what has been done in the past.

Your organization doesn't have the tools to develop the activities in the format that you think is best.

- If you can, use a trial version of the tool to build your prototype. If your stakeholders agree that the tool is necessary, you'll have a stronger argument for investing in it.

- If you're sure that it will be impossible to get the tool, look for ways to replicate the most important aspects of the format in some other way. For example, if you wanted a custom animated drawing showing how a widget is assembled but there's no budget for it, consider recording a simple video instead and adding annotations in common video editing software.

Chapter 9. Activity design: Choose an activity and interview the SME

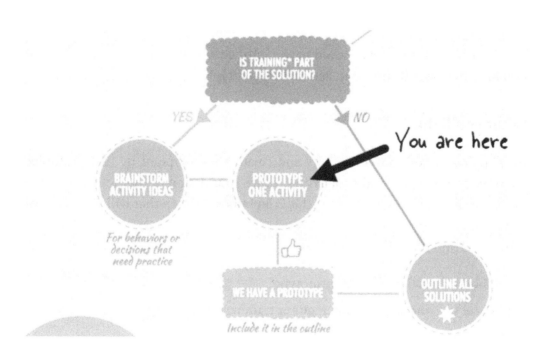

Task	Who does it	How long it might take
Choose one activity idea for development as a prototype. The activity will serve as a model for the rest. The activity could be a stand-alone mini-scenario or one typical decision point in a longer branching scenario. Interview the SME to get the nuanced understanding you need to write a challenging activity.	You'll choose the activity to be prototyped. The SME will help you understand the task and its barriers.	This could take minutes or hours, depending on the complexity of the activity and your understanding of the job context.

Tool: Activity planning document (see map-it-book.com)

Results: You'll get a deep understanding of the task that people need to practice. Information you'll collect includes:

- A detailed example of a realistic challenge that people face when performing the task
- The most common mistake, why people make it, and what happens as a result
- Other common mistakes and their causes and consequences
- The correct choice, why it's hard to make, and its consequences

What you've done

You've noted ideas for activities and have identified which format might be best for each one. Now you'll choose an activity to prototype.

What you'll do

You're going to flesh out an activity and create a prototype of it. The prototype will serve as a model for other activities. Since your design of this activity sets the precedent for many more activities, this is an important step that will take up most of the book.

In this chapter, you'll do the following.

1. Choose an action for your prototype
2. Make sure the action really requires training
3. Schedule a meeting with the SME
4. Plan to get the right details from the SME, which are probably not the details you're used to getting
5. Get the details from the SME, focusing on context, "why," and consequences
6. Carefully ask what information is required to make the decision
7. Take notes. In subsequent chapters, you'll continue to create the prototype.
8. Write the question and options
9. Design the feedback

10. Identify how you'll provide the supporting information

11. Create and test the prototype

You're still in the activities ring of the map, and you're focusing on one activity.

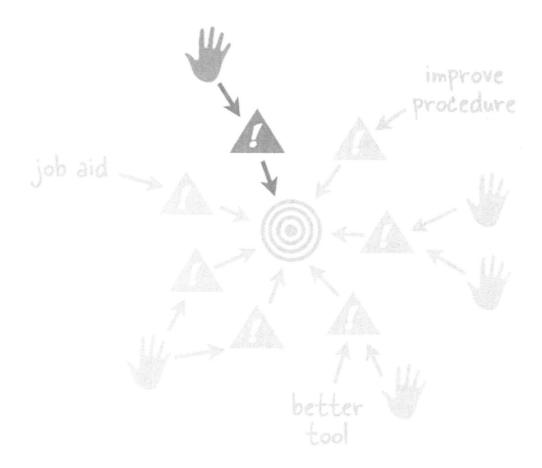

Who's involved?

You should probably be the one who writes the activity. However, you'll need your SME's help to identify the best options to use and add realistic details. A practice activity requires more from the SME than conventional test questions, so stock up on "Hello Kitty" cupcakes or whatever else makes the SME happy, and bring them to every meeting.

Should the SME write content?

It might be common in your organization for SMEs to hand you a slide deck that has "what they need to know." Some organizations ask the SME to write the course content for you, and then you're supposed to apply retroactive instructional design to it.

However, you're trying to move the focus from presenting content to having people practice what they need to do. Also, as SMEs spend time writing scripts or designing slides, they become attached to their work and reluctant to change it.

If your SME is used to writing materials, sidestep any suggestion that they create content. You might position the change as a way to make life easier for the SME. "I just need to interview you," you might say. "You don't have to write anything or create slides."

On the other hand, if your SME is enthusiastic about designing activities and eager to abandon the school model, then you're on a dream team. In that case, you might consider having the SME write some activities – **after** you write the prototype that you're going to create now. Your prototype will serve as a model for other activities.

What type of activity?

We're going to design a type of practice activity that can be used in any format, from elearning to face-to-face sessions to immersive games.

At first, it looks like "just" a multiple-choice question, but it's designed to simulate the kind of decision-making that people have to do on the job. It sets a scene, asks the learner to make a realistic decision, and provides options that have been carefully designed to tempt the learner to make a common mistake.

In its most basic form, it might look like this:

> Bill needs to pass a scalpel to Sara during surgery. What should he do?
>
> a) Put the scalpel in a sterile kidney dish and hold the dish out to Sara.
>
> b) Hold it by the neck and place the handle in Sara's palm.
>
> c) Put it on the surgical drape for her to pick up herself.
>
> d) Toss it gently in her direction, handle first.

You might be thinking, "That looks like elearning." But the type of activity we're going to create can be used in any format, including live training, as we saw in the previous chapter.

A multiple-choice question provides discipline

We're using the multiple-choice format to structure a deep examination of the decision and its consequences. The format requires us to analyze the context, decision, common mistakes, best approach, and, importantly, the consequences of each option. A multiple-choice question is a handy, familiar way to store a ton of information about each decision.

A good multiple-choice question can be turned into anything from an informal discussion to an immersive world where avatars face challenges. Because it stores so much information about the decision and possible consequences, it's going to be our default activity for now. Later, you can turn it into anything you want.

The humble multiple-choice question, when it's used as we're about to use it, becomes a surprisingly powerful tool for analysis. The most common mistake I see in training is a lack of analysis. This includes skipping the broad analysis of the performance problem as well as failing to closely examine the decisions the learner has to make on the job. This lack of analysis is why we have so much boring training.

Writing a challenging, realistic multiple-choice question requires exactly the kind of analysis that we often skip. That's why we're going to spend several chapters writing just one question, its options, and feedback for each option. Once you have that process down, you'll repeat it for your other activities. **You'll also end up with all the context and information you need to turn your multiple-choice questions into any other type of activity.**

Be sure to write options and consequences, not just the questions

In live training, the facilitator might just ask the question and not present the options. However, the discipline of writing the options and feedback is essential.

First, by writing the options and feedback, you'll develop a much deeper understanding of the performance problem that will inform the rest of your design. Also, the facilitator needs to know what are the common mistakes and what would happen for each one, so they can elicit that knowledge from participants during the discussion.

Some people say we shouldn't use multiple-choice questions, because having people select pre-written options makes the question too easy. "They should generate the answer on their own," they argue. Interestingly, research cited by Ruth Clark in *Scenario-based e-Learning* (2013) suggests that, in elearning, at least, "Selecting preformatted responses imposes less mental load than constructing a response from scratch and has been found to lead to better learning."

This doesn't mean that you shouldn't ask an open-ended question in a live session and wait for answers. It's a great way to make people think and to surface misunderstandings. However, you should design multiple-choice options beforehand so you know what are the most common mistakes and what's the best response, and you also shouldn't let stakeholders talk you out of providing challenging multiple-choice questions if you think it will be more effective. A multiple-choice question can actually inspire more discussion than an open-ended question if it includes appealing distractors.

Elearning: Make sure your tool handles contextual feedback

If you plan to develop an online activity, make sure your software lets you provide different feedback for each option.

A disturbing percentage of question-building tools let you provide only two types of feedback: correct and incorrect. Instead, you need to be able to provide different feedback for each option. In addition, your feedback might be more extensive than the tool assumes. If your tool provides one tiny box for you to enter your feedback, you'll get frustrated.

If you think you'll be designing a branching scenario, look for a tool specifically for that. Twine is an open-source solution for interactive fiction writers. It's free but, like any open-source project, it expects you to do some of the heavy lifting yourself.

"But I don't want my activity to be a multiple-choice question."

Again, I'm not saying that the final format of your activity should be a multiple-choice question. You can turn a multiple-choice question into practically anything. I'm saying that the discipline of writing a good multiple-choice question is a great way to quickly but deeply learn about a decision and store information about common mistakes and their consequences.

Also, if you look closely at the final format you have in mind, you might discover that a multiple-choice question lurks within. For example, the following common activities are multiple-choice questions in disguise:

- Branching scenario: Each decision point is a multiple-choice question.

- Structured roleplay: If you give role players some guidelines (as you should!), those guidelines reduce what people can say from "anything at all" to "things that match these criteria."

- Activity that has people apply a job aid: The job aid reduces potential actions from "I could do anything at this point!" to "This reference says I should check X and then, based on the result, decide between Y or Z."

Don't try to cover everything in one activity

If you want your practice activity to be, essentially, "Do the entire task," you might be getting ahead of yourself.

For example, if you plan to put new printer repair people in front of malfunctioning printers and say, "Fix the printer," you've skipped a few steps. "Fix the printer" would be a great later activity, but leading up to it, you should probably include more focused activities.

For example, an earlier activity could be, "This printer has a problem in its feed mechanism. Can you find it?" You'd include a job aid that, for example, lists steps that diagnose paper-feeding issues. This structure makes it a multiple-choice activity: The technicians think, "Which of these steps should I do next, based on the results I got from the previous step?" and not "What, out of all the possible things I could do to this printer, shall I do now?"

These more focused, scaffolding activities make the final "Fix the printer" activity a multiple-choice question. The new technicians have gone through a series of activities that included lists of diagnostic steps, so they now have a repertoire of steps to choose from. As a result, the final "Fix the printer" activity becomes, essentially, a multiple-choice question with many, but not infinite, options.

What about branching?

Should your prototype activity be a one-scene, standalone decision or a branching scenario? I'd suggest you first develop just one decision point, such as a self-contained mini-scenario: The learner makes a decision and sees the consequence, the end. Once you've established how you'll write and develop a typical decision, you can take on the additional challenge of plotting a branching scenario if you decide that's appropriate.

If you don't have any activities that can stand alone as one decision, choose a typical decision from the larger story and develop just that decision. Plan to help reviewers imagine the story that would precede and follow the decision. Your goal at this point is to establish how you'll present a specific challenge, options, feedback, and information. Once you've established that, you can apply it to all decisions in the scenario and write the plot.

1. Choose an action for your prototype

Your prototype activity will serve as a model for others, so choose an action (behavior) from your map that's typical of the others. If you anticipate having some very different types of activities, you'll probably want to create a prototype for each type.

2. Make sure the action really requires training

You should already have identified which behaviors require practice activities and which can be supported in other ways, such as through a job aid or an improvement to a procedure. That happened during the analysis with the flowchart.

Now, take a second look at the action you've chosen for your prototype and double-check that it ended up on the correct path in the flowchart and really requires a practice activity. Practice activities help people practice making decisions on the job that **require judgment**.

For example, which of the following actions do you think justify the development of what I call a practice activity? If a practice activity isn't appropriate, what could you do instead?

a) Memorize the correct dosage for a horse (for a veterinarian who usually works with cats and dogs but occasionally sees horses)

b) Apply the three-step Difficult Conversation Model (for managers who meet frequently with team members)

c) Follow these eight steps to set up the equipment the same way every day

d) Troubleshoot the printer in different settings (for printer repair people who travel to customers' offices)

e) When a caller asks for Nigel, connect them to line 3 (for receptionists)

Here's my take on them:

a) Memorize the correct dosage for a horse: This shouldn't require memorization because the vet is only occasionally confronted with a horse. A reference on a smartphone might be a better solution. A practice activity probably isn't necessary unless the information provided by the reference is tricky to apply.

b) Apply the 3-step Difficult Conversation Model: This is a complex, frequent behavior that requires judgment and can't rely completely on a job aid, so it's a good candidate for a practice activity.

c) Follow these 8 steps to set up the equipment the same way every day: If the steps require no judgment — they're just things like "Push the blue button and then move the green lever up" — there's probably no need for training. Maybe we could just put a sign on the wall next to the equipment that lists the steps.

d) Troubleshoot the printer in different settings: This requires judgment and is a good candidate for practice activities, as are most behaviors that involve diagnosing a problem.

e) When a caller asks for Nigel, connect them to line 3: This is a simple rule, so it's doubtful that it requires training. If the receptionist doesn't have to respond within milliseconds, we could just provide a current list of staff names and their lines. If the receptionist must memorize this information for some reason, we might design drills. Drills are simple memorization activities, not the complex decision-making activities we're focusing on here.

The behaviors we're focusing on **require judgment.** They don't expect people to robotically complete one step after another. So, make sure that the behavior you're about to turn into a practice activity requires some independent judgment and can't be solved with a simple job aid or memorized with a drill. The more grey areas the decision has, the better.

3. Schedule a meeting with the SME

To get the insight you need, you'll need to talk to your SME, not send emails back and forth or ask them for their PowerPoint deck. Tell the SME you'd like to interview them so you can understand what's happening when people need to perform the action that you've chosen for your practice activity.

This conversation could take anywhere from 15 minutes to more than an hour, depending on the complexity of the real-world task and activity you've planned. You could do this in person or over the phone.

When you set up the interview, make sure the SME understands the following.

- They don't need to prepare anything. You'll just ask some questions. It will be easy for them.
- You're going to talk about Specific Task X – not the entire project, and not "the course."

4. Plan to get the right details from the SME – not the details you're used to getting

Once you're sure a practice activity is necessary, you need to collect a lot of information. But what information is most useful?

In the traditional approach to training design, you'd ask the SME the following:

- What should people do in this situation? (That would become the "correct" answer.)
- What might they do wrong? (These would become your distractors.)
- What rules guide how people should make this decision? (You'd describe the rules in your feedback, after saying "Correct!" or "Incorrect," of course.)

This approach creates generic questions with obvious answers and preachy feedback. To add depth and challenge, we need to get different information, including:

- What's happening when people make this decision? Where are they? Who are they talking to?
- Why is the decision hard?
- What are the common mistakes people make, and **why do they make them**?

- What happens when someone makes each common mistake? What specifically are the consequences?
- What should people do instead of the common mistakes, and why?
- What happens when people make the best decision? What specifically are the consequences?

We're asking for three types of information that are overlooked in the traditional approach: what is the **context** of the decision, what are the **consequences** of each choice, and **why** are people struggling in the first place?

And that's only some of the information we need to gather. But what's the best way to get it? Let's look at an example.

Example: Arno and the "trusted advisors"

Imagine that you and I work for a performance improvement firm, analyzing and solving problems for a range of clients.

Remember Bob and Luisa's project from the chapter on setting goals? They helped their widget salespeople listen to customers and find them the best widget. In fact, they did such a good job that their competition, Weeber Widgets, has gotten nervous.

Now we're in a meeting with Arno, a manager from Weeber.

"We're changing our brand personality," Arno says. "Instead of doing what most widget companies do and focus on how great our features are, we want to create an emotional connection with our customers. We want to become their trusted advisors for all their widget needs."

"Trusted advisors?" I say.

"If we just talk about our features," Arno explains, "then we're always scrambling to stay ahead of the competition. For example, if we say our widget is the fastest, a competitor will come out with a faster one. But if we build an emotional connection with our customers, the competition won't be able to pull them away with a slightly better feature."

"So you'd like to change how your staff talk with customers and represent the brand?"

"Yes," Arno says. "They need to understand emotional branding."

During the meeting that follows, we move Arno from his original goal of "Salespeople will understand emotional branding" to "Weeber market share will increase

20% by the end of the year as all salespeople implement the Trusted Advisor sales model."

Arno helps us list what the salespeople need to do and why they aren't doing it. There are several actions on the list, including:

- Ask questions designed to uncover the emotional benefits that matter most to the customer (we break this down into sub-actions, one for each major type of question)

Salespeople haven't been doing this because the emphasis on emotional benefits is new. Most of them have experience only in technical sales, where it isn't common to identify emotional benefits.

- When a customer shows concern about the heat generated by some of our widgets, respond in a way that builds trust

Salespeople think that industry publications have unfairly criticized Weeber widgets for this issue. As a result, the salespeople interpret a customer's objection as unfair criticism and respond defensively.

During the meeting with Arno, we build the action map out to the "action" ring. Then we say goodbye to Arno and brainstorm activity ideas for the actions that appear to need training.

We decide that most activities should simulate a conversation between the salesperson and a customer, since most actions take place during that conversation.

Aim for flexibility in formats

Arno has told us that the sales staff are all sociable people who prefer to learn as a group, but he'd like to avoid travel expenses. A virtual meeting with a shared screen could be the way to go if we decide an event is useful. Maybe we'll have people complete some group activities in a kickoff event, do other activities on their own over a few weeks, and then have another online event to discuss the controversial points and main takeaways.

The types of scenarios we've brainstormed could be used in a live session in two ways.

1. The facilitator could display the question with its options, and participants could debate the options, vote for one, and then see the consequences of their choice.

2. The facilitator could display just the question, not the options, and have a more open discussion. We'd make sure that the facilitator's guide included the options and their feedback so the leader would know how to respond to the decisions that participants are likely to suggest.

The question with its options could also be used as a self-paced online activity. For example, it could be one of a bank of practice activities used for spaced practice after a live session.

Choose an activity to prototype

Our next step is to choose a typical activity to be our prototype. We decide to prototype the activity that helps salespeople respond to objections about how hot some widgets get. Most of our activities focus on changing how people talk with customers, so this is a good representative for prototyping. Also, responding to an objection is a little trickier than asking customers for information, so it will be a good challenge for us.

Schedule a meeting with the SME

Arno is both the client and SME on this project, so we've scheduled a meeting to get the details we need for our prototype activity. When we called him, we made clear that we're going to focus on the one behavior that we've chosen for development.

"We'd like to help people respond to objections about the heat generated by some widgets," we said. "Do you have a few minutes to help us understand what happens in that situation?"

What do we need to know?

Now we're meeting with Arno, who is happily munching on the vegan dark chocolate bar that he loves and we provided, because we know it's always a good idea to make your SME happy.

Now, what should we ask to get the information we need for our activity?

How about this question: "How do you respond when a customer is worried about a widget getting hot?"

Here's the response we're likely to get from Arno: "I tell them that the heat is a harmless byproduct of high performance. I show them that I'm familiar with how widgets work and what our industry publications say about the heat."

Could you write a detailed question, at least three tempting options, and feedback for each option with only that information? I couldn't.

How about the following questions? Would they give us what we need?

- When does the decision happen? What's going on at that point?
- Why is the decision difficult?
- What's the most common mistake, and why do people make it?
- What happens as a result of that mistake?
- What are some other common mistakes and their consequences?
- What should people do instead?
- Why don't they do it?
- What principles or rules of thumb help guide this decision?

That's a much longer list of questions. Should we run through the list with Arno? Let's try it.

"What's the most common mistake?" we ask Arno.

"They get defensive," he says. Does that give us enough information to write a good option?

If we accept his answer, the draft of our activity question could look like this:

"I'm concerned about the heat generated..."[Customer raises objection about heat]

What do you do next?

A. Get defensive

B. ...

Although the questions listed above are a good start, they're too generic. Generic questions get generic answers that lack the detail we need.

"This type of general question serves to divorce the practitioner's knowledge and skills from their lived experience," write Beth Crandall et al. in *Working Minds: A Practitioner's Guide to Cognitive Task Analysis (2006)*.

So how do we get the details we need?

5. Get the details from the SME, focusing on context, "why," and consequences

Rather than ask generic questions, encourage the SME to tell about a specific incident, or ask them to perform the task in its real context and explain how they make each decision.

Ask for a story

The critical decision model described in *Working Minds,* mentioned above, asks the SME to tell about a specific time when the decision was especially difficult or memorable.

"Tell us about a time when you responded to an objection about heat in a really good or bad way," we might say. Then we'd ask additional questions to get the information we need, such as:

- What was happening? Who was there, and what did they say?
- What did you conclude about the customer? Why?
- What did you say in response? Why?
- What happened as a result?
- What would a novice have done in the same situation? Why?
- What would happen as a result?
- What's another common decision a novice might make in that situation? Why? What would happen?
- How did you make your decision? What information did you base it on? Is there a rule of thumb?

Because our story about Arno is simple, our discussion is likely to be short and easy. We could ask a few more questions and quickly be done.

This approach really shows its power in more complex decisions, such as diagnosing a medical condition, predicting the weather, or deciding how to respond to a natural disaster. For such complex decisions, the authors of *Working Minds* suggest walking the SME through the story in four levels.

1. Get a brief overview of the incident, so you can get a sense of the decisions involved and make sure it's an appropriate incident. Typically, the incident is a non-routine, challenging event that, although it's unusual, shows how experts make decisions and what impacts those decisions have.

2. Build a timeline of the incident, marking when major decisions or realizations occurred.

3. Deepen the story, going beyond the facts of what happened to find out, as the *Working Minds* authors write, "what did they know, when did they know it, how did they know, and what did they do with what they knew?" What were they concerned about at each point? What options did they consider? What information did they look for, and where did they find it? This is a good time to elicit the mental models or rules of thumb that the expert uses.

4. Finally, ask "what if?" questions, such as, "How could you have gotten a different outcome? What might have happened if a novice had been in charge at this point? What training, if any, might have helped you make the decision?"

For more ideas, I recommend you read *Working Minds*, which describes this and other research-supported methods in clear, practical detail.

Have the SME complete the task while thinking aloud

Another option is to have the SME perform the task while thinking out loud. This won't work well with Arno unless we happen to have a customer handy who's worried about hot widgets. However, for many types of tasks, this can be an efficient way to get what you need.

For example, if I were to teach someone to drive in the southern Mexican city where I used to live, I'd first have them ride along in the passenger seat. I'd drive through a confusing intersection while describing what my brain is doing.

"Technically, we have the right of way," I'd say. "But I'm waiting for that bus because in reality, the bigger vehicle gets the right of way. Now we've got an opening! I'm going to zoom across two lanes because otherwise I'll never get a chance to turn left at the next intersection. "

Once we're safely through the intersection, you could ask me what common mistakes a novice would have made, why they would make them, and what other rules of thumb or principles apply in addition to "the bigger vehicle gets the right of way."

A variation on this is to videotape the expert performing then task, and then show them the video and ask them to explain their thinking. "What were you thinking at this point?" you might ask. "Why did you do that? What would a novice have done instead?"

This can be the most efficient way to get the information you need for a realistic practice activity. You'll also need to ask several "what if" questions to learn about the common mistakes and understand their consequences.

Ask lots of "dumb" questions

In your discussion, encourage the SME to surface the beliefs or assumptions that can interfere with good choices. You might use your outsider status to ask "dumb" questions, to make sure the SME identifies the common mistakes.

For example, let's say your client is a government agency, and the task is to approach a possibly mentally ill homeless person and encourage them to move their belongings so construction can start where they've camped.

As the SME tells a successful story about such a conversation, they describe how one employee of the agency walked over alone to talk to an upset man.

"Wouldn't it be safer to bring a colleague with you?" you ask.

The SME explains that you're more likely to persuade the person if you approach them alone, so you don't seem like you're bullying them. It's best for you to have a colleague keep an eye on you, but talk to the person alone.

"It's a common mistake for people to do this in twos or even threes," the SME says, giving you an idea for a useful distractor.

Your SME might not think of these questions on their own, so don't hesitate to ask them.

Consider approaching additional SMEs

Whether you use a story- or task-based approach, you might discover that your SME doesn't have experience in a specific task or area. Consider asking for help from people who have the necessary experience, rather than relying on generic information that your current SME might have.

Also, some decisions are made by teams, not by lone experts. In that case, you'll want to interview a team that was involved in a specific incident, so you can understand the challenges faced at each point and gather the details necessary to translate them into meaningful activities.

6. Carefully ask what information is required to make the decision

When you're confident you have a good understanding of the task and decision, ask questions like the following.

- What's the **minimum** information people need to know to make this decision?
- What should they memorize, and what could they look up?
- Where is that information now?

As we saw during the analysis, it's common for a SME to make two problematic assumptions:

- People need more information to make the decision than they really do.
- People should memorize more information than they really need to memorize.

Here are four ways to help the SME avoid sinking into the quicksand of information.

Save the information discussion for last

The SME might want to first tell you everything people need to know. Instead, ask them to tell you a story or complete the task while thinking out loud, and only then ask about the necessary knowledge. This will help remind the SME that your goal is to help people to make good decisions, not just to get information into their heads.

Remind the SME that this activity will be one of a series

The SME might be concerned about the many basic concepts and other prerequisite knowledge that people should have before they can make the decision in your activity. Reassure the SME that this won't be the only activity and that people will have plenty of opportunity to learn the basics through other activities.

However, if you're planning to make your prototype the first activity and the SME has a long list of what people legitimately need to know before they can make the decision, you might want to rethink your prototype. You'll want to organize your activities so the earlier ones help people learn (or confirm their pre-existing knowledge of) basic concepts, one at a time, before you put them in situations that require them to apply several concepts at once.

Maybe your prototype is more difficult that you thought and should appear somewhere in the middle of the materials, after easier activities. Or maybe your prototype requires people to apply too many variables or make too many decisions at once. Can you eliminate some of the complexity?

Use the mini-flowchart

If you're designing an activity for a task that didn't get a detailed look during your original analysis, you might use the "Memorize or job aid?" flowchart we first saw there. Here it is again.

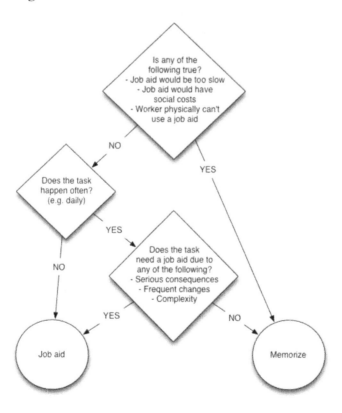

This might help the SME see more clearly that the expert knowledge that's in their head doesn't necessarily have to be put in everyone's heads.

Play a game

In *Working Minds*, the authors describe a "20 questions" game that I think could be adapted to determine the information required for an activity. It's normally used to understand how experts think, and it works like this:

1. Give the expert a problem to be solved, but provide little or no information about it.
2. Make the expert ask you for each bit of information they need to solve the problem.
3. Note the information that the expert requests and when they request it, which can tell you a lot about how they make decisions.

We could adapt this game to help identify the information we should supply with an activity. First, we could play the game with an expert. Next, we could try it with a novice, who's probably going to ask for a lot more information. The difference between the two gives you an idea of what the expert has in their head that the novice doesn't. This helps identify what information you should provide during the activity and begin to identify information that might need to be memorized.

Of course, it's likely that the expert's information doesn't all need to be memorized, so you'll want to take a close look at that, possibly using the flowchart above.

7. Take notes

As you interview the SME, make sure your notes include the following:

- The context of the decision, especially what makes it hard
- The three most common or problematic mistakes and their separate consequences — these should be specific and detailed, such as the words that people actually say in a conversation, not vague descriptions like "get defensive"
- Why people make each mistake; what makes it appealing
- The best choice and its consequence, in detail
- A basic idea of the information required to make a good choice

You'll use these notes to write the activity in the next chapters.

Instead of relying on notes, another option is to record the conversation, which has the additional benefit of capturing how people in the organization talk.

Example: Notes from our talk with Arno

For our prototype activity about responding to customer's objections about heat, we've added notes reminding ourselves of the common mistake ("Get defensive"), another common mistake ("Distract them with another widget"), and the correct response ("Show willingness to talk frankly about the issue and show broad expertise in the field of widgets").

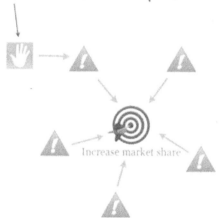

Scenario: A well-informed customer brings up bad reviews about heat.
Options: defend; distract; show expertise

With those reminders and our more detailed notes, we're ready to write our first draft. We thank Arno and go off to write on our own, which we'll see in the next chapter.

Common challenges

The SME just keeps telling you what people need to know.

- Ask them to tell you a specific story instead. These could be stories from the SME's own experience (best) or stories about what other people in the organization did.

- Have the SME perform the task while you watch or record them on video. Ask them during or after the task what they were thinking at key points and what a novice would have done instead.

- Consider finding an additional SME who might be more open to this approach, positioning it as "It's helpful to have as many perspectives as possible" or "This is a lot of work for one person."

The SME just wants to write something and send it to you.

- Suggest that having an interview would be less work for them, and make clear that you're going to ask them to tell interesting stories about things they've done. Most people enjoy talking about themselves.

- If you suspect the SME wants to control how the content is written out of a concern for accuracy, remind them that they'll review every activity you write. They'll have lots of opportunity to catch any errors.

- If the SME wants to send you content because that's how it's always been done, remind them that this project is different. If you haven't already, show them some activities like the ones you plan to prototype. Point out that to create that type of activity, you need to use a different process and collect different information than usual. This is one reason why I strongly recommend you include the SME from the beginning, starting with the business goal.

The SME is happy to talk but doesn't say anything specific.

- If you're using the story-based approach, don't stop at "Tell me about a time..." Also ask very specific questions like, "What were you thinking at this point? Why?" and "What would a novice say instead of what you said?"

- If you're watching them perform the task or reviewing a video, stop the action as necessary to ask questions like, "Why did you do that?" and "How did you know that the widget was about to wobble? What did you see? What did you hear?"

The SME doesn't want to participate at the level required by the project.

- Ideally, your SME became enthusiastic during the goal-setting and analysis phase. If this isn't true of your SME, try showing them some activities like the ones you plan to prototype, if you haven't already. Sometimes a reluctant SME can get inspired by cool activities.

- If your SME still resists contributing much, consider finding an additional SME. Position it as, "It's helpful to have as many perspectives as possible" or "This is a lot of work for one person."

The SME keeps disappearing.

- If your SME is interested in the project but is slow to respond to your requests for interviews, politely point out to them how their timely response is important to staying on schedule. If this doesn't work, you might escalate it to the client, saying that you're going to have trouble delivering on time because it seems the SME has too much on their plate. That might be enough for the client to clarify priorities for the SME.

- If the SME continues to delay things despite seeming enthusiastic about the project, consider finding an additional SME. Position it as, "It's helpful to have as many perspectives as possible" or "This is a lot of work for one person."

Chapter 10. Activity design: Stem and options

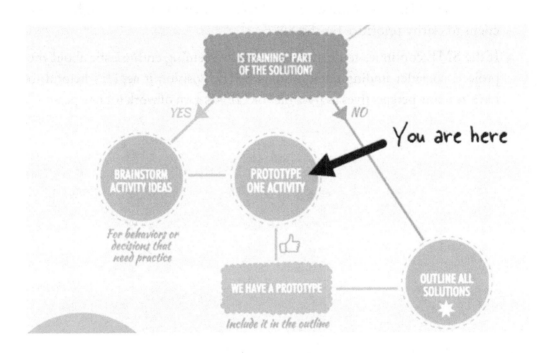

Task	Who does it	How long it might take

For the activity you've chosen to prototype, write the stem (question) and options.
In the stem, you'll do this:
   - Give people names or say "you"
   - Show, don't tell
   - Include details, both relevant and distracting
   - Avoid drama
In the options, you'll cover the following:
   - The most common mistake as identified by the SME
   - Other mistakes the SME identified
   - The best option
	You do the writing, checking with the SME if you need more information.	20 minutes? How quickly do you write and revise?

Results: You'll have a realistic question and subtle, challenging options. The question could stand alone as a one-scene scenario, or it could be a typical question in what will become a branching scenario.

What you've done

In the previous step, you chose an action from your map for which you'll design a prototype activity. You interviewed your SME to get the details you need to write a strong activity.

What you'll do

Now you'll use the information from your SME to write the stem (question) and options for your prototype activity. You won't write the feedback yet. That's in the next chapter.

Remember, you're writing a multiple-choice question because it's a good way to make sure you cover the major mistakes, and it can be used or adapted in many ways. It might not always be a multiple-choice question. It could be used in any format from self-paced elearning to face-to-face discussion.

In this chapter, you'll:

1. Assume the activity **isn't** preceded by an information presentation. You can always change this later.
2. Write a rough draft of the stem
3. Give people names or say "you"
4. Show, don't tell
5. Include details, both relevant and distracting
6. Delete drama
7. Write the option for the most common mistake
8. Write the other incorrect options
9. Write the best option
10. Revise the options to make them more subtle
11. Don't write the feedback yet

Who's involved?

You should probably do the writing. You might need to check again with your SME if you discover you don't have enough information from them about the context, common mistakes, and consequences.

1. Assume there's no information presentation

For now, write the activity with the assumption that people will be plunged into the challenge without preparation. In other words, you're not going to present everything they need to know and then have them "practice applying it" with this activity. Instead, they'll go directly to the activity and learn through the challenge.

Later, you'll decide if people need to have information or other help before they make a decision. If so, you'll identify the best way to provide that information, whether it's before the activity or during it. You're setting the bar high right now because it's easier to lower a high bar than to raise a low one.

2. Write a rough draft of the stem

We'll continue the work we started with Arno in the previous chapter. We're going to write an activity that will help his widget salespeople overcome customer's objections about the heat that some widgets generate.

First, we'll write a strong stem, which is the setup and question. We're going to put a lot of work into the stem because once we have a good stem, it's much easier to write options.

Here's our first attempt:

> A salesperson is meeting with a new customer. The customer points out that a recent review said the J-12 runs hot.
>
> What should the salesperson do?

Is this stem interesting? Do you care what happens?

Even if I were a widget salesperson, I wouldn't care. First, who is "a salesperson?" Nobody I know or care about. And "the customer?" Another nobody. Plus, the whole thing is generic and boring. It sounds like a training person wrote it.

3. Give people names or say "you"

First, let's fix the nobodies:

> Carla, a salesperson, is meeting with Ravi, a new customer. Ravi points out that a recent review said the J-12 runs hot.
>
> What should Carla do?

Did you notice that the names help you "see" the people? I think we have databases in our heads of names and faces. The person filed under "Carla" in my head has dark straight hair to her shoulders, so now I "see" her.

But do our salespeople really care about some fictional Carla? Who do they care about the most? Themselves.

> You're meeting with Ravi, a new customer. Ravi points out that a recent review said the J-12 runs hot.
>
> What do you do?

It seems like common sense to use "you," because it makes the experience more immediate and interesting. And I'd say that we should use "you" more often than not. However, there are a couple of situations in which we might want to create a Carla instead.

- **The situation is highly charged.** For example, Kognito Interactive created a simulation for the families of returned soldiers. In the scenario, a husband and wife are having an argument. The husband is a soldier with post-traumatic stress disorder and a head injury that has limited his short-term memory. He forgets things and gets angry easily, and he's a big, strong guy. In the simulation, you choose what the wife should say to defuse the argument. Even though most of the learners are probably wives, too, the wife in the scenario isn't "you," and I think that's a good choice. It helps avoid overloading learners with emotion. (Look for "Family of Heroes" at www.kognito.com.)

- **The "you" doesn't represent every learner.** If resources are limited and the client insists on having activities that apply to "everyone," you might use characters like Carla to reduce complaints like, "But I don't do exactly that on my

241

job!" (However, your best solution is to create targeted activities and control which learners receive which activities.)

"But it's risky to say 'you.'"

"If they make a mistake, they'll feel bad," too many clients have said. "You could damage their self-esteem." This concern comes from the school mindset, which views all "learners" as fragile children with empty brains.

First, neither children nor adults are fragile beings whose self-worth will be crushed by one poor choice in a fictional, 20-second training activity.

Second, how could games be so popular if a mistake destroyed the player's ego? In a game, your character could die a gruesome death due to your poor choices, and you'd probably just say, "Darn," and immediately try again.

Instead of crushing our self-worth, the possibility of making a mistake makes the game challenging and addictive.

You might want to reassure your client that people using the activity will be clearly told that their answers aren't being tracked. If the activity will be done in a live session, the facilitator will make clear that mistakes are actually encouraged, or, if necessary, the participants' choices can be anonymized by technology, such as by using clickers to vote.

Our sales scenario isn't emotionally charged, and it's targeted well, so we'll keep using "you." But even though adding names made it slightly more interesting, it's still boring. What else could we do?

4. Show, don't tell

Let's make another change. Instead of telling what happened, we'll show it.

> You're meeting with Ravi, a new customer.
>
> "I might be interested in your J-12 widget," Ravi says. "At 79 wiga-bits, it has enough power for spurdling. But I've read that it runs hot."
>
> What do you say?

Did you find yourself "seeing" the scene more clearly? By making words come out of Ravi's mouth, we can almost see his lips moving. It's like a movie.

Also, Ravi sounds like a real customer. The scene no longer sounds like it was written by a trainer. We've caught the attention of the salespeople.

Cheap trick: The simplest way to "show, don't tell" is to have characters say things in quotation marks. Once you've made yourself write dialog, other "showing" techniques come naturally.

This is a short, basic stem, but we've snuck in one detail that will help us write good options.

5. Include details, both relevant and distracting

In the scene, Ravi says that the J-12 has 79 wigabits, which is enough for the spurdling he needs to do. However, Ravi is wrong. The J-12 has only 60 wigabits, which isn't enough for spurdling. This will drive our feature-obsessed salespeople crazy, which is exactly what we want.

We planted that detail because it will make one of the incorrect options much more appealing, which makes the question more challenging. You'll see what I mean in a minute.

6. Delete drama

Let's look at another example. Here's a common approach to writing a stem. Why did the writer use this technique, and what effect does it have?

> You're in charge of today's meeting. So far, three people are there, all of them men. You're waiting for the last person, Lori, who is a woman in her early thirties.
>
> Ralph, a middle-aged man, looks pointedly at his watch. "Lori's late again," he snarls. "Probably planning a dramatic entrance on those ridiculous heels of hers."
>
> What do you say?

This is way over the top. The writer thought they needed to exaggerate the problematic behavior to make the activity "interesting." They've instead made it unbelievable. It's unlikely that such a statement would be made in any halfway functioning workplace or that anyone would "snarl." The writer also relied on stereotypes.

243

It's common for the first draft of a stem to be over-dramatic. Even though your stem probably isn't as far gone as my example, you might step back and check it for unnecessary drama. Some things to look for:

- Any dialog attribution other than "said." No one should "sneer," "cry," or "exclaim" their lines. Limit yourself to "said" and "ask."

- Exclamation points

- Stereotypes like the angry man or emotional woman

- Any situation that you don't see at least once a week in a typical workplace, unless the point of the activity is to help people respond to unusual events

You don't need fake drama to make a stem interesting. You just need a subtle, realistic challenge that the learners face often and want to handle better.

We've just applied my rather arbitrary four rules of stems.

> **Four rules for strong stems**
>
> 1. Give people names
> 2. Show, don't tell
> 3. Include details, both relevant and distracting
> 4. Delete drama

7. Write the option for the most common mistake

Once we have a strong stem, it's much easier to write subtle options. However, that doesn't mean that we should just dive in and get creative, listing all the possible choices a person could make. We have specific mistakes that we want to **encourage** people to make.

We go back to our action map for Arno's activity to remind ourselves what we're trying to do. The first mistake on our list is the most common one, "get defensive."

How could we write that option? Arno said that one thing salespeople do is say that the company's research doesn't show any issues, so let's use that as option A.

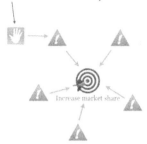

Scenario: A well-informed customer brings up bad reviews about heat.
Options: defend; distract; show expertise

You're meeting with Ravi, a new customer.

"I might be interested in your J-12 widget," Ravi says. "At 79 wiga-bits, it has enough power for spurdling. But I've read that it runs hot."

What do you say?

a) "Our studies show that heat doesn't cause issues for the J-12. Would you like to see the test results?"

We check that option off our map and move on to the next.

Scenario: A well-informed customer brings up bad reviews about heat.
Options: defend; distract; show expertise

8. Write other incorrect options

Next up is "distract the customer with another widget." We were thinking ahead to this option when we made Ravi wrong about the wigabits. Now we use that detail to make this incorrect choice more appealing.

> You're meeting with Ravi, a new customer.
>
> "I might be interested in your J-12 widget," Ravi says. "At 79 wiga-bits, it has enough power for spurdling. But I've read that it runs hot."
>
> What do you say?
>
> a) "Our studies show that heat doesn't cause issues for the J-12. Would you like to see the test results?"
>
> b) "Actually, the J-12 has only 60 wigabits. If you're going to be spurdling, I'd recommend the K-77."

We check that one off the list on the map. Most activities have more incorrect options, which we'd also write now, but we're keeping our example simple, so we move on to the last (and correct) option.

9. Write the best option

Our notes say the correct option is to "show expertise." Arno described that as showing knowledge of what the industry is saying and being willing to talk about the heat.

> You're meeting with Ravi, a new customer.
>
> "I might be interested in your J-12 widget," Ravi says. "At 79 wiga-bits, it has enough power for spurdling. But I've read that it runs hot."
>
> What do you say?
>
> a) "Our studies show that heat doesn't cause issues for the J-12. Would you like to see the test results?"
>
> b) "Actually, the J-12 has only 60 wigabits. If you're going to be spurdling, I'd recommend the K-77."
>
> c) "Are you referring to the *Widget World* review?"

Obviously, this is the first scene in a longer scenario, but you get the idea. Our discussion with the SME elicited the realistic details we needed to turn a vague idea into a specific situation with realistic words coming out of realistic people's mouths. We included a detail that makes one of the incorrect options more appealing, and we included wording that the SME says people use on the job.

We wrote the incorrect options first because they're usually hardest to write. **I'm not saying that we should leave the options in this order.** We should rearrange them, and we might not even display them, depending on how we use the final activity.

10. Revise the options to make them more subtle

Like the first draft of your stem, the first draft of each option might be too simple. If your options seem too obvious, first consider whether you've included enough of the challenge that comes from the real-world context of the task.

Look for challenge in the context

It can be easy to focus too much on the decision and not enough on the context that makes it challenging.

For example, in one of my scenario design classes, a participant was designing activities to help midwives in West Africa use a new approach called kangaroo care with pre-term babies. In kangaroo care, if the baby weighs less than 1500 grams, it shouldn't be wrapped in its own blanket. Instead, it should be placed naked on the mother's bare chest, so it can benefit from her warmth, and then both should be wrapped together.

We decided to write a practice activity for this as a group. Our first draft looked something like this:

> Your patient has just given birth to a baby boy. You've cleaned the baby and weighed him. He weighs 1430g and is breathing well on his own. You've put a diaper on him. What do you do next?
>
> a) Swaddle him with a clean blanket to keep him warm
> b) Put him on the mother's bare stomach and wrap them together

We could think of only two options: Either use kangaroo care, or don't. At this point, the activity just tests whether the learner remembers the weight at which kangaroo care should be used. It's a simple knowledge check.

We took a step back and asked, "Why aren't midwives doing this?" The weight that requires kangaroo care is easy to memorize, so why do they need training?

The answer was that the midwife isn't alone in a room with a completely passive mother. There are likely to be other family members present, and they and the mother are likely to support generations of tradition. There are cherished, local ways to take care of a new baby that don't include kangaroo care.

The difficulty isn't in remembering the weight at which the care should be used. The difficulty is introducing a new approach during an emotional situation — it's the **context** that's challenging.

First, we rewrote the stem.

> Your patient, a shy young woman named Mary, has just given birth to a boy who weighs 1430g and is breathing well. As soon as you've cleaned and diapered him, Mary's aunt reaches for him with joy.
>
> "He's so small!" she says. "Let me wrap him!" She indicates the blanket she brought, smiling.
>
> What do you do?

By adding the context to the stem, we've opened up many possibilities for options. None of us was a subject matter expert, so our ideas would definitely need to be checked, but thanks to having a stronger stem, we quickly brainstormed the following draft options.

> a) Wrap the baby in the blanket and put it on Mary's stomach so it has contact with her.
>
> b) Help the aunt swaddle the baby so it's done correctly.
>
> c) Say, "The baby will be warmest on his mother's stomach. Let me show you."
>
> d) Ask the aunt to go for some more warm water and put the naked baby on Mary's stomach when she's out of sight.
>
> e) Say, "Mothers in Village X have found that such tiny babies are happiest on the mother's stomach."

Again, we'd need a SME's help, but our new activity is already more challenging than the original. It checks for the proper knowledge (that a baby weighing less than 1500 grams needs kangaroo care) but also has the midwife identify the best way to introduce the new technique. We're helping midwives practice a difficult conversation that has grey areas, not just asking them to remember a number.

"My options are still too obvious."

If you have trouble writing subtle options even after considering the context, you might try the following.

- Make sure the action you've chosen from your map represents a decision that includes grey areas. As we saw in the previous chapter, simple decisions aren't good candidates for practice activities and might need just a job aid, not training.

- Make sure the SME has identified several mistakes that people make, not just the right choice. Those mistakes are your distractors. If you forgot to get mistakes from the SME, talk to them again.

- Check your stem again. Can you include some details that will make one of the incorrect options more appealing? In the example stem, that's why we had Ravi make a mistake about the wigabits.

- Make sure you've asked, "Why aren't they doing this?" or "What makes this hard?" and have gotten a detailed response beyond, "They don't know it." Consider asking again what's going on during the decision that makes it difficult to carry out.

- Check for drama: If an option seems extreme, it will stand out as incorrect. If necessary, ask your SME for the exact wording of poor choices. For example, would someone really say, "Not my problem!" to a customer? Probably not.

11. Don't write the feedback yet

You'll write feedback in the next chapter. For now, admire your stem and options, and consider if there are still some ways that you could make them more realistic and challenging. Read on for some more ideas.

Unless your SME has shown that they want to reject the school model and design realistic practice activities, don't show them your draft yet.

Example of a more complex problem: Noah and Brian

Let's look at another situation that's more nuanced. How could a more complex decision be turned into a multiple-choice question?

This time, we're working on a project tentatively called, "How to Manage Project Managers." Our audience is managers who are in charge of several projects at a time. Each project has a project manager (PM). We want to help learners manage their project managers and keep everything on track.

Thanks to the SME, we have a list of the common mistakes for the activity we're about to write, and we understand what tempts people to make poor choices. First, we need to write a strong stem that gives us enough material to inspire subtle options.

Stem

Here's the first draft of a stem. What kind of options might it inspire?

> A member of your team, Brian, is occasionally a few days late with his deliverables. Today, his project manager complained to you that Brian hasn't completed part of the project that the PM needs to meet the deadline.
>
> What do you do?

If we wrote options at this point, they'd probably be something like this:

a) Talk to Brian to find out what's wrong.

b) Ask the PM to help Brian.

c) Email Brian telling him to meet his deadlines.

Our weak stem inspired weak options. It's nearly impossible to write interesting options for a vague, generic stem.

First, let's improve the stem by giving everyone names, showing rather than telling, and adding some details.

> Noah, one of your project managers, emailed you earlier today to ask for a 10-minute meeting. Now he's arrived for the meeting and looks flustered.
>
> "It's Brian," he says. "He's always been a procrastinator, but now it's affecting my ability to meet my deadlines. He was supposed to give me Phase 1 three days ago, and when I ask about it, he only says, 'I just need another day.'"
>
> What do you do?

That's better, but there's still a problem. In real life, the manager would have a history with Noah and Brian that would affect the decision. Our options would be much stronger if we knew that history. How can we provide that background without making people read a novel?

Backstory links

Here's an approach I stole from the world of interactive fiction. First, we add links to some important elements. I'm assuming this is on a shared screen in a live session, or it's self-paced elearning.

> <u>Noah</u>, one of your project managers, emailed you earlier today to ask for a 10-minute meeting. Now he's arrived for the meeting and looks flustered.
>
> "It's <u>Brian</u>," he says. "He's always been a procrastinator, but now it's affecting my ability to meet my deadlines. He was supposed to give me <u>Phase 1</u> three days ago, and when I ask about it, he only says, 'I just need another day.'"
>
> What do you do?

Here's what you see when you click Noah:

> Noah transferred to your department three months ago, citing personality differences in his previous department. He's reliable and does solid work.

> He can look impatient in meetings, glancing often at his watch, and when someone offers a new idea, he's likely to point out problems with it.
>
> He seems committed to meeting the unit's goals and has proposed changes that improved efficiency. He's the team lead for the project.

Here's what you see when you click Brian:

> Brian has been working with you for two years. He's possibly your quietest staff member, rarely speaking out in meetings.
>
> In performance reviews, he rarely identifies goals for himself and instead asks for your suggestions. He's occasionally a little late with his deliverables, but they're always error-free.
>
> He recently asked to be moved to a quieter cubicle, away from a coworker who talks loudly on the phone, and you've noticed lately that he looks tired.

The question just got a lot more nuanced. It sounds like there could be personality issues, and what's up with Brian? While we haven't added a ton of details, there's enough here to give us ideas for several tempting options, more than we had before.

The links are optional

If this is self-paced elearning, I'd strongly suggest making the links optional. That way, people who explore more are rewarded with more information to support their decision, and no one feels forced.

"No one will read that much!"

I've used this example in several in-person workshops. Every time, people lean forward intently to read about Noah and Brian. They want to figure it out. They don't fiddle with their phones or stare out the windows.

The myth that "learners" won't read is pervasive but easily disproven. The same person who supposedly refuses to read more than three bullet points in the compliance training goes home, gets online, and spends hours reading political blogs (or fan fiction or...). **The problem isn't that the training contains text; the problem is that the text is boring.**

We're still showing rather than telling

While there's no dialog in the backstory, the text still shows rather than tells. For example, it describes what Noah does instead of just telling us, "Noah can come across as a bit of a jerk."

What about Phase 1?

The last link in the stem serves a different purpose. Here's what you see if you click Phase 1:

> You've just started your second project for a major client, TamCo. Your first project with them went so far over budget that it lost money for your employer.
>
> If you don't keep this project on track, you could lose all the TamCo work to your colleague Samantha, who seems to delight in pointing out your team's delays at every meeting.

This increases the urgency, which makes the decision feel important and (I hope) engages the learner more.

Options

Thanks to the backstory, we've now got much more material for the options. Here are some ideas.

> Noah, one of your project managers, emailed you earlier today to ask for a 10-minute meeting. Now he's arrived for the meeting and looks flustered.
>
> "It's Brian," he says. "He's always been a procrastinator, but now it's affecting my ability to meet my deadlines. He was supposed to give me Phase 1 three days ago and when I ask about it, he only says, 'I just need another day.'"
>
> What do you do?

a) Open the schedule for the project to confirm that Noah is correct about the deadline.

b) Tell Noah, "I appreciate you coming to me with this. I'll look into it today."

c) Call Brian to see if he can come into your office.

d) Ask Noah, "Was the input that Brian needed delivered on time?"

e) Ask Noah, "Has there been any friction between you two?"

It's probably not immediately obvious which option is correct. That's mostly because we've added subtlety to the story, but it's also because we're keeping a secret.

Keep secrets

The Noah and Brian scenario will come first in the training. We're not going to list a bunch of tips or describe correct management techniques before the activity. We're just going to send people into the scenario and have them learn from experience.

That's where our secret comes in. The managers currently micromanage their project managers, slowing everything down. The client wants them to instead help the PMs become more independent. We've failed to mention that to the learners.

Look at those options again. Some are micromanaging, such as calling Brian or promising to fix the problem yourself. Other options help Noah improve his own project management skills, such as asking him if the input Brian needed was delivered on time.

In the scenario, the micromanaging options lead to branches in which delays and other bad things happen. The skill-building options go down paths with better results.

What if we told them everything first?

The "secret" — the fact that we don't want people to micromanage — makes the scenario more challenging. What would happen if we used the conventional approach instead?

The conventional approach would be this: First, we give a presentation telling managers that they shouldn't involve themselves in their PMs' projects. We say their job is to stay out of the details and help the PM build their own skills. We present tips like, "Don't act as referee" and "Encourage your PM identify bottle-necks."

Then, finally, we send them into the scenario. The same stem and options that were interesting before are now much more predictable.

Plunging people into the activity is a version of the "stream of activities" approach, which we'll look more closely at in later chapters. Instead of first "teaching" them, we sent people directly into an activity to learn from experience. In this case, we were hardcore: We not only didn't prepare them, we also didn't link to any tips in the activity, because our goal was for people to **see for themselves** what works and what doesn't. The "how-to" information will come after the decision, most of it in feedback and some in short presentations or job aids.

"But they have to KNOW stuff!"

If you don't want to keep secrets and make your activity more challenging, then you'll want to give people some information so they can make a good decision. For example, you could offer the information as optional help, or you could use the feedback to tell people exactly what they're doing right or wrong instead of just showing them the consequences of their choices. We'll look more closely at these techniques later.

Some people will argue that keeping secrets isn't fair to learners, who supposedly need to feel perfect in every way and should therefore never struggle. I'd respond that our activity with Noah and Brian lets people experiment. The learners, who are grownups with decades of life experience, can do what they'd normally do (micro-manage) or try something new. They aren't publicly shamed, they aren't punished, and they're not even told "Incorrect!" They just notice that the story isn't going well, they start to see a connection between their decisions and the problems, and at any time they can start again and choose a different path to confirm their conclusions.

Importantly, **we're not asking people to make decisions about something they know nothing about**. They already manage project managers; we're just helping them see that there might be a better way to do it. If the secret we're keeping is something they know nothing about, such a new, counter-intuitive law they've never even heard of, then our scenario would just frustrate them.

We'll look more closely at this technique and the concerns it can raise in the chapters on providing feedback and information. I've touched on it here because withholding some information is one way to make the stem and options more challenging and interesting.

Consider having them defend their choice

In scenarios with lots of grey areas, you can help people see the concepts that they might be applying intuitively by having them explain their choice.

For example, let's say that a learner in the Brian and Noah scenario chooses option e: They want to ask Noah, "Has there been any friction between you two?" That's not the best choice, but before we show the learner a negative consequence, let's find out what they were thinking.

Before we show the consequence, we ask another question:

> Why did you say this?
>
> a) Brian and Noah have very different personalities and maybe I shouldn't keep them on the same project.
>
> b) I want to help Noah see that he can come across a little strong to quieter people like Brian.
>
> c) I plan to suggest that Noah ask Brian why he's struggling, but first I need to know if they're getting along.
>
> d) I want to figure out if I should talk to Brian and help him work better with Noah.

We could use their answer to this question in a number of ways. Here are two possibilities.

If we want to provide guidance and stop keeping our secret, we could provide a bit of telling feedback here. For example, if the learner picks a micro-managing reason, such as **d**, we could say, "This won't help Noah become a better project manager. It will just make more work for you." Then we could send them back to the original question (not the defense), where they'll be able to make a better choice thanks to the insight they got from defending a not-so-good choice.

Or, if we're using elearning, we could tailor the next scene depending on the defense chosen. For example, if the learner said they want to help Noah build his PM skills (defense options **b** or **c**), which is what we want people to do, we could show a mostly good consequence. If the learner chose a micro-managing defense, such as **a** or **d**, the next scene could show a mostly bad consequence.

If you take this approach, the plot could get seriously complicated fast, so you might reserve this technique only for important decisions.

Avoid storyfied presentations

It's common to create the following type of activity. What's wrong with it?

> Your company's web site is ranked 147th in Google results for "microwidgets." You want to move up in the ranking as much as possible, but how can you do that? To find out, you jump on GuruChat and connect with Gloria, the search engine optimization (SEO) guru.
>
> "I'll be happy to help," Gloria says. "I see that you want people to find you when they type 'microwidgets.' First, in SEO terms, what is 'microwidget?'"
>
> a) search term
>
> b) keyword
>
> c) targeted product
>
> d) Boolean operator

At first, this looks like the other activities. We've put the learner in a realistic problem and we have a character with a name. But the question we've asked is a quiz question. We're asking people to recognize or guess a term, not make real decisions. We've also created a seriously annoying guru.

If we continue in this pattern, Gloria will undoubtedly present some information. "Here's a graphic showing good places to put your keywords," she might say, displaying a generic web site with spots highlighted. "You should go to the HTML chat room to learn how to put your keywords there."

In the next scene, you're in the HTML chat room talking to Zhang, the HTML guru. "Here's how you edit the title tag," he says, displaying a screen shot of some HTML with "microwidget" highlighted.

"You'll also want to edit the ALT tags," Zhang says. "Where do you think you'll find those?" Now you have to choose an answer, such as "footer," "image," and "header."

This isn't a practice activity. This is a storyfied presentation with quiz questions. The quiz questions are marginally more interesting than conventional ones because they ask you to guess based on pre-existing knowledge, but they're still quiz questions.

It's often easier to create this sort of presentation than it is to create a real practice activity. For example, to turn the SEO presentation into a real practice activity, we'd want to have the learners actually edit a simulated web page and try to put keywords in the right places, which is trickier than having fake people present screenshots. But even though it would be harder to design, a realistic activity would give learners valuable practice in a safe place, where they couldn't break the company website. It would also treat them with more respect.

Common challenges

Your question is too easy.

- Make sure you're asking people to make a decision that requires judgment. Don't ask them to make a basic if-then decision like, "When a caller asks for Nigel, connect them to line 3." Instead, choose a behavior that has grey areas.

- Are you planning to tell everyone how to answer the question before you ask it? Instead, aim for plunging people in without preparation. Your goal is to help them practice **thinking on their feet**, not to test their short-term memory. You can add optional help later.

- Does the stem include realistic details about the context? Does it include the aspects of the situation that make the decision hard?

- Do the options include the most common mistake? Did you make that mistake tempting by adding details to the stem?

- Are the stem or options over-dramatic? For example, do characters show unrealistic levels of anger? The more subtle you can make the situation, the more challenging the question will seem.

- Are you "teaching" something that's a variation on common sense? If so, have you considered keeping it secret? Instead of offering the model as optional help, consider letting people discover the rules of the model as they make decisions and see the consequences. You'll want to make the model very clear in a debrief after the activity, as we'll see in later chapters.

You can't think of enough options.

- Look again at your stem. Are you asking a "binary" question, such as testing nurses to see if they remember the weight at which they should use kangaroo

258

care? If so, look at the context instead. What makes it hard for people to apply this knowledge? If there's nothing difficult about the context, maybe you don't need a practice activity. A job aid or memorization activity might be better.

- Have the SME tell you about several mistakes that people make, or ask recent or future learners what makes the situation difficult and what choices they've tried in the real world. Don't let them describe only the right choice.

There's no clear right or wrong answer; everything is grey.

- If in the real world the situation is grey, then your question should be grey, too. This is a good thing. However, one or two options should lead to a better result, either immediately or in the long term, and the other options should lead to slightly worse results. Encourage your SME to identify which choices lead to better outcomes.

- If no best practice has been identified yet, you're probably not ready to design training. However, you could approach the project as a way to identify the best choices, using the activities to promote discussion. You could even have groups of learners and SMEs write the activities themselves, debating how to write and score the options, and identify best practices that way.

- If you're developing online materials, avoid using software that requires you to identify one "correct" option. Instead, just use contextual feedback (unique feedback for each option). If you must score the choices for some reason, consider applying relative scores to them, such as having two options that are worth 2 points, one that's worth 1, and one that's worth 0.

- If you're creating a branching scenario, consider the impact of the endings more than the individual options. For example, aim to create one "best" ending, some "fair" endings, and some "poor" endings. Design paths that sometimes cross, so if I'm heading toward a bad ending and realize it, I can get onto a better path by making better decisions. If you need to score the activity, it's easier to assign scores to the endings than to the many options at each decision point.

Your question is boring.

- Does your activity focus on a real problem that people face on their jobs, or is it a disguised quiz question? If the activity helps people solve a problem that they care about, it's less likely to be boring.

- Does everyone in the activity have a name? Are they speaking in quotation marks?

- Is there an emotional component to the challenge, or is it just a logic puzzle? Consider adding some non-dramatic emotional pressure. For example, you could have the problem arise at the end of the fictional day, when the "you" in the problem just wants to go home. This will both add some urgency and tempt people to choose an incorrect but time-saving option.

- Are you using direct, informal language? Consider replacing bureaucratic phrasing with more direct versions, such as saying "now" instead of "at this point in time."

You're concerned that there's too much text.

- Can you cut some descriptive text? It's common for the first draft of an activity to be wordier than necessary. Good targets for deletion include adjectives, adverbs, and small talk like, "Hi, Noah, how's it going?"

- Make sure the dialog is super-efficient. Often, people try to make dialog "realistic" by writing details like, "Good morning, Jan. Thank you for agreeing to meet with me. I'm hoping to gain some clarity about why the Pandon project seems to have slipped in its timeline. As you know, it's very important for us to blah blah blah." Instead, take a scriptwriter's approach and sketch the dialog: "I'm concerned about the Pandon project slipping. What's going on?" We know that in real life there's usually more verbal padding, but we don't want to read it.

- Look at how you've provided the backstory. Could it be optional links, like in the Noah and Brian example? Could you summarize it more? Make sure every detail provides realistic context or makes distractors more tempting. There's no need to describe the weather or the music that the guy in the next cubicle is listening to unless that detail could help sway the player's decision.

- Once you've cut everything you can, don't show the draft to stakeholders until it's in prototype form. It's often best for stakeholders to see the text in a working prototype instead of as a Word document, because you're probably creating something different from what they're used to, and it's likely they can't picture it yet.

The dialog sounds fake.

- First, cut all small talk, as described above. Follow the example set by movie scriptwriters. Movie dialog isn't a transcription of a real-life conversation; it's a very condensed version.

- Have people speak in short sentences. Even ungrammatical ones, like this one. And keep the vocabulary informal.

- Read the dialog out loud, or have someone else read it to you, and listen for unnatural phrasing.

- If you're not familiar with how people in the organization talk, consider sitting in on a meeting and taking notes of the terms they use.

- Make sure you're not trying to inject too much drama, which can make the dialog sound false.

Chapter 11. Activity design: Feedback

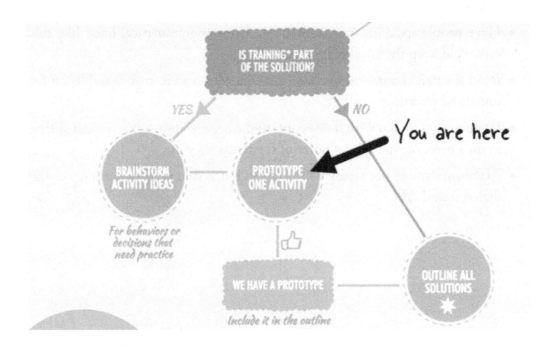

Task	Who does it	How long it might take

For the activity you've chosen to prototype, write unique feedback for each option. The feedback will:
  - Show the consequence of the choice (continue the story)
  - Let the learner draw conclusions
It might also:
  - Offer optional telling feedback
  - Include a snippet of a job aid or other reference
  - Send the learner to information or remediation that they appear to need
	You do the writing, checking with the SME if you need more information.	20 minutes?

What you've done

You're writing an activity that's going to become your prototype. You've met with your SME to get the details you need, and in the previous chapter you wrote the stem and options.

What you'll do

Now you'll write feedback for each option. Since feedback and information are so closely intertwined, you might want to read both this chapter and the following one before you apply the ideas to your project.

Remember, your activity should require judgment — it should help people practice making a decision in a complex situation; it's not a drill question or fact check. As a result, your feedback will be more nuanced than you might be used to writing.

To get that nuance, you'll make several decisions before you write a word. In this chapter, you'll:

1. Commit to showing, not telling: In the feedback for each option, you'll continue the story to show the consequence of the choice and let the learner draw conclusions

2. Consider ways to respond to, "But our learners can't draw conclusions!"

3. Decide if the feedback should be delayed or immediate

4. Decide who, if anyone, should provide the feedback

5. If you're planning a longer scenario, consider how the structure affects feedback

6. Draft your feedback

1. Commit to showing, not telling

Let's write feedback for our widget activity. Here it is again:

> You're meeting with Ravi, a new customer.
>
> "I might be interested in your J-12 widget," Ravi says. "At 79 wigabits, it has enough power for spurdling. But I've read that it runs hot."

> What do you say?
>
> a) "Our studies show that heat doesn't cause issues for the J-12. Would you like to see the test results?"
>
> b) "Actually, the J-12 has only 60 wigabits. If you're going to be spurdling, I'd recommend the K-77."
>
> c) "Are you referring to the *Widget World* review?"

Let's say that a salesperson chooses **a**, the most common mistake, and says that Weeber research doesn't show any problems with heat. What feedback could we provide?

Here's one approach. What happens in your brain when you read it? How much thinking do you do?

> Incorrect. This response could make you seem defensive and increase Ravi's skepticism. It would be better for you to show that you're familiar with what the industry is saying about the heat of our widgets. Try again.

When I read that feedback, nothing happens in my brain. I don't need to think because the teacherly Omniscient One has jumped in and told me what to think. And how well do I learn if I don't think?

Here's another approach. What happens in your brain this time?

> "I'm not surprised that **your** studies don't show any problems," Ravi says, sounding a little annoyed. "But *Widget World* does rigorous, independent testing, and they found heat issues. What can you tell me about the heat?"

Now my brain is working. It's having to draw a conclusion. It has also noticed that I've annoyed the customer, so alarm bells are ringing. I'm more likely to remember what I just learned because I had to think about it, and my emotions got involved.

It's show vs. tell again

My guideline for feedback is the same as it was for writing stems: show, don't tell.

The "incorrect" feedback that came from, apparently, a voice in the sky is "telling" feedback. The feedback that continued the story, showing Ravi's reaction, is "showing" feedback.

In Instructional Design Land, telling and showing are called "instructive" and "intrinsic," but the result is the same. Telling feedback simply inserts knowledge into our heads or tells us what to do (that's why it's "instructive"). Showing lets us learn from experience by continuing the story ("intrinsic").

As Julie Dirksen points out in *Design for How People Learn* (2011), showing feedback creates desirable friction. "One of the reasons this is important," she says, "is that *telling* is smooth, but *showing* has friction: it requires learners to make some of their own connections to interpret what's going on." This friction helps people learn, she says. "Learning is messy, and interacting with and resolving that messiness can help embed the information into long-term memory."

> *We're easily seduced into believing that learning is better when it's easier, but the research shows the opposite: when the mind has to work, learning sticks better.*
>
> *Peter Brown, et al. in Make It Stick (2014)*

Set the training wheels high

If you learned to ride a bike with training wheels, you might remember a certain sensation: The bike is tipping! If you didn't correct it on your own, the training wheels touched the ground and saved you from falling over.

At first, you might have set the training wheels really low, so they saved you from the slightest tipping. You often felt them support you as you tottered. As your skills improved, you might have raised the little wheels. That developed your ability to notice when you were off balance and adjust on your own.

Feedback in training should be like those little wheels.

When you're a novice just finding your balance, the feedback stays close and frequently nudges you upright. But then, as you develop your skills, the feedback should retreat. It should let you feel that tipping sensation more often, because the best way to improve in the real world is to **notice when you're tipping and adjust accordingly**.

"Telling" feedback: permanent training wheels

A lot of training, especially elearning, uses only telling feedback, provided immediately. "Incorrect," it says the minute we start to tip. "Straighten up by doing X, Y, and Z right now."

And then it never backs off. No matter how much we might improve, the feedback never lets us notice on our own that we're tipping, and it never lets us figure out how to straighten up. It's constantly interrupting and "fixing" us, like the world's most annoying parent.

If that's how we're trained, how are we going to ride solo on the job?

"Showing" feedback: feel the tipping and adjust on your own

"Showing" feedback lets people feel that tipping sensation. Carefully written, it also hints at what they should do to straighten up.

Here's Ravi's feedback again. How does it hint at the error and the better choice?

> "I'm not surprised that **your** studies don't show any problems," Ravi says, sounding a little annoyed. "But *Widget World* does rigorous, independent testing, and they found heat issues. What can you tell me about the heat?"

Instead of telling learners that their choice could "increase Ravi's skepticism," we have Ravi express it for himself. People can feel the bike tipping as Ravi gets annoyed. And instead of telling learners that they should talk about the heat, we have Ravi suggest it.

> *Our feedback should help people sense when the bike is tipping and correct it on their own.*

Live training: showing and telling through discussion

How does the showing vs. telling battle play out in a live event?

In the chapter on activity ideas, we looked at one way to run the activity about needle safety in live training, whether it's in person or online. Here's the activity again. How is the feedback provided? Is it showing or telling?

Tell the group, "Let's say that a clinician named Magda has just jabbed herself with a needle that she took out of a patient's artery. What should she do first?"

Let people call out or type their recommendations, and choose one. You might selectively hear a recommendation of Betadine, the most common mistake.

"Okay, Magda washes the wound with Betadine," you say. "The patient has hepatitis C. What are the chances that Magda has it now?"

If the participants don't mention the consequence on their own, report the consequence of the choice: "Magda doesn't know it yet, but she just caught hepatitis C."

Finally, remind them of the job aid: "What should she have looked at before she made her decision?"

Through discussion, the facilitator helps people see the consequence of their choice — that's showing feedback. The correct procedure, the telling feedback, is provided by the job aid. This would be a good time to have everyone look at the job aid again.

Example: Branching scenario on paper + debrief

A more complex situation requires more finesse in the feedback discussion. Here's an example.

I worked on a project that helped US soldiers prepare for culture shock in the Middle East. We mostly designed classroom sessions because that's what the learners preferred. The sessions were part of a longer series of classes on how cultures differ.

Here's a typical session: First, without preparation, the soldiers formed small groups to go through a branching scenario. It was printed on paper, and they debated each choice in their small groups.

One scenario was based in Iraq, where a US officer worked as an advisor to an Iraqi commander. Someone had started a small bombing campaign to scare civilians in the village. It appeared to be another incident of harassment in the longstanding friction between tribes.

Because he had the low tolerance for ambiguity common to Americans, the US officer felt an urgent need to find and publicly punish the bombers. He told the Iraqi commander to act immediately. However, the local people used a slower and more collaborative approach to solve the problem. The US officer's urgent demands made the Iraqi commander ignore him and damaged their already problematic relationship.

In the scenario, the soldiers played the role of the US officer. They tried to make sure the bombings would be stopped without damaging the American's relationship with the Iraqi. There was no "telling" feedback in the scenario; players just saw the consequences of their choices and reached one of several endings.

After the small groups went through the scenario, the facilitator led a large-group discussion. Debrief questions in the facilitator's guide helped the facilitator elicit the points that the scenario was designed to make.

Here's a snippet of the discussion guide. First, you'll see the question the facilitator asked, followed by the points to be elicited in the discussion. **The facilitator didn't just read out those points.** Instead, they tried to guide the discussion so the soldiers would raise the points on their own, and then the facilitator would confirm them.

If one group started a bombing campaign against another group in a US town, how would the authorities respond?

Immediately try to publicly identify the bombers and stop them

Why are the Iraqi and US approaches so different?

The US is a low context culture while Iraq is high context

In high context cultures, community connections and face are important, so solutions are likely to involve more of the community and be less cut and dried

Iraq has a long, complex history of tribal issues

What could the US officer have done to handle his need for immediate answers when the Iraqis seemed to be working slowly?

Recognize that his need comes from his cultural background and that the people around him don't feel the same urgency; pushing them will damage his relationships

Recognize that the Iraqis might already be resolving the situation in quiet, subtle ways that he doesn't know about [that's what happened in real life]

Ask his translator to help him understand what may be happening and how he should respond to it, keeping in mind that the translator might favor one side in the conflict

Ask soldiers with more experience in Iraq what they recommend

The facilitator also presented one slide that had tips on how to manage an American sense of urgency in a different culture.

According to one facilitator, when the class bell rang, the students didn't want to leave. They wanted to keep discussing the scenario and the issues it raised.

What if we had used a conventional design instead, presenting information and then using "telling" feedback? Let's try it. Here's our lesson plan.

Conventional lesson plan

1. Present slides with definitions of terms, including "cross-cultural competency," "high context," "low context," and "tolerance for ambiguity." Explain that Iraq is high context and the US is low context. Point out that Americans tend to have a low tolerance for ambiguity, which can make them want immediate solutions to problems.

2. Present slides with do's and don'ts for responding to problems as an American in a high-context culture. Point out that a common error is to push local individuals to act decisively when the culture requires more collaborative approaches.

3. Go through the scenario as a large group. Provide telling feedback at every point, such as, "This is not the best choice. You can't rely on your translator to be objective. You should gather other perspectives as well." Always suggest what they should do next, referring to the do's and don'ts slides as necessary.

4. When the bell rings, watch the students flee.

The less we wag our fingers at people, the more we show our respect for their intelligence. The more they're "allowed" to think for themselves, the more involved they get.

Of course, we want to avoid overloading newbies. One reason you'll test your prototype is to make sure your interesting challenge isn't actually a frustrating impossibility. You might also decide to provide the kind of help that we'll look at in the next chapter.

At the same time, we don't want to redundantly present information that people already know. That's why in the original version of the lesson plan, the facilitator didn't push the "high context / low context" concept but waited first to see if a participant volunteered it as an explanation. The participants were preparing for work abroad and had already spent a long time in training. They could easily have learned the concept already.

2. Consider ways to respond to, "But our learners can't draw conclusions!"

Even if you think your audience will be fine with "showing" feedback, your SME or client might be concerned. They might still have the school mindset, which encourages them to think that the minute we put an adult in the "learner" category, they become a clueless child.

That's one reason you're developing a prototype. You'll test it on learners, and then you'll be able to say with confidence that your learners are indeed adults with functioning brains who can tell by Ravi's annoyance that they made a bad choice.

Show, then tell

However, even the results from a prototype might not be enough to calm a worried stakeholder. Here's a solution that can make everyone happy:

First show what happened, and then provide optional "telling" feedback.

This is also a safe approach if you can't avoid including people with a range of expertise in your audience, including newbies who need the clarity and reassurance provided by the "telling" feedback.

Here's how it could look in its most basic form, using our widget sales example.

> "I'm not surprised that **your** studies don't show any problems," Ravi says, sounding a little annoyed. "But *Widget World* does rigorous, independent testing, and they found heat issues. What can you tell me about the heat?"
>
> *This response could make you seem defensive and increase Ravi's skepticism. It would be better for you to show that you're familiar with what the industry is saying about the heat of our widgets. Try again.*

Here's a less intrusive variation for elearning:

> "I'm not surprised that **your** studies don't show any problems," Ravi says, sounding a little annoyed. "But *Widget World* does rigorous, independent testing, and they found heat issues. What can you tell me about the heat?"
>
> Why did this happen?

The "Why did this happen?" link displays the "telling" feedback. I use it sometimes in branching scenarios. The default feedback just continues the story, but people who are confused can also see optional "telling" feedback.

Of course, "showing" feedback can appear in many variations, not just as scenes in a story. For example, in software training, the most appropriate feedback is whatever the software does in response to the learner's command, whether that's to complete a calculation or delete all records in the database.

3. Decide if feedback should be delayed or immediate

Should you immediately jump in to provide feedback, or should you let people flounder a bit?

The original Iraq scenario described in the live training section above had two types of feedback: immediate showing feedback, and delayed telling. At each decision point in the story, the soldiers saw the consequences of their decision. They didn't get any corrective "telling" feedback until the debrief discussion, after the scenario ended.

Let's look at another example. When does the instructor provide immediate feedback, and when is it delayed? What's the effect of delaying feedback?

Example: Widget diagnostics

You're in a live classroom session, learning how to diagnose wobble in widgets. The widgets aren't supposed to move when they operate, but sometimes they develop a wobble. What causes it? How can you fix it?

The instructor has put a widget in front of you. When you turn it on, it wobbles.

"You've got a chart of symptoms and their causes," the instructor says. "Let's see if you can use the chart to diagnose this widget's wobble."

Not sure what to do first, you check the widget's feet. They're all there and firmly attached.

Next, you pick up the widget and shake it gently. You hear a rattle. Should you hear a rattle? You're not sure. The chart doesn't mention a rattle.

You get out your screwdriver and open the belly of the widget. You start to reach inside when the instructor suddenly appears at your shoulder.

"Wait!" he says. "The widget is still plugged in. Are you sure you want to stick your hand in it?"

You quickly unplug the widget and turn to ask the instructor what to do next but he's off talking to someone else.

The chart mentions that a loose fan housing can make a widget wobble, so you carefully wiggle the little box that has the fan inside. It seems firmly attached.

You continue poking around in the widget, checking things that are on the chart and temporarily knocking a wire loose, until finally you notice that the housing of the widget is loose in one corner. When you tighten those screws, plug the widget back in, and test it, the wobble is gone.

The instructor appears at your shoulder again and asks you to describe the steps you just went through.

"You checked useful things," he says, "but you could have found the problem sooner, without having to open the widget. I saw you check the feet. What could you have done at about the same time?"

You realize that you could have held the widget on the table and tried to wiggle it, to make sure its housing was sturdy, and you tell the instructor that.

"Right," he says. "It's a good idea to check everything you can before you open up the widget. Opening the widget can be risky."

When everyone has diagnosed their widgets, the instructor leads a discussion of the major lessons learned. As a group, the participants improve the diagnostic chart so it lists all the symptoms to check in order, reinforcing what they've just learned. The chart becomes the job aid that they'll use back at work.

Was that immediate or delayed feedback?

For the most part, the instructor provided delayed feedback. He let you poke around in the widget rather inefficiently instead of standing at your shoulder and correcting you every time you tried something that wasn't perfect.

However, at one point he provided immediate feedback, when you were about to electrocute yourself.

This is an example of providing instant feedback for errors that could seriously throw the learner off track, while delaying feedback for other items. It's what I recommend when you have moderately experienced or independent learners, for several reasons.

First, a lesson is probably more memorable when it's learned through experience. The main lesson you drew from the widget-diagnosis activity was, "When diagnosing issues with widgets, check all the external possibilities before opening the widget." Do you think you would have remembered that lesson as well if the instructor had constantly stood at your shoulder and stopped you the minute you got out your screwdriver? "No, don't do that yet!" he might say. "You should check everything on the outside before opening the widget."

Immediate correction can lessen the impact of a lesson. Instead, if you live with your mistake for a while and then realize it was a mistake, the realization can be more memorable. You'll look back at the fan-wiggling and all the other checks you did, plus the risk of electrocution and the wire you knocked loose, and see that they all could have been avoided. "I'll never open a widget again without first wiggling it!" you vow.

Second, how would you have felt if you had instant feedback at every step? What if the instructor stood constantly at your side, interrupting every time you started to do something, telling you to do something else instead? I would have felt like the victim of a control freak, or at least I would have suspected that the instructor thought I was a child.

Letting people make non-serious mistakes and then improve their performance could increase motivation, because it lets people feel autonomy and builds their competence. Along with relatedness, autonomy and competence are two of the three psychological needs that create motivation, according to several researchers and authors, including Susan Fowler in *Why Motivating People Doesn't Work ... and What Does* (2014). If I struggle with something on my own and then conquer it, I feel a surge of motivation and pride. If instead my hand is constantly held and I'm carefully shown how to do every little thing, I don't feel competent or respected.

Another type of delayed feedback: Compare your work

If the learner completed a work product as part of the activity, they could compare it to the same product that an expert created. For example, in the widget-diagnostics activity, you could make your diagnosis and fix the problem, and then compare the steps you took to the steps an expert would have taken.

Consider the level of expertise

Obviously, the timing of the feedback should match the learners' level of expertise. Complete novices will appreciate more frequent feedback. People who have some experience with the topic will feel more respected and might have a more memorable experience with delayed feedback.

When considering the level of expertise, consider the topic as well. As I've mentioned before, a lot of corporate training isn't difficult to understand. Much of it is common sense or represents decisions that most adults would make on their own with a nudge or two.

So even if the topic is new to the learners, if the training is just modifying what a reasonable adult would do with minimal prodding, then people might not need instant feedback or other handholding.

> *Most corporate training I've seen underestimates the intelligence of the learners and over-estimates the difficulty of the challenge.*

Also consider how learners' expertise improves as they go through the training. If you're presenting challenging material, people will appreciate quick feedback more when they're brand new. As they develop their expertise, delayed feedback might be more appropriate.

4. Decide who, if anyone, should provide the feedback

In live training, the facilitator is usually on hand to help with activities. In elearning, that role is often given to one of the following characters. Which, if any, do you think is useful?

- **The Omniscient One:** This is the faceless, disembodied voice that provides telling feedback in most elearning. The One has no personality or gender, unless you're using a narrator, in which case I'd say, "Why are you using a narrator?"

- **A fictional SME or mentor:** This is a stock photo or illustrated character who claims to be an employee of the organization but who is often too perfect to be believable. This person pops in to provide telling feedback during activities, or is always in the corner ready to help with one click. They usually have no personality except for an irksome perkiness.

- **A wizard, superhero, or other stereotypical savior:** This is usually an illustrated character, almost always male, whose presence is supposed to "lighten things up" while he tells you what you did wrong.

You can probably tell that I'm not a big fan of any of those approaches. What are some alternatives?

- **A real-life Omniscient One:** At the beginning of the material, make clear that a real person with a name wrote the feedback. This might be your SME, if they're willing, or you. For example, in the scenarios I write for my own business, people know that I'm the one giving feedback. The feedback needs to occasionally use "I" and sound like a human being for this to work. It should always use "you."

- **A real-life SME:** Instead of using a too-perfect stock photo, use a photo of your real-life SME, if they're willing, and make clear as above that they're providing the feedback.

- **A character from the story:** If you're using a branching scenario or a series of scenarios based on the same characters, you could give one of those characters enough expertise to provide telling feedback when needed (and only when needed). For example, in the Iraqi scenario described earlier, a more experienced officer who works in a neighboring town could provide telling feedback in a self-paced version of the activity.

  An interesting extension of this was suggested by a participant in one of my scenario design workshops: At the end of a branching scenario, have the character you were interacting with step a little bit out of their role and tell you why they responded as they did to your choices.

If (in the next chapter) you decide that you should provide optional help when the learner needs to make the decision, the same "person" who provides feedback could provide the help. For example, if we wanted to provide optional help during the cross-cultural scenario, we could have the more experienced officer who provides feedback also be available to provide hints at the decision points.

The expert could also show how they would solve the problem, either as help or as telling feedback available after you show the consequences of the learner's choice. For example, if you challenge learners to fix a squealing widget, you could have them make their attempt first, and then show how an expert would do it, so they could compare the steps they took to the expert's approach. Or, you could provide optional help during the activity, in which the expert shows how they diagnosed a similar problem, to give learners a model to follow.

5. If you're planning a longer scenario, consider how the structure affects feedback

If you're planning a branching scenario, you might find yourself considering two basic structures that take different approaches to feedback.

Teaching scenario: Lots of telling

The simplest structure is what I call a "teaching" scenario. I've seen it presented as a branching scenario, but it isn't really one by my definition.

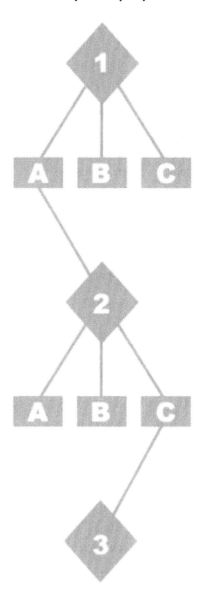

The scenario usually works like this: You're presented with the first scene of a story and choose an option, let's say B. You see immediate feedback that tells you that you chose incorrectly, and that you should really do what's described in option

A. The scenario sends you back to the same scene and this time you obediently choose A.

Now you see the second scene, and the process repeats. If you choose correctly, the story advances. If you choose incorrectly, you have to go back and do it right.

To play an example of this kind of scenario, see the sample activity for this chapter at map-it-book.com.

Unlike a true branching scenario, a teaching scenario doesn't have different plot lines. Everyone sees the same scenes. That's because the designer uses telling feedback to make their points, instead of letting the story show you.

Our activity with Ravi and the widgets could be the first scene in a teaching scenario. If the learner makes the mistake of getting defensive when Ravi asks about heat, most designers using this structure provide immediate telling feedback, like this:

> Incorrect. This response could make you seem defensive and increase Ravi's skepticism. It would be better for you to show that you're familiar with what the industry is saying about the heat of our widgets. Try again.

The learner is required to go back and has to stay on the original scene until they choose the correct option, C: "Are you referring to the *Widget World* review?" Then they finally see the next scene, in which Ravi says, "Yeah, *Widget World* said the heat was pretty noticeable. How would that affect my spurdling?" Now the learner chooses what to say next, and the process repeats.

A slight improvement on this approach is to add some showing to the feedback. As we saw earlier in this chapter, you could first show what happened, and then tell the learner what they did wrong and send them back to do it again.

However, the entire structure is so controlling that the overall experience is that of being constantly told what to do. That's why I call it a "teaching" scenario, or when I'm cranky, a "control freak" scenario.

Even though it feels controlling, I can imagine situations in which this structure would be useful. If you're introducing novices to a subtle and counter-intuitive process, this type of constant correction could be a good way to start out. In that case, the teaching scenario could be the first in a series of increasingly complex scenarios. Feedback could be delayed in the later scenarios as the learners gain expertise.

Also, if you're not willing to take on the design of a truly branching scenario, this structure could be a compromise. If it's well written, it will be more engaging and probably more memorable than an information presentation. To make it feel less controlling, I'd strongly recommend that you emphasize the showing feedback and make the telling feedback optional.

Although I can see times in which you might consider this structure, make sure that you aren't underestimating your audience or overestimating the difficulty of the material. In most situations that require multiple, related decisions, a truly branching scenario is probably more effective and interesting.

Branching scenario: Lots of showing; delayed telling

The "teaching" scenario made its points through telling feedback, and it required players to redo every wrong decision. In contrast, a truly branching scenario **shows** people what works and what doesn't, different choices lead down different paths, and telling feedback is usually delayed until the end of a storyline.

You can recognize a branching scenario immediately by its plot diagram, because it has different storylines. Instead of everyone seeing the same scenes, some people see scenes that others don't as they go down different paths.

In the following simple example, some players go directly from 1 to 4, while others see scenes 2 and 3 and may never see 4.

The feedback is usually all showing: The player makes a choice and immediately sees a new scene. That new scene shows the consequences of the choice, moving the story along, and requires a new choice. Included in the options are choices that can help the player recover from a mistake and get onto a better path, as well as options that send them down bad paths.

Let's go back to Ravi's concern about the hot widget. Here's what the learner could see after they say, "Our studies show that heat doesn't cause issues for the J-12. Would you like to see the test results?"

> "I'm not surprised that **your** studies don't show any problems," Ravi says, sounding a little annoyed. "But *Widget World* does rigorous, independent testing, and they found heat issues. What can you tell me about the heat?"
>
> What do you say?

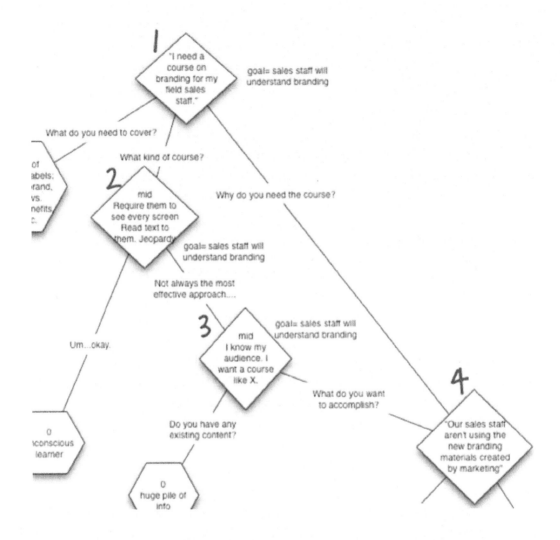

a) "The J-12 does run warmer than some other widgets, but if I remember right, the *Widget World* testers didn't see any impact on performance. Is there another reason you're concerned about heat?"

b) "It's true that the J-12 gets a little warm, but if you're going to be spurdling, you'll actually want the K-77. It's also one of the coolest-running widgets in the industry. Can I show you the specs?"

c) "All widgets generate heat, thanks to the transmogrification of inductability. However, that heat doesn't affect performance, and ceramic heat-reducers just add cost. Can I ask what budget you're working with?"

There's no telling feedback. We trust our learners, who are all adults with experience in sales, to notice that Ravi has gotten annoyed and that they need to adapt their approach. We do have telling feedback planned, but we're saving it for the end of the storyline.

The story structure is part of the feedback

In a branching scenario, learners know that some paths are better than others. When they realize they're on a not-good path, they'll try to imagine what the best path looks like, and they'll look for ways to get there. This requires a higher level of thinking than simple telling feedback allows, and I'd argue that it helps people develop a more complete understanding of the issue. This is what I mean by "the story structure is part of the feedback."

This is a great feature of branching scenarios, but it requires some careful planning, so here are some tips. At this point, you're still focusing on creating one decision point as a prototype, but you'll also need to consider the bigger picture that will surround that decision point.

When you want to create a branching scenario, **plot it first** using flowcharting software or by entering notes in an interactive fiction tool like Twine. As you write your high-level plot, keep the following in mind.

- **What's the best path?** Plot that first.

- **What are the common mistakes?** Each one could be a major path in the story. For example, there could be a "defensive" branch and a "distract them with another product" branch, in addition to the best "trusted advisor" branch.

- **What are the endings?** You might aim for one "best" ending, a few "fair" endings, and a few bad endings or quick failures.

- **How do the branches connect?** People should be able to cross from one branch to the other. This lets them recover realistically from mistakes, and it keeps the branching from growing out of control.

  For example, if I originally get defensive with Ravi but realize it isn't working, I should be able to choose a "trusted advisor" option in a later scene and cross over to the better path. This ability to cross paths is one of the great benefits of branching scenarios — people practice recognizing and recovering from mistakes.

Telling feedback happens at the end

In a truly branching scenario, I recommend saving telling feedback for the end of a plot line to avoid interrupting the story.

The simplest approach is to write feedback that addresses how the learner got to that end. You don't need software that tracks every choice; you just need to build the branches and connections in such a way that you can provide meaningful feedback at each ending.

The end point should show the final scene of that storyline, to complete the story. Then the telling feedback could appear, or you could offer it optionally.

When I create an ending for an online scenario, I often describe the final scene and then include a link that says, "Why did this happen?" When people click it, I explain how they ended up at that point and suggest what might have worked better.

It's a good idea to clearly label the ending, saying, for example, "You've reached a good ending, but not the best one." Here's an example from the end of a path in the widget sales scenario.

> "Okay, I'll take the Q-35," Ravi says, taking out his credit card.
>
> Three months later, Ravi comes back. "My Q-35 seems to draw a lot of power," he says. "You said it was the best model for the type of spurdling I do, but the guys at Acme Widgets say it's oversized. Now I'm not sure who to believe."
>
> You've reached a mediocre ending. Why did this happen?

If learners could make egregious mistakes in your story, such as electrocuting their fictional selves, consider having the mistakes result in short failure paths. Show the ending scene, provide telling feedback so people understand what they did wrong, and encourage or require them to try again. If instead you let an egregious mistake continue for several scenes, people might be less likely to start over and succeed.

When you design a short and sudden failure, there's no need to say, "FAIL." It's already obvious by the result that they did something seriously wrong.

Ongoing feedback: Make it part of the story

If you have good reason to think that people will need minor correction all through the story, you might consider providing what Ruth Clark calls "invisible feedback." This is easiest to do in an elearning scenario.

The most common version I've seen is telepathy: You're in a conversation with someone, and you're not sure how they're reacting to your statements. So, you click the person's head and a thought bubble appears, letting you read their thoughts.

Another technique is to use a meter. For example, a gauge in a sales scenario could show how "warm" the prospect is to what you're trying to sell.

I'm not a huge fan of these techniques, because part of what we want people to practice is reading other people. In real life, I can't click your head to see what you're thinking. I have to interpret your body language and speech. If I'm practicing how to talk to you, I should also practice how to interpret your actions and statements.

However, if you're using elearning and there's no budget for the level of production that would show a person's reactions, and you're not confident that you can provide good cues in the story, I could see how mechanisms like mind-reading and gauges could be useful. They're less intrusive than telling feedback that interrupts the story.

Optional help or nudges

If the branching scenario has people apply complex skills that are new to them, you might consider providing optional, contextual help at useful points.

By "contextual" I mean a bit of help that applies to the decision that the person just made, not a generic how-to guide, which is discussed in the next chapter.

For example, in the Iraqi scenario, I might ask my translator for advice. In the consequence for that choice, the translator says I should stop demanding that the bombers be identified. A "Should you believe him?" link also appears, so I click it. The "telling" feedback that appears reminds me that my translator is a member of the same tribe that's probably responsible for the bombing, so I should consider his advice with that in mind.

6. Draft your feedback

Note what you'd probably show and what, if anything, you'd like to tell in the feedback for your prototype activity. Use the consequences for each option that the SME described in your interview. Make sure to write a unique consequence for each option, not one "incorrect" result and one "correct" result.

Since feedback often provides or links to supporting information, you'll probably tweak or add to your feedback in the next chapter.

Common challenges

You're concerned that people won't draw the right conclusions without being told what to think or do.

- In your feedback, plan to first show the consequences of the learner's choice, and then offer optional telling feedback. Resist the urge to force people to see telling feedback until after you've tested your prototype on actual learners and you've seen that they need it.

- You'll add optional information in the next chapter, so hold off on telling people a lot right now.

You suspect that a stakeholder will want all feedback to be "telling."

- If you suspect that the SME or client will want to force telling feedback on everyone, suggest they wait and see how the prototype test goes. Also, don't show your draft to the stakeholders until it's a prototype and they can see how the feedback is provided.

You're concerned that if you let people make mistakes, they'll just remember the wrong choice instead of the right one.

- Research summarized in *Make It Stick* (2014) suggests that when people make mistakes and are given corrective feedback, they don't "learn" the mistake. Instead, they're more likely to learn the right way **better**.

Chapter 12. Activity design: Add the information

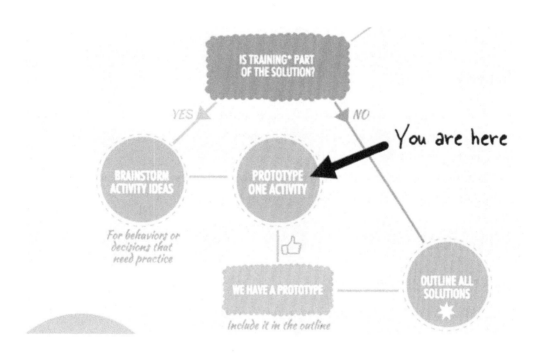

Task	Who does it	How long it might take
For the activity you've chosen to prototype, identify how you'll provide the information needed to make a good decision. Recommended: 　- Limit the info to what's absolutely required. 　- Divide it into "can look up" and "must memorize." 　- Link to the info from the activity. Don't present it first; instead, let people pull what they need. 　- Plan to make activities increase in difficulty. 　- Plan to use a debrief to help people see overarching concepts.	You make the decisions. The SME and recent or future learners can help you determine the best format for the information.	The time you'll need will depend on the current state of the information. For example, if there's already a good job aid, you'll spend very little time. If you need to create a reference from scratch, you'll need a lot more time.

Big idea: Create a standalone activity that links to the required information. Then it can become part of a **stream of activities**.

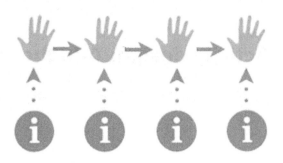

What you've done

You're designing a prototype activity. You've drafted the stem, options, and feedback for each option. Now you'll consider how to provide the information that people need to complete the activity.

This is a big step, because it can affect how the activities relate to each other and how they fit into any training event you might be planning.

What you'll do

You're about to do the following:

1. Choose one of three approaches to providing information
2. Confirm what information is really required for your prototype activity
3. Divide that information into "can look up on the job" and "must memorize"
4. Add the information to your map
5. Put the "can look up" info into a job aid or other reference
6. Plan to put the "must memorize" information into people's brains
7. Plan your scaffolding
8. Consider including worked examples
9. Decide when to make the information available
10. Consider how you might fade the help

11. Decide how you'll help people see over-arching concepts

12. Choose the format for the information

You're still focusing on your prototype activity, but you're moving out to the "information" ring of the map.

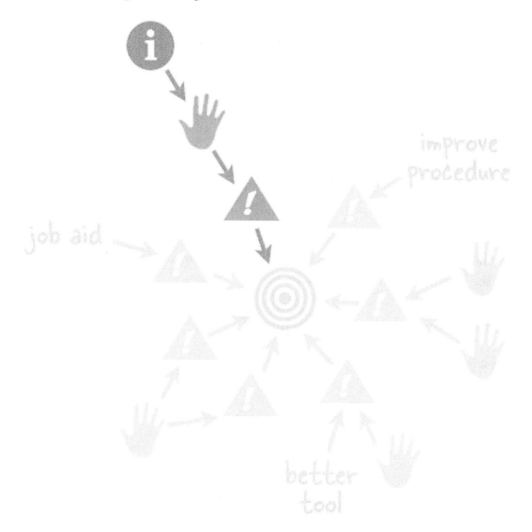

Why are we looking at the information last?

Finally, near the end of our process, we're looking at the material that most designers begin with: the information. We're finally going to tell people what they need to know — sort of.

It's common for designers to first gather all the content and then create activities that deliver that content. Instead, we jumped "ahead" to designing activities, asking, "What do they need to do?" and designing activities around that. We're considering the information only now, very late in the process. Why did we leave the information for last?

I see a couple of advantages:

- We make sure that we design activities that support what people actually do on the job. Content-based design often ignores what people really do because the designer is too distracted by what people supposedly need to know.

- Designing the activity first makes clear what people really need to know. If the activity is realistic, then the information that people need for the activity is the information they need to know in real life, and it's probably less than the SME thinks.

When we look at how to provide information, we also need to consider the organization of the project. Let's look at possible approaches to organization and how the information plugs into them.

1. Choose one of three approaches

How and when could you provide the information related to an activity? I see three basic approaches.

Tell, then test

The "tell, then test" school model uses this approach:

First, you tell them everything they might need to know, and then you give them a test or activity so they can apply what you just told them.

If we redesigned our sharps safety course with this approach, the presenter could go through the following slides:

Slide: Dangers posed by injuries from infected sharps; list of infections

Slide: Costs to the hospital of testing for these infections

Slide: Do's and don'ts of responding to a needlestick injury and a reminder to look at the job aid on the wall

Activity, probably without the optional help we used before because we've just told everyone everything they need to know and we want to see if they "remember" it

Most designers who use the tell-then-test approach don't include optional help in the activity, because they view the activity as a test to see if people remember what they were told. So first they'd tell everyone everything, and then their version of the Magda activity would look like this:

Magda has pricked herself with a needle she removed from a patient's artery. What should she do first?

☐ Let the wound bleed freely.

☐ Suck blood from the wound with a syringe.

☐ Pour Betadine on the wound.

☐ Report the injury to the Infection Control Team.

The conventional lesson plan for the soldiers shown in the previous chapter is also a tell-then-test approach. The facilitator first told them all about the cultural concepts they might need, not caring whether they had already learned them elsewhere. Next, he described how to solve the problem they were about to be given, and finally he gave them the problem scenario, interrupting often to correct them when they made a mistake and tell them what they should do instead. Telling feedback is a natural partner to "tell, then test."

A variation of "tell, then test" is the common "tell, show, do." First you tell them what they're going to do, then you demonstrate the task, and then you have them do it themselves. When people finally get to try the task, they're probably relying on their short-term memory more than their deeper processing skills. They're imitating what they just saw. Also, in most applications of this approach, everyone has to sit through the same telling and showing regardless of their pre-existing knowledge.

"Tell, then test" is by far the most common approach in workplace training, but that doesn't make it the best choice. It's common because it's based on the familiar school model, but that model assumes that learners have empty heads, can't be trusted to think, and wilt like fragile flowers at the slightest whiff of challenge.

It assumes ignorance or even stupidity

The main argument in support of this approach is that it supposedly reduces frustration. Learners are very thoroughly prepared before they're asked to try something, reducing the chance that they could make a mistake.

Ironically, this approach could actually increase frustration. Corporate training rarely teaches anything approaching rocket science. The content is often common sense or requires only minor adjustments to what an adult would probably decide to do on their own.

When I'm in typical corporate training about topics like data privacy or being nice to each other, a tell-then-test design suggests that the designer thinks I'm dumb. I'm an adult with decades of experience, but the designer is making me listen to stuff that I already know or could figure out in a lot less time than their presentation is taking. I get insulted and frustrated, which is not the best state of mind for learning.

Even if I know nothing about the subject and need a lot of information, "tell, then test" delays my application of my new knowledge. The designer's desire to tell me everything I might possibly need to know before letting me try it can mean that what feels like an eternity passes before I get to do anything. I also, usually, have little or no control over the pace at which the information is delivered.

It just toys with our short-term memory

Most "tell, then test" experiences put a few factoids in our brains and then ask us to take them out again five minutes later. There's rarely any attempt to get the important information into our long-term memory or to have us process it in any way that could make it stickier. Spaced practice would help this a bit by having us retrieve the factoid repeatedly, maybe over several weeks.

Test, then tell

If we move the "tell" to the end, we get "test, then tell." It's probably the easiest alternative to the school-style "tell, then test." You lead with the activity and then provide the information.

For example, in our needle safety training, we could open with the Magda scenario and view it as a motivational activity — it shows people their knowledge gaps and, if they choose incorrectly, dramatizes the reason they're taking the training.

Our approach could look like this:

Activity: The Magda decision, probably without the optional information because we're going to present it in a few seconds

Slide: Magda risked getting the following infections: list of infections

Slide: Cost to the hospital of testing for these infections

Slide: Do's and don'ts of responding to a needlestick injury and a reminder to look at the job aid on the wall

Activity: Another activity to introduce the next topic

This is an easy change for most designers, because they're still presenting information in the familiar way, with slides and discussion. They're just doing the presentation after the activity, instead of before.

One advantage of this approach is that it doesn't just poke learners' short-term memory. Instead, by putting the activity first, it challenges them to dig around in the dusty corners of past lessons learned, evaluating existing knowledge to see if it applies in this situation. If they don't pull up the correct knowledge, this approach shows them their own knowledge gaps, making them more receptive to the information they're about to hear.

Even this minor change can make stakeholders nervous, because you're asking people to do something before you've told them how to do it. "You're setting them up to fail" is the most common protest. However, you have an easy answer that usually works: "If people struggle a bit in the activity, it motivates them to pay attention to the teaching that immediately follows." You still promise that there will be plenty of information presentation, that the knowledge will still rain down from the sky as everyone expects. No one will feel challenged or frustrated for more than a few seconds.

Drawbacks

While the change seems minor — just put the activity before the information — the training "feels" significantly different and could be more appealing. However, this approach has some drawbacks.

First, it could train people to not think very hard. As soon as I notice that a torrent of information follows every activity, I begin to tune out the activities. Why should I try to make the right decision if I'm going to be told every possible thing I should know the minute I make my choice?

Second, if the activity doesn't act as a filter for the information, my cynicism will only increase. Let's say I'm in a webinar. The facilitator posts an activity and we all vote for our choice. I picked the right choice but that's irrelevant. The presenter has used the activity just to motivate us before an information dump. Now she's talking and talking, presenting information that I already know and proved that I know by making the right choice in the activity, and soon I'm in another window watching a cat play the piano.

Use the activity to determine what the learner should see next

One way to avoid the cynicism I just described is to make the activity act as a placement test. People who make the correct decision see a quick confirmation of the knowledge that they've just shown they possess, and they go on to the next activity. The people who choose less expertly get more information before they go on.

This is easy to do in elearning but hard in live training. The webinar presenter usually can't say, "Okay, those of you who correctly chose B, go ahead and do this other activity while I talk to the others."

One solution to this problem is the third approach: create a stream of activities that optionally include the necessary information, and let learners pull the different levels of information they need.

Stream of activities

This is the most challenging approach to design, but I think it can create the best experience. Instead of alternating activities with information presentation, you make the necessary information available in the activity itself and let people pull what they need.

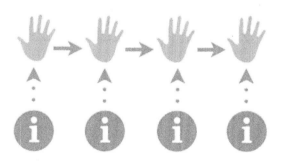

There are many ways to include the information. We saw one approach earlier, in the sharps safety course. We didn't present any information; we just plunged people into the activity. However, in the activity, we gave them optional access to the information they needed to make a good choice. For example, they could look at the real-world job aid before they made their decision.

After they made their choice, we showed them the consequences and included the job aid that they should have looked at.

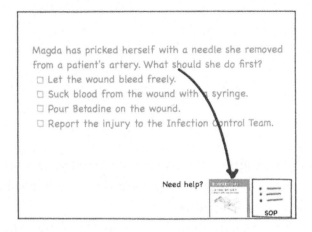

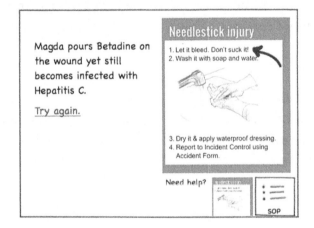

The information was provided optionally during the decision-making phase, and a quick confirmation or correction was provided in the feedback. **This activity could be immediately followed by another,** with no information presentation in between, because the information is included in the activity itself.

How might this work in a live session?

The live version of providing the information in the activity could look like the following. Let's make it a low-tech, face-to-face workshop in an empty room with no slides or laptops, which is the most challenging situation in which to try this approach.

> On the wall of the room, the facilitator tapes a copy of the sign that appears in every room of the hospital. It tells you how to respond if you jab yourself with a contaminated needle.
>
> The facilitator doesn't present a list of do's and don'ts. She just mentions that people might want to look at the sign if they're not sure what to do.
>
> Then she describes Magda's challenge: "Let's say that a clinician named Magda has just jabbed herself with a needle that she took out of a patient's artery. What should she do?"
>
> Participants call out their recommendations. Some look at the sign first, and some don't.
>
> The facilitator selectively hears a recommendation of Betadine, the most common mistake.
>
> "Okay, Magda washes the wound with Betadine," she says. "The patient has hepatitis C. What are the chances that Magda has it now?"
>
> If the participants don't mention the consequence on their own, the facilitator reports the consequences of the choice: "Magda doesn't know it yet, but she just caught hepatitis C."
>
> Finally, the facilitator asks, "What should she have looked at before she made her decision?"
>
> After confirming that the job aid had the answer, the facilitator immediately moves on to another challenge: "I need to give an unconscious patient an injection. Imagine that they're lying right there. What should I do first?"
>
> This time, the optional help for this activity is a quick reference that all participants have on their smartphones. They can look at the reference or not before they answer.

Again, in live training, it's hard to have the activity act as a filter, letting the people who answered correctly skip ahead. But at least in this format, the information presentation is reduced and put under the learners' control, and in the example above, the "feedback" is in the form of a discussion rather than an information dump.

We've just seen one simple example of how this could work. We'll look at more ways later in this chapter, but first let's consider why we're doing this.

Advantages of the stream of activities

Learners are in control

In the first two approaches shown above, we **pushed** information at people. Whether we did it before or after the activity, we stopped everything and said, "Everyone, listen to this."

However, in the stream-of-activities approach, we're encouraging people to **pull** information. We let people decide what they need to know in order to solve the problem, and we provide optional access to that information.

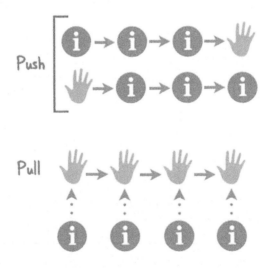

People who already have some expertise might not pull any information and just make the decision. People with less experience might look at all the information before they decide.

This means that people with slightly different levels of expertise can complete the same activity, with no one being told what they already know, except for quick confirmations of correct choices. The more experienced get confirmation that they can make that decision. The newer people catch up to the more experienced by learning what they need to know before making the decision, or by choosing incorrectly and then being sent back to try again or receiving remedial information.

As I hope is obvious, I'm not saying that we should design the same activity for everyone in the company, from newbies to experts. **Our training should be pitched at specific groups.** I'm saying that within each group there is guaranteed to be a range of pre-existing knowledge as well as different preferences for risk-taking, and we're accommodating those differences by letting people determine how much they need to know before making a decision.

We're saying to the learners, "We recognize that you're all adults with brains and life experience." We avoid a motivation-killing, one-size-fits-all presentation.

> *In the end, autonomy is about choice and agency. The ability to consciously choose what we do and how we do it is central to our concept of personal independence. It is the core of something deeper, our sense of agency. Agency is the idea that we can make conscious decisions that will lead to a hoped-for outcome — essentially, that we can determine our fate. We are not pawns of a deterministic system, powerless to decide where we end up.*
>
> *— Tracy Maylett and Paul Warner in MAGIC: Five Keys to Unlock the Power of Employee Engagement (2014)*

The activities are more challenging

As we saw earlier with the example of Noah and Brian, an activity is more challenging if we're plunged into it without first being told all the do's and don'ts. The same activity that's too easy after a presentation becomes more challenging when the information isn't presented first. It's more challenging because we're not just treating our short-term memory as a trampoline. Instead, we dig through prior knowledge, evaluate whether it applies, and build or reinforce connections.

Many designers are concerned about making training "engaging." In the search for engagement, they often reach for elearning bling or cringe-inducing games. But instead of entertaining people, we should be engaging their brains. **Challenge is motivating** and helps people feel engaged.

> *People crave work experiences that challenge their minds and their skills, that are intellectually stimulating, and that offer them the*

> *chance to rise to the occasion and excel even in high-stress situations.... People, in general, not only want challenge — they **need** challenge.*
>
> *— Tracy Maylett and Paul Warner in MAGIC: Five Keys to Unlock the Power of Employee Engagement (2014)*

By giving learners control over challenging activities, we show that we're confident that they can handle it. Our higher expectation can lead them to perform better, Nik Kinley and Shlomo Ben-Hur say in *Changing Employee Behavior* (2015): "Essentially, the higher the expectations we place on people and the more we tell them we believe in them, the better they tend to do."

Struggle creates deeper learning

The stream-of-activities approach doesn't present a lot of information before the activity. We just start the activity, and people pull information if they need it. This means they might struggle a bit and then look for help. How much they struggle depends on how much support we provide, but struggle is baked in to the activity.

"It's not fair to just throw them into an activity!" some clients might say. "You're setting them up to fail!" Actually, we may be setting them up to succeed.

> *Trying to solve a problem before being taught the solution leads to better learning, even when errors are made in the attempt.*
>
> *—Peter Brown, et al. in Make It Stick (2014)*

Research into "productive failure" suggests that when people are asked to solve a problem before they're 100% prepared, they can not only figure out the solution to the current problem but also see more clearly how to solve different but related problems. They appear to understand the underlying concepts better than people who were first told, step by step, how to solve the original problem.

This type of transfer is what we want in workplace learning. We want people to not only know how to solve a specific problem, but to also confidently solve different but related problems on their own.

For this to work, people should have enough prior knowledge to see how to approach the problem. As described later in this chapter, they could get this prior knowledge through a series of increasingly challenging activities rather than through a presentation, or we could provide help during the activity.

We should also make sure that people eventually see the correct solution and how it's reached. This could be provided as optional help, depending on how difficult you feel the problem will be, and in my opinion, it should definitely be provided in the feedback. For example, if I flounder briefly and sort-of see that I need to do A before B, I want to see in the feedback a crystal-clear confirmation that yes, I should do A before B, and **here's why**.

Some clients worry that if we let people make bad choices, they'll remember only the bad choices and not the better ones. This might be true if learners never see why their choice was bad and what the better choice would have been, and they're never given a chance to fix the problem. But we're going to give rich, contextual feedback rather than just saying, "Incorrect." And when people make a choice or ask for the solution, we'll show them the solution clearly.

> *"When learners commit errors and are given corrective feedback, the errors are not learned. Even strategies that are highly likely to result in errors, like asking someone to try to solve a problem before being shown how to do it, produce stronger learning and retention of the correct information than more passive learning strategies, provided there is corrective feedback."*
>
> *—Peter Brown, et al. in Make It Stick (2014)*

For links to research summaries about this approach, search for "productive failure" at my blog at cathy-moore.com and on the web. You might also explore publications on "desirable difficulties" in learning and see the useful research summaries in Ruth Clark's *Scenario-based e-Learning* (2013) and in *Make It Stick* (2014) by Peter Brown, Henry Roediger, and Mark McDaniel.

Finally, if you still have stakeholders saying, "It's not fair!" ask them which of the following is really more fair to learners.

Fair? Make everyone sit through the same presentation whether they already know the information or not. Then ask them a question that has them rely on their short-term memory of that information. Don't let them prove that they already know the material or even give them time to consider their pre-existing knowledge. Treat them all as equally ignorant children who must be told what to think.

Fair? Immediately challenge people to make an interesting decision. Let them consider their prior experience and existing knowledge without interruption. Let them easily pull the information they need, whether it's a lot or a little. Show them the consequence of their choice so they can see for themselves if they "get" it, and let them pull more information if they need it. Let each person manage the experience in the way that works best for them.

We have more delivery options

The stream-of-activities approach embeds support and information in the activity. So rather than being a minor distraction in a lengthy presentation, **your activities could stand alone.** This gives you more options for delivery.

As we saw in the earlier section on formats, you might want to ask whether the activities really need to be part of a training event. For example, maybe they could be provided on demand, as short practice sessions before doing a task in real life. Or they could be emailed to people in small doses, spread out over time, to space out the learning and practice retrieval.

I recommend grouping activities by context if necessary and including a debrief of some sort, as described below, to avoid creating atomized bits of learning that don't relate to each other. But even with that caveat, creating self-contained activities opens up many possibilities.

We inspire deeper discussion

We saw this in the example of Tanya and the salary data. If we first told everyone the safest way to carry data home and then asked, "What's the safest way to carry data?" there would be zero discussion. Instead, if we don't present all the information first and just ask the question, we get much more discussion and probably deeper learning.

Choose your approach

We just looked at three ways to organize information and activities. You can probably guess which one I prefer, and if you can even dimly imagine using the stream of activities, I strongly suggest you give it a try right now.

In the next steps, you'll decide which bits of information are required and how you'll provide them.

2. Confirm what's really required

Look at your notes from the interview you did with the SME. Which information did they say was required? Now that you've written the activity, how do you feel about the information that the SME said is required? Does it feel complete, incomplete, or excessive? If you're not sure, get another opinion.

You might talk to someone who's less expert than your SME but who regularly does the task to the required standards. The most useful person might be someone who recently learned the task, because they'll remember more clearly whether they really had to memorize some information from the beginning, or whether they just ended up memorizing it because they used it so much.

Be sure to ask the recent learner about concepts. Was there a particular view of the big picture that helped them remember how to make the decision? What rules of thumb or principles come into play?

3. Divide the information into "can look up" and "must memorize"

When you're confident that you've identified the information that's really necessary, split it into two piles:

- Information that people could look up on the job before or during the task
- Information that people really must memorize in order to make a good decision on the job

During your interview with the SME about this activity, you might have used a small flowchart to make the "Job aid or memory?" decision as shown in chapter 6. (If you skipped that step, go back!) If you've talked with a recent learner as described above, you might have adjusted that division, probably putting more information into the "can look up" category.

4. Add the information to your action map

It's a good idea to add notes about the information to your map, so you'll end up with a central record of everything that's included in the project. If you're using mind-mapping software that lets you link to documents or web pages, use that feature to link to the actual references.

Here's an illegibly high-level view of one action on my "how to use action mapping" map. From left to right:

- Green: The main action ("For each action that will benefit from practice, brainstorm practice activities that can be used in any format.")
- Plain text: Notes answering, "What makes this hard to do?"
- Green: Sub-actions; below them a note about a non-training solution
- Yellow: Activity ideas
- Blue-grey: Information

Here's a closer look at how the info relates to the activities.

Ignore, for now, what the client wants — You're the expert in how people learn; you'll recommend formats

Focus on the idea, not the format — How could you develop this activity idea in formats X, Y, and Z? — Examples of the same activity in multiple formats

Brainstorm realistic activities that help people practice, not knowledge checks — Are these examples practice activities, or knowledge checks? Why? — Examples & non-examples with explanation

How would you design a practice activity for this task? — Tips & how to: Identify the decision that people have to make; have them practice making that decision

Don't get distracted by trends from education — Fads like problem-based or discovery learning can be misapplied; often over-focus on absorbing information & don't provide enough scaffolding

L&D leadership: Make clear designers' job is to find best solution to performance problem; not a course factory

Some actions just have information attached to them. In this project, these are notes about messages we want the learners to hear; they're not activities. We could elicit these messages through group discussion or, maybe, deliver them through activities (and maybe connect them to the relevant activity with a line).

Other actions have practice activities, which will link to the information shown in blue.

5. Put the "can look up" info in a job aid

The information that helps people make a good decision might already be in a job aid or other reference. If that job aid needs improvement, work with its owner to create a new version.

If no job aid or reference exists, you'll want to make one. Ideally, you'll design the aid for use on the job or at least as a publication on the intranet for others to use, and you'll also include it in your activity.

Determine the best format for the job aid

What I'm calling a "job aid" is a reference or reminder in any format that helps people follow a process or apply concepts to their job. Some examples:

- Help screens in software
- "Cheat sheets" that summarize processes
- Standard operating procedures
- Checklists
- Decision tables
- Tip sheets
- Lists of things to say
- Reminders that pop up at the time you need them
- Signs on the wall
- Policies, preferably made easy to understand
- Labels, arrows, and other indicators on equipment
- Sticky notes on your computer
- The dinging bell that reminds you to buckle your seatbelt

Designing job aids is outside the scope of this book. Instead, I'll point you to *Job Aids and Performance Support* by Allison Rossett and Lisa Schafer.

Your main goal should be to design a job aid for use in the real world. Once that reference exists, you'll include or link to it in your activity. You're solving a real-world need while simultaneously creating useful training material.

Make the job aid available in your activity

Your activity focuses on a decision that people have to make on the job. Your job aid contains the information or tips that will help them make that decision. Ideally, you'll include the job aid in the same format that it's used in real life.

For example, in our sharps safety example, the real-life job aid is a sign on the wall. In live training, we can stick that sign on the wall of the training room. In elearning, we can take a photo of that sign and link to it. We avoid recreating the sign, which saves time.

You might make the job aid available as an optional reference during the activity. I suggest you definitely include it in feedback, maybe displaying the appropriate snippet of it to provide corrective or confirming feedback after you've shown the consequence of the choice. Finally, the job aid might also be included during a debrief discussion, which happens after several activities or one big, complex activity, as we'll see later.

Condense as necessary

Your supporting information should be concise and provide just what people need to solve the problem. For example, instead of providing the 10-page, painfully verbose version of the anti-harassment policy, work with the owners of the policy to create a concise, scannable version that could be used in your materials and provided as a reference on the job. You don't want people to waste time and brain power searching through information.

6. Plan to put the "must memorize" info into people's brains

If your SME and recent learner have convinced you that people really do need to memorize some information, you've got a decision to make: Do they need separate memorization drills, or can they memorize the information just by using it in practice activities? The answer depends on the amount and nature of the information and how it's used on the job.

Example: Learning basic HTML

Let's say that some marketing staff in your firm need to learn enough HTML to change the text of existing web sites, so they don't have to rely on slow outside firms. The SME gives you a list of the HTML and CSS codes that staff should be able to enter and troubleshoot many times a day. It lists only the most common formatting codes.

Your client wants you to create online activities that are available on demand. That way, as the outsourced work is gradually brought in house, staff can learn the necessary skills right before they start editing online. What would you do?

If you know basic HTML, I'd bet you learned it the same way I did: By editing or creating a simple web page while looking often at a reference for the codes. There was no separate memorization step — you probably didn't make HTML flashcards. Instead, you learned the codes by heart because you used them often to create something that mattered to you.

I'd suggest trying the same approach to the HTML project: Create a reference showing how to use the most common formatting codes. Then give people a safe place to practice using that reference.

Start with simple activities, such as having people enter the codes to make normal text bold, and let them rely on the job aid to learn the codes at first. In feedback, show the consequence of an incorrectly entered code, such as the entire paragraph now being in boldface, and point to the spot in the reference that shows the properly formatted code.

Increase the complexity of the activities until people are making the kinds of edits they need to make on the job. Because they'll use the codes often in the activities, they'll naturally stop depending on the reference, taking off their own training wheels. They'll still have the reference for use in the real task, if they need it, and they'll already be used to working with it.

In this case, we provided a reference during the activity and also showed snippets of the reference in the feedback. We didn't create separate memorization activities.

Of course, we could skip the training altogether and just turn people loose on the actual web sites with a reference, but their mistakes could cause major problems. Instead, we had them practice first on fictional sites that they couldn't break.

Are drills useful?

It can be tempting to skip creating the kinds of contextual activities I've just described and use drills, because drills are a lot easier to design. For example, you can buy an elearning drill template and fill it questions like, "Which HTML code creates a line break?" And if people really do need to memorize a big collection of data, such as when learning a language, drills are useful.

However, in corporate training people often don't need to memorize vast amounts of information. The popularity of drills in corporate elearning reflects our unhealthy obsession with information, not a widespread need for memorization.

For example, we could use a game-show quiz to see if people know the year that the anti-harassment law was passed. However, the fact that the quiz tool makes this easy doesn't mean that our learners need to memorize that date.

Drills are useful for embedding the knowledge necessary to make skills automatic. For example, if you memorize the 1,000 most common words in a foreign language, you'll have much more fluid conversations than if you have to constantly look things up. The problem is that many designers stop at the drills. They don't design activities that help people **apply** the memorized knowledge.

One solution is to mix the drills and contextual practice activities, as described in the following example.

Example: Technical specifications

Let's say that Weeber Widget's manufacturing plant regularly buys loribdenum from various suppliers. Loribdenum is a natural product that contains varying amounts of xypheon. For making widgets, the more xypheon the loribdenum contains, the less loribdenum you need to buy. Unfortunately, the price increases as the xypheon percentage increases.

Loribdenum salespeople memorize several calculations and technical details so they can have uninterrupted conversations with their buyers without the social costs of having to look everything up on their smartphones.

For example, the prospective customer might say, "We're planning a run of 3,000 megawidgets. We don't want the weight of the loribdenum to exceed 200 grams per widget, and we need at least 76 filots of xypheon per unit. What's the best price you can give me?"

Because they've memorized many specifications and formulas, the salesperson can quickly use any calculator to identify which grade of loribdenum would be necessary, how much the customer would need, and what it would cost, without having to look up values and calculations.

To train these salespeople, we could mix drills with contextual practice activities. For example, we could first use a game to help them memorize the different grades of loribdenum based on the xypheon percentage. Then we could have them practice applying this in simple simulated conversations, where the questions focus on the loribdenum grades, such as, "I need the highest grade you've got. How much xypheon is in it?"

We could continue mixing drills and practice activities, increasing the complexity of the activities until the salespeople are answering the questions that come up in real life. We could support long-term memorization with spaced practice, such as new activities delivered periodically, or review activities that salespeople can access before meeting a client.

7. Plan your scaffolding

"Scaffolding" refers to designing activities that become harder as the learner develops their skills. This could mean that each activity becomes more difficult, or we slowly take away the help we've been providing, or a combination of the two.

It's like raising the training wheels. It helps the learner think, "I can do this hard thing!" and not, "This is impossible."

Scaffolding reduces frustration but lets you challenge people. The traditional approach to reducing frustration is to not challenge people at all. The tell-then-test model is an example — we tell them everything they might possibly need to know before asking them to try anything.

In the stream-of-activities approach, we want to challenge people enough to make them feel competent and get them to the next activity with a minimum of presentation. To do this, we need to carefully organize our activities, provide the right amount of optional help, and design feedback that's concise but thorough.

If you want to try for a stream of activities, you'll want to ask yourself some questions.

- **How should I order the activities?** You might start with activities that aren't very hard and that build the foundation for later, more difficult challenges. We saw an example of this in the loribdenum sales activities. The earliest activities just required learners to recommend the correct grade of loribdenum, while later activities had them combine that information with other data in calculations to answer more complex questions.

- **How much optional help should I make available during the activity, and in what format?** The help is often the same information that traditional trainers present before an activity. It could be provided as the real-life job aid, as handouts or links, or in as simple a format as, "If you get stuck, raise your hand and I'll come help you."

- **Should people attempt the activities alone or in groups?** If you're designing a live event that makes group work easy, consider having people work in groups. They'll combine their different knowledge, and their discussion could lead to deeper learning.

- **How will the optional help and the feedback relate to each other?** We saw an example of one approach earlier, with the needlestick activity. The optional help was the real-life job aid, and the feedback highlighted the part of the job aid that contained the correct answer. The optional help was detailed, showing the entire job aid, while the feedback quoted only the most relevant part of the optional help.

Example: Learning Zeko

Let's say that we're sure our audience knows nothing about the topic. In fact, let's teach them a language that I just made up. We couldn't possibly expect people to use a language they don't know without any preparation. Or could we?

Our (fictional) learners are part of a news organization that works in several countries. When they arrive in a country, they need to quickly navigate to the site of a disaster or other newsworthy event. Translators aren't always available. As a result, the learners need to know basic navigational terms like "left" and "right" and words like "yes" and "no."

Our learners want to learn some navigational Zeko in their spare time so they're always ready for an assignment in Zekostan. They want to use self-paced elearning. If we took the conventional approach, what would we do?

Here's a typical approach, based on about a billion language-learning programs I've used:

1. Present several words on the screen. Show them in Zeko and English at the same time. Learners click the Zeko word to hear it pronounced.

2. Test the learners' memory of those words with a game-like drill. First show each word in Zeko and require people to choose the English translation. Then show each word in English and have people choose the Zeko word.

3. Next, give them some audio drills. Play the Zeko word in audio and have learners choose the English translation. Finally, display

the English word and have them choose the Zeko word based only on its audio.

4. We're done!

Unfortunately, here's what we've done:

- We've loaded up the learners' short-term memory with isolated bits of knowledge. "Right" flashed on the screen, then "hello," and then "car."

- We've left it up to the learners to store that abstract information somehow. We probably expect them to come back to the software and run the drills again.

- We've trained our audience to translate in their head, which is inefficient. For example, the only way they interacted with the Zeko word for "left" was to translate it into English.

Let's try another approach. What would happen if we didn't teach people any Zeko and just threw them into a problem that they had to solve using the language? And what if we didn't even give them a dictionary? I designed a short branching scenario to test this idea.

You've just landed in Zekostan to cover the report of a crashed UFO. You have to navigate to the alleged crash site before a competing news agency gets there, using Zeko words that you haven't learned or even heard before. Try it now, if you can. You'll find the link in the sample activities at map-it-book.com.

The scenario is a prototype, not a full-fledged activity. At the very least, all the Zeko words should have audio pronunciations. More advanced activities later in the story should probably be in video or at least audio-only to help people reduce their dependence on written words.

I designed the activity to answer critics who say it's "not fair" to make people solve a challenge without first telling them everything they need to know. I wanted to show that not only is it "fair," it can be more interesting and memorable.

I also wanted to explore how to help people learn vocabulary the same way they learn it in the real world — by observation, trial, and error. I wanted to do the following:

- Make the words more memorable by associating them with specific scenes and emotion

- Avoid the inefficiency of in-the-head translation by making the meaning of the word clear in context, rather than just attaching it to an English word

- Have learners apply new vocabulary in a (somewhat!) realistic setting as soon as possible, so retrieval practice happens in a context similar to the real-world situation

- Give the learners a visual reminder of several words' meaning, in the form of the sketch at the end of the story, to reinforce what they learned and offer another non-translating way to store the words

This would be a seriously inefficient way to teach a lot of vocabulary, so in the real world we'd probably start with this scenario, then use more efficient activities to teach more words, and then have a more advanced scenario, and so forth. What might those more efficient activities look like?

I'd vote for staying in the story but in a much more condensed way. For example, we could build on the sketch that ended the scenario and show a drawing of the entire crash site. Labels in Zeko only could identify useful items and concepts, such as "mountain" along with "up" and "down," "car" vs. "bus," a compass with the four directions labeled, and so forth. Maybe Ludo makes the drawing for us. The labels could be clickable so we hear the pronunciation as well.

Then, armed with that sketch as an optional reference, the learner could go through another chapter of the story, this time applying the new vocabulary from the sketch, the words they learned in the first chapter, and a few new words that they learn as the story continues.

This would keep the vocabulary in context, continue the emphasis on immediate application, and give people several options for memory storage, not just abstract translation.

Of course, in the real world we could provide any number of job aids, including a quick reference that reporters could carry on their smartphones. It would be interesting to experiment with a visual quick reference, something like the site sketch, in addition to a traditional dictionary application.

Many designers would give learners access to these job aids during the scenario. That way, people wouldn't have to figure things out during the story and could just look up the word. However, I wanted to test a more "pure" approach in which the only scaffolding is a careful introduction of new information in the story. I also suspect that people who have to figure out a word in context build stronger connections to it than the people who immediately grab the dictionary.

The Zeko activity was easy and quick to develop. You can read more about the development in the blog post linked above.

8. Consider including worked examples

A worked example shows how an expert would solve the problem, step by step. It's such an efficient way to learn that it can reduce the number of activities you need.

A worked example could be a simple demonstration that's provided as an optional link, or something far more complex. It might show how someone completes the entire thing, or it might show how they would complete the first, say, five steps and then have the learner take over.

If you're helping people learn a longer and more complex process, consider threading one example through all the activities. My scenario design course includes a fictional project with a fictional SME. As people progress through the course, they can practice on the fictional project and see how I would complete the step for that material. This serves as a suggested model. Then they apply the techniques their own, real-life project.

Examples are so powerful that they can reduce the number of practice activities you need, Ruth Clark writes.

> *When working memory capacity is tied up solving problems, there is little resource left over for learning. However, imagine that instead of working a problem, you are reviewing an example. Your working memory is free to carefully study the example and learn from it. In fact, by providing an example as a model, the student has an opportunity to build her own mental model from it.*
>
> *— Ruth Colvin Clark in Evidence-Based Training Methods (2015)*

9. Decide when to make the information available

If you're using the stream-of-activities approach, you have three buckets in which to put the supporting information.

1. Optional information made available during an activity

2. Confirming or correcting information in feedback or a debrief

3. Principles and summary concepts elicited during a debrief

If you want the activity to be more challenging, you might skip bucket 1 and focus on 2 and 3. For example, no optional help was provided in the Zeko activity. Instead, Ludo provides confirming or correcting feedback by reacting to what you said (bucket 2), and the new terms are summarized in a debrief sketch at the end of the activity (bucket 3).

If you use bucket 1 and provide information during the activity, that information might include the same material that you put in bucket 2. For example, if people can look at a job aid before making their decision (bucket 1), that job aid might also appear in your feedback (bucket 2).

I'd strongly recommend you never skip bucket 2. After you show the consequence of the choice, you should somehow confirm or correct the choice. That information might be optional "telling" feedback, it might be "showing" feedback delivered through the story, or it might be delayed until a debrief at the end of the story, but it needs to be available for the people who need it.

Recommended approach: For most projects, I recommend you try creating a stream of activities, not a presentation that's interrupted by occasional activities. For each activity, you could consider providing the information in the following ways.

- **Decision point:** Make information available optionally, such as the real-world job aid. The info is available in the decision point itself, to be pulled by the people who need it.

- **Feedback (unique for each choice!):** First show the consequence of the choice, and then make correcting or confirming information available. That information might be the relevant part of the job aid, or some "telling" feedback delivered in a non-patronizing way or through group discussion. I recommend making this confirming information optional, but worried stakeholders or user testing might convince you to deliver it automatically, after showing the consequence of the choice.

- **Debrief after a series of activities or a complex branching scenario:** Provide a debrief to help people see the principles or concepts that connect the activities. If people are learning how to deal with grey areas, a live discussion might be best. Otherwise, try to provide the debrief as thought-provoking questions, not just a list of bullet points.

10. Consider how you might fade the help

Should the information you've identified always be available, or should you gradually take it away so people have to rely on their memory?

If the activities have people use a real-world job aid that they'd also be able to use on their jobs, there's no reason for them to memorize the information. They'd even be able to use it during assessment activities, as shown below. The question mark represents an activity, while the document represents the real-world job aid. It's always available, just like in the real world. (The path goes down one column and then the other.)

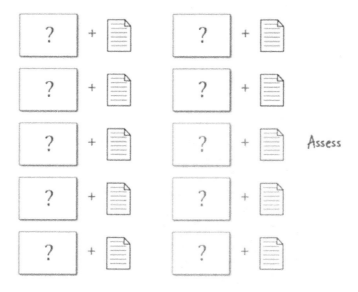

On the other hand, if your supporting information should eventually be memorized, you could gradually withdraw ("fade") the help during the stream of activities. For example, if the help is a worked example, you'd complete less of the example each time until participants are completing the entire task on their own.

11. Decide how you'll help people see overarching concepts

We've been focusing on the information required to make a good decision. At this point it's easy to focus on the specifics, such as the steps of a procedure. It's easy to overlook the underlying principles, rules of thumb, and other non-data that people also need to master.

To avoid information overload, we have to make some hard choices about the information we require people to memorize. For example, if learners could memorize only one of the following bits of info, which would you choose?

> a) "We need to avoid even the appearance of unethical behavior. We should avoid actions that are technically correct but that are easily misinterpreted."

> b) "We should reject gifts that are valued at 50€ or more."

If I had to choose only one to be memorized, I'd pick **a**. The principle is more universally applicable than the specific rule, the rule probably changes occasionally, and **the rule can easily be looked up**. Also, someone who remembers only the rule and forgets the principle could find themselves in this situation:

> "Hugh, the other company bidding on this project has filed a complaint about that watch their competition gave you."

"But they said it was a 48€ watch! It's under the 50€ limit."

"It doesn't look like a 48€ watch, and you shouldn't be accepting gifts at all when tensions are so high."

The 50€ rule is easy to look up. The principle is harder to apply, so in my opinion it should get more attention in the training. Unfortunately, the popularity of drills means the 50€ rule gets all the love.

As we've already seen, my favorite way to help people see principles is with a series of practice activities followed by a debrief. We saw an example earlier in the training for future officers in Iraq.

Another approach is to move the concept-learning earlier, such as through a hint in the activity itself. For example, in the Iraq activity, we could have included printed hint cards that each had one useful principle or rule of thumb. At any point in the activity, the learners could stop and pull a hint card at random. Some hints we could have used are:

- In high-context societies, even military leaders might step back and let collective decision-making take place.

- Which is likelier to work: Getting everyone around you to change how they make decisions, or adapting to their technique?

- Your translator can help you understand local culture, but his primary allegiance might be to his tribe.

While these tips aren't contextual — they aren't tailored to a specific decision point — they'd help the players consider decisions from a different angle and begin to learn the higher-level principles they'll need in the field.

A debrief ties it together

If you use the stream-of-activities approach, you create self-contained activities that could be delivered in several ways — online, self-paced, face-to-face... This flexibility has all sorts of advantages, but it also makes it easy for us to create what seems like a random collection of unrelated challenges. That's why I strongly suggest you include a debrief after any stream or collection of activities.

The debrief helps people see the higher-level concepts that connect the activities — it helps them move from the concrete to the conceptual and back again.

For example, in the Iraq military scenario described in chapter 11, the facilitator led a debrief discussion that encouraged people to identify the cultural concepts and basic recommendations that the scenario was designed to elicit. The discussion pulled the focus up from the specific story to the more globally useful concepts.

In our simpler course on sharps safety, we could go through several decision-making activities, and then ask participants to identify the common situations or errors that underlie the mistakes they saw. For example, we could get participants to point out that in three of the activities, the scenario characters ran into trouble because they let themselves be distracted and skipped steps of the procedure.

Debrief formats

Carefully led discussions are great for debriefs, but they're not always possible.

For example, in self-paced elearning, the debrief might be limited to a very short presentation highlighting the concepts or higher-level lessons delivered by the activities. In the needlestick course, this could be a very short summary of the common errors underlying specific mistakes. A slightly better approach would be to display open-ended questions that ask people to elicit some concepts, and then summarize the concepts when learners click to reveal the answer.

A further step for elearning would be to encourage participation in an asynchronous discussion forum. You could seed this forum with questions that ask people to identify the concepts and conclusions they drew from the activities. The more controversial your questions, the more participation and thinking you're likely to elicit.

Invite critiques of the activity

If you're using a complex branching scenario or a shorter but controversial activity, one sure way to get a discussion going is to ask people to provide feedback on the design. For example, you could ask, "Which options do you wish you had at this point?" and "Why do you think the designers left them out?"

Have learners create or improve job aids

If you had people use job aids or other references during the activity, ask for feedback about them in the debrief. You could even go a step further and provide less-than-perfect job aids for the activity, knowing that people will want to improve them.

A more advanced step is to provide no job aid during the activity and ask the learners to create one when they're done. Obviously, you'll want to use this last option with care, with people who have enough expertise to complete the activity without serious frustration, and you might position creating the job aid as, "How would you help a complete novice do what you just did?"

Make sure that the job aid includes the rules of thumb or other principles that underlie the steps of the procedure.

12. Choose the format for the information

The information we want to provide could include everything from specific procedural steps to high-level concepts. If we want to design a stream of activities, in what format should we supply this information? Here are some ideas out of the many, many possibilities.

Job aids

As we've seen, if a job aid is useful on the job, it's a good idea to include it in the activity. It's probably most efficient for you to link to or distribute the real-life job aid, rather than reproducing it in your activity.

Worked examples

A "worked example" shows how an expert solves the problem. You could show just a few steps to help people get started, show just the tricky steps, or show the whole thing. Seeing an example like this can be far more efficient than listening to a trainer describe how to do it. Probably the ideal approach is to let the learner decide how much of the example solution they need to see and when they need to see it.

Hints

Hints can take any number of forms. A worked example or job aid could be a hint. The paper cards I described above could be hints, though they aren't contextual.

A contextual hint provides the help that the learner probably needs at that point. For example, if I'm entering information into a database and I'm stuck at one field, wondering what I'm supposed to enter, a contextual hint would focus on just that field.

Mini-presentations from repurposed slides

If there are already slides that explain how to perform the task, maybe slides that were used in a conventional workshop, you could recycle them as **optional** help or remedial information in your activity.

For example, if I'm not sure what to do in your webinar activity, I could click a link you've provided and see a **short** mini-presentation that tells me what I need to know.

> If one of your stakeholders is nervous about not using traditional training, this can help relieve their anxieties. The slides they're used to seeing are still there; it's just that they won't be forced on everyone. They'll appear to the people who ask for them or who clearly need them, such as people who made a bad choice in an activity.

Because the slides are optional and the attention is on the activity, people will expect less bling. You can reserve animations for the situations that really benefit from them, rather than using them to make boring content more "interesting."

In face-to-face sessions, you could provide the mini-presentations online, if participants are expected to bring their own laptops, or on a laptop provided on each table. Since most conventional slides are just text documents, you could even print them out and leave them on each table to be referenced as necessary, though it would be best to design a more easily skimmed conventional document.

Peer-generated content

Forums, internal blogs, quick videos that show how to do something — all of these might already be available, created by your learners' colleagues. It can sometimes be problematic to link to specific items, since this type of material tends to come and go quickly, but if the content is organized by topic you could at least send learners to a useful collection of information. And if it's hard to link to specific items, this is your chance to be proactive — you could research and propose a solution and help get it implemented.

Manuals, books, other publications

Any type of publication can be used to support activities, from short articles to entire books.

If you're trying to teach something deep and complex, like I'm trying to teach training design, then a long publication might be your best option. This book is an example. I use it to support my courses and workshops.

Before I wrote the book, clients wanted me to "teach them action mapping" in a day (or an hour!). They wanted the traditional shot in the arm, and in my attempt to deliver that, I crammed too much information into the workshop. The result wasn't as activity-rich as I would have liked.

When you can provide a separate publication, whether it's a book, well-organized site, or something else, then you can design practice activities that focus on the challenging areas and let the publication cover the rest. The publication could serve as optional help during the activity ("If you need help, see the chart on page 27"), people could read it afterward to more clearly see the bigger picture that they glimpsed during the activity, or it could be distributed as preparatory material.

The drawback, of course, is that participants have to read more than they might be used to reading for the typical one-day workshop or short course. However, I'd argue that many workshops or courses are stuck at the "high-level overview" stage precisely because they try to deliver information that should be provided separately. If we "flip" our training so the information is delivered separately from the event, we can use the event to dig deep into practice activities, and the learners can go through the other materials at their own pace.

Let research guide your information design

In this book, we're focusing entirely on activity design. Information design is a huge topic that would require an additional book. Luckily, several people have already written that book.

I'd suggest you look for publications that offer recommendations supported by research. You might look for works by Ruth Colvin Clark, Richard Mayer, Connie Malamed, and Allison Rossett.

Don't have time for an entire book? A web search for "multimedia design principles" will give you a good summary of research that's relevant not just to elearning but to any presentation of information. These are important principles that many designers have never been taught, so it's worth taking 30 minutes to get acquainted with them.

Stream-of-activity principles

Here's a summary of the principles that guide the stream-of-activities approach.

Principles of the "stream of activities" approach

1. Activities help people practice making the decisions that they make on the job, in a realistic context.

2. Activities target common mistakes and support behaviors that will achieve the business goal.

3. Activities target specific job roles and levels of expertise. They aren't expected to apply to everyone.

4. Instead of pushing information, we let people pull it. For example, activities aren't preceded by a lot of information. Instead, the information is offered during the activity as optional help, afterwards in feedback, or both.

5. The activity models the real-world use of information. For example, if a job aid is useful in the real world, it's included as optional information in the activity. No one is required to memorize information that doesn't need to be memorized on the job.

6. Feedback shows the consequence of the choice first. Each choice has a unique consequence.

7. "Telling" feedback is made available after the consequence to confirm or correct the choice. The telling includes the relevant part of the supporting information, such as part of the job aid. It can appear immediately or be delayed, and it can be optional.

8. Earlier activities build foundational skills used in later activities.

9. Complex activities or groups of activities are followed by a debrief that helps people see connections and concepts.

10. Activities are designed for flexible delivery, at different times and in different formats. They can be included in an event, made available for on-demand use, delivered over time as spaced practice, or made available in many other ways.

Examples of projects

Below are a few examples of fictional and real projects that show how the above principles could be applied. As you read about each example, consider whether it addresses all the principles. Which ones does it skip?

Sharps safety

We've already discussed one fictional example in the sharps safety course, which included the real-world job aid as optional help. That optional information is scaffolding.

A snippet of the job aid appears in the feedback to confirm or correct the choice. The feedback both shows what happens (Magda gets infected) and tells us what we should have done (the highlighted spot on the job aid).

Other activities in the project follow the same format: Optional information in the form of the real-world job aid or procedure supports the decision. The feedback shows the result of the decision and shows the relevant portion of the job aid or reference.

If we deliver these activities as an event, such as an online course, we could start with the easier challenges, such as the activity with Magda, and increase the complexity of the decision. Or, we could group the activities by concept, such as all activities in which distraction is an element, to help people see connections. Either way, learners would see only the activities that applied to their jobs, and we'd wrap up the course with a debrief to highlight the main points.

At first, the client wasn't interested in principle 10, flexible delivery. He wanted a formal online course. However, as the course showed results, he agreed to provide spaced practice in the form of stand-alone activities delivered over time.

Widget sales

Let's go back to our project with Arno in which salespeople are supposed to become "trusted advisors" to widget buyers. We were designing an activity to help people overcome objections about heat. How could we include supporting information?

We don't plan to precede this activity with a presentation that lists do's and don'ts. We have a short, inspiring message at the beginning about our change to being "trusted advisors" and why that will be a good thing **for the salespeople,** and then we start the activity. People learn the techniques as they complete the stream of activities, and a debrief pulls it all together at the end.

First, let's say we're using elearning, because that's easiest to show here. Here's a mockup of the start of the activity. How could we add scaffolding to help unprepared salespeople choose the "trusted advisor" option and not the common mistakes?

You're meeting with Ravi, a new customer.

"I might be interested in your J-12 widget," Ravi says. "At 79 wigabits, it has enough power for spurdling. But I've read that it runs hot."

What do you say?

- ☐ "Our studies show that heat doesn't cause issues for the J-12. Would you like to see the test results?"
- ☐ "Actually, the J-12 has only 60 wigabits. If you're going to be spurdling, I'd recommend the K-77."
- ☐ "Are you referring to the Widget World review?"

One simple approach would be to create a list of tips that help salespeople move from a feature focus to the more emotional "trust" focus. The list would become a real-world review aid to help people remember what to do, and we'd also link to it in the activity.

How could we confirm the information in the feedback? One approach is to display the appropriate snippet of the tips document. This could be optional (which I'd recommend), or we could make the bit of the document open automatically on the feedback screen.

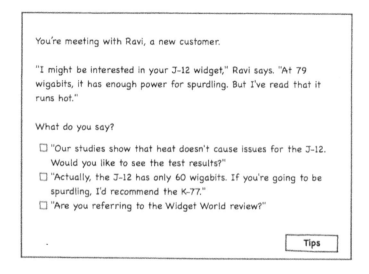

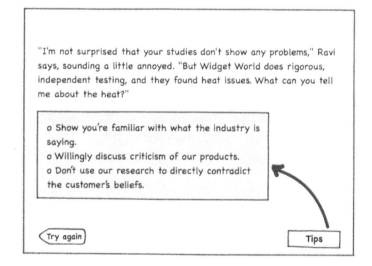

Since this training focuses on changing the brand's personality, I'd strongly recommend that it include face-to-face sessions, preferably several spaced over time. A shot-in-the-arm online course or one-day workshop isn't likely to have much effect.

Live version

How could we use the same approach in live training?

Let's take the most difficult situation in which to tailor information to each

learner: a face-to-face workshop with one facilitator and several participants.

All our salespeople have gathered in one room for the "training." They're aware that they're supposed to adjust what they're doing but haven't been told exactly how. If we don't first present all the do's and don'ts, how can we provide optional help in the activity?

Many trainers would reach into their bag of tricks for a roleplay. Let's go along with them see what happens. What do you think about the following idea for a roleplay?

> Participants are paired off. One participant pretends to be a customer concerned about the heat of the J-12. The other needs to overcome the objection using the "trusted advisor" model described on a printed sheet of tips. Okay, everyone, go!

What will happen? The fictional conversations will go off in all directions, because both the fake customers and the salespeople are making choices from an infinite selection. There's not enough structure to make our points.

For example, we haven't restricted what the customer can say, and since they don't know what points we're trying to make, they'll say whatever occurs to them. All that analysis we did to identify the common mistakes, the consequences of those mistakes, the best choice — we've thrown all that out. In the resulting barrage of possibilities, we might end up making no clear points at all.

As we've seen, one solution is to create scenarios with limited options that are designed to represent the most common mistakes, distribute or share the scenarios, and debate the options. During that debate, some people might look at the list of tips and some might not.

Those who use the optional information and as a result argue for a different choice can explain to the others why they've made that decision, which both reinforces their own understanding of the tips and propagates them throughout the group.

After several structured, focused activities like these scenarios, then it might be appropriate to use freewheeling roleplays. People will then have a much clearer idea of what they're trying to accomplish.

Earlier we looked at an example for the other widget company. Their salespeople went through several branching scenarios and discussed them asynchronously, and then they got together for roleplays. In those roleplays, we gave each fictional customer a document describing of their needs, their past experience with widgets, and the price they were willing to pay, which kept the conversation focused.

Noah and Brian

Earlier, we looked at an activity that intentionally provided no help during the decision. This was the "how to manage project managers" material that was intended to help learners stop micro-managing and instead build their project managers' skills.

During the first branching scenario, we kept a secret. We didn't tell the learners that we wanted them to change what they did. We just presented a situation designed to tempt them to micro-manage, and we included several micro-managing options as well as a more skill-building option.

The only feedback that people received during most of the scenario was the consequences of their choices. There was no telling feedback until the end of a storyline, as in the following plot diagram.

Each diamond represents a decision point in the scenario. Each decision leads to a new decision point that describes the consequence of the previous decision and requires the next decision. No "telling" information appears until the end of each story line.

The Noah and Brian storylines were connected at certain points: People who chose micro-managing options saw their projects get delayed. They had the chance to realize they were going the wrong way and begin to choose more skill-building options. This is what I mean when I say that the branching structure is part of the feedback — people know that the story is going badly and that there are better paths, so they start choosing different options to try to get to those paths.

At the end of a storyline, we describe the final scene and finally provide telling feedback. Here's an example. After we describe a poor ending that resulted in a

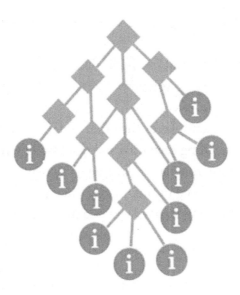

late project and friction between Noah and Brian, we provide a link: Why did this happen? Here's what it shows.

> **Why did this happen?**
>
> You intervened twice between Noah and Brian, which gave them the message that you're willing to be their referee. As a result, they kept coming to you with issues that they should have been able to handle on their own. You also gave Noah the impression that he doesn't have to connect with people personally and can simply insist that they deliver on time. This won't help him succeed on future projects.
>
> Instead, you could have built Noah's skills and taken yourself out of the dispute. Learn more.

The "learn more" link launches a **short, extremely concise** presentation of the model, focusing on a few key points. Then another scenario starts that helps illustrate those first few points. With each scenario, we get deeper into the model, learning more about it and applying it in more situations.

After a few scenarios, we offer a debrief, preferably in live discussion, that helps people digest what they've learned, debate how the scenarios worked, and consider how they could apply the model to their projects.

To provide reinforcement and deeper learning, we'd occasionally send the learners additional scenarios or take advantage of regular meetings to run live scenarios with a summary of the model as support.

Cross-cultural projects

We've also looked at some cross-cultural training for soldiers. The activities in that project were branching scenarios, and none of them offered optional help or telling feedback. The feedback and information were delayed, coming only in the debrief. Why do you think we delayed it?

One reason is that delaying the feedback made the scenarios feel more realistic and game-like. When you're having a real-life conversation, no one interrupts to tell you that you're doing it wrong.

We also chose this approach because it fit what the soldiers preferred. When we interviewed them, they made clear that they liked to learn in groups, from other soldiers, and they didn't like having outsiders come in and tell them what to do. Since we were outsiders, it seemed best to make any information or telling feedback come from another soldier.

As a result, the scenarios included only showing feedback that continued the story, and we relied on the discussion and debrief, led by other soldiers, to provide information and highlight connecting concepts. No outside expert lectured the soldiers.

The scenarios in this project were used in classroom training far from the field. I'd recommend that the client expand their use of the scenarios to provide them in the field or at least online during deployment, to reinforce the learning and to act as just-in-time practice. For example, an officer who's about to meet with a tribal leader for the first time could practice a similar interaction before going to the meeting. This would address principle 10.

Practice: What would you do?

Below are two projects that analysis shows would be helped by some training. How would you organize the activities and information to apply the "stream of activities" principles?

> a) A chain of hotels in a region that's popular with sex tourists wants their staff to recognize and appropriately respond to possible child trafficking.

Since the hotels are spread over a wide region, the client wants an online solution. To make managing the material simple, they want one course for all employees, covering jobs that include housekeeping, reception, and security. What type of activities and information would you create, and how would you cover such a wide range of job roles?

b) A chain of sporting goods stores wants managers to be more support-ive of their team members. The client has a new management model they'd like managers to use, and they think they'd like a combination of elearning and face-to-face sessions. What kind of solution would you propose?

First, of course, in both cases we'd work with the client to identify a business goal, list and prioritize what people need to do, and examine why they aren't doing it. Then, **for the behaviors that can be helped with training,** we might take the fol-lowing approaches.

- **a) Recognize and respond to possible child trafficking:** In this real-life project, we created a bank of mini-scenarios. Each scene described a possibly suspicious situation, such as a male foreigner checking in to the hotel with a local girl who may or may not be over the age of consent. The learners had to decide whether the situation was suspicious enough to act, and what that action should be. When action was required, it was usually simple: tell your boss or call a hotline.

  The activities were packaged in an online course at the request of the client. The first screen of the course didn't present information; instead, it motivated people to take on the challenge of responding to child trafficking. The learners chose their job from a short list, and then they immediately started scenarios that were appropriate to their job.

  Some scenarios applied to more than one job. For example, suspicious behavior in the hallway could be seen by a housekeeper or security staff, so a hallway scenario was made available to both job roles. Other scenarios were job-specific, such as a housekeeper seeing an unusual number of photographs of children in a room.

  A short debrief after the scenarios highlighted the principles that the sce-narios illustrated and encouraged learners to take the appropriate actions.

  I'd recommend that additional scenarios be delivered at spaced intervals after the course, to remind people of the principles and keep the message in front of them. It might also be helpful to create scenarios based on real events, to show the real-world outcome of decisions made by learners' peers.

There were some environmental issues to overcome, such as a cultural reluctance to challenge a hotel guest. In addition to making sure managers support the anti-trafficking message, one approach would be to have a formerly trafficked child describe how they were helped by hotel staff who were willing to act. This could be part of the course, probably as part of the debrief, to end on a motivating note, or, more memorably, the person could tell their story at a face-to-face gathering.

- b) **Help store managers become more supportive:** I worked on a similar project. The most prominent problem was that employees were submitting falsified performance reports. During the analysis, the client recognized that people were doing this to stay afloat in a competitive culture in which they received little support from their managers. The client decided to try to change the culture by helping managers become more supportive.

Some managers had few problems on their team, while others had several issues. The client interviewed managers to identify what the successful managers were doing differently. Using that information, the client wrote branching scenarios that helped all managers see the consequences of their treatment of team members and apply a new management model. They also scheduled face-to-face sessions for the managers, limiting attendance to specific roles to make sure sensitive issues could be discussed freely.

I'd suggest having the managers go through a longish and ideally controversial branching scenario before meeting in person, without knowing anything about the new management model. The scenario would help spark and structure the in-person conversation about cultural issues and the managers' role in changing that culture.

Then, during the live session, the managers could go through the scenario again, or a similar scenario, as a large group, this time applying the new management model when making decisions. This would help them recognize which choices the model recommends and see how they shape the outcome and give them the chance to discuss any resistance they had to the model.

Then I'd put the managers in groups of four and distribute another scenario, either on a laptop or on paper. Each group would also have a summary of the new model as a reference. I'd steal an idea that worked well in our military projects: I'd have each participant adopt a choice and always have to defend that choice, whether they agreed with it or not. So, for example, Steve would always have to defend option B as well as he could, no matter what option B was.

Requiring people to defend "bad" options helps create a much deeper discussion and uncover the problematic beliefs that affect decisions. It also helps more expert people put themselves in a less expert person's shoes, improving their ability to help colleagues.

I'd recommend a large-group debrief in which everyone discusses the issues raised by the new scenario, the ways that the new management model applied to the story, and how the story was similar (or not) to the challenges participants faced on the job. This could be followed by small-group discussion in which people shared the challenges they're currently facing, followed by structured roleplays in which they practice applying the new model to those challenges. I'd also suggest following up with additional scenarios spaced over time and more face-to-face discussions at their regular regional meetings, where company leaders would make clear that they support the change.

Common challenges

Your client or SME expects conventional "tell, then test" training.

- Ignore their expectations for now, and avoid showing your activity drafts to any stakeholders who are still using the school model. Create your prototype and then get their reaction.

You're concerned that the culture of the learners or organization will make an activity-first approach fail.

- People in some cultures are reluctant to try a new activity without preparation, especially in public, so this is a legitimate concern. However, before you let assumptions limit your ideas, create and test a prototype.

You're sure that a stakeholder will insist that all people be exposed to the information.

- If you're 100% sure that you will be required to "expose" people to specific information and track their exposure, even though you included stakeholders in the analysis of the problem and "information exposure" is unlikely to be a solution, consider taking the approach that Anna took in the story with which I opened the book. Every time a learner made a choice about what to do with a sharp object, the feedback displayed not only the consequence of that choice but also the correct information. That way, everyone was "exposed" to all the information. They just saw it in feedback after making a choice, instead of in a conventional presentation.

- Depending on the type of the information, another approach is to put the required information into a simple reference, such as a PDF. If necessary, have learners sign or click a confirmation saying that they've been properly exposed to the information. Make that reference available as optional help in activities that require people to apply the information by making decisions in realistic situations. This way, you avoid having to make an information presentation halfway interesting with bling or training games and can focus instead on designing activities that have people **apply** the information.

Chapter 13. Prototype and refine

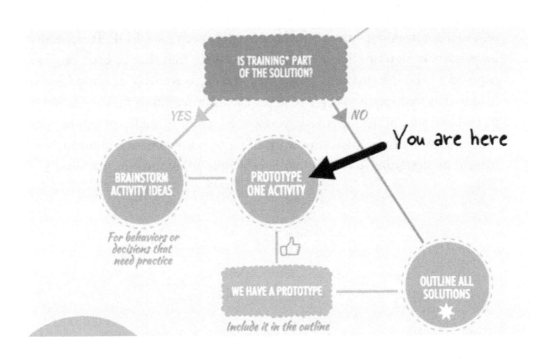

Task	Who does it	How long it might take
Create a usable mockup of your activity with minimal graphics and no bling. Have the SME check it. Get the client's reaction. Test it on learners.	You create the prototype or oversee its creation. You'll get feedback from your SME, client, and future learners.	Depends on the complexity of the prototype and the amount of rework it requires

Big idea: By creating a very plain mockup, you'll:

- Make testers focus on the cognitive challenge, not the bling

- Let stakeholders see for themselves that you don't need time-wasting bling when the challenge is interesting

What you've done

You've spent the last several chapters designing a representative activity. Now you'll turn that activity into a functional prototype for testing in the format that you think is best, whether it's elearning, live training, or some other format.

Once the prototype is improved and approved, you'll use it as a guide to write and produce the other activities and materials.

What you'll do

You're going to:

1. Create a prototype of the activity (even if it's a face-to-face activity)
2. Prepare for questions from the SME and client
3. Have the SME check the activity
4. Get the client's reaction
5. Test it on learners

Who's involved?

You'll need the following:

- Your client and SME
- Anyone else who might have veto power over your idea
- A handful of learners
- The technology or environment that you'll use to deliver the final activity (a laptop, a room, etc.)

1. Create your prototype

In this book, I've focused relentlessly on multiple-choice decision-making activities, so you probably have a multiple-choice scenario question. Now you'll create a functional draft of it in the format you intend to use with learners.

A prototype is a working example of the type of activity that you think will help learners. It looks like a draft but acts the way the real activity will act. I strongly encourage you to prototype all types of activities, even if you're planning something low tech.

Most people think of elearning when I say "prototype." In elearning, a prototype is a very basic, sort-of functional version of the final activity, minus distracting colors or bling. For example, below is an elearning prototype. Everything that would be clickable in the final activity is clickable in this prototype. You could create it in PowerPoint, or create the image in a mockup tool like Balsamiq and then add buttons in PowerPoint. I used Balsamiq and a quick sketch on my smartphone to create the example shown here. To make it interactive, I'd overlay transparent buttons using a slide design or elearning tool.

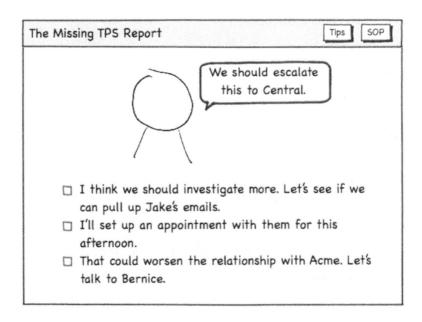

It's not just for elearning

As we've seen, you could leave your question in multiple-choice format and use it in face-to-face training, a live webinar, or self-paced elearning. You'll test the format of your choice during this step.

Another approach is to move the options from the question into the facilitator's materials. Then, in the live session the facilitator could use question on its own, as an open-ended discussion instigator, and they'd use the options in their notes to guide the discussion to the common mistakes and their consequences.

It works but isn't pretty

Your goal is a working version of the activity but one that's very obviously a draft.

If there are slides or other visuals, make them look like a black-and-white sketch. This keeps the focus on the challenge, how the information is provided, and how the feedback works. It avoids detours like, "You'll have to change that blue to the brand blue — what is it called, cerulean or something? And the logo should be bigger, and..."

If your activity is just discussion, write a suggested script or detailed talking points for the facilitator.

If you're creating an elearning activity, create clickable slides so your reviewers can experience how they ask for help, what happens when they click a choice, and whether they can go back and try again. Again, these slides probably should look like black-and-white sketches.

I've seen designers create prototypes using free photos or cartoons from clipart sites. It can be distracting to see a cheesy stock image in what is supposed to be a challenging, professional activity, so my preference is to stick to grayscale and sketches.

Consider getting separate feedback for visual ideas

If your activity will be developed in a strongly visual medium, consider creating a few mood boards showing the different colors and "feels" you're considering. After reviewers go through the prototype activity, show them the mood boards and get their reaction.

A typical mood board is a collage showing examples of the illustration or photographic style, colors, fonts, and maybe layout that you're considering using. It's a "mood" board because all these elements put together create an emotional reaction. You can pull the examples from the web or magazines. They aren't the actual images you plan to create; they just have the same "feel." You arrange them informally on a poster board or virtual board like Mural.ly, creating one board for each "mood."

For example, if you're planning to create a visually rich branching scenario, you might create two or three mood boards showing different approaches to the visual design. One might feature graphic-novel style illustrations in a muted range of colors, while the other might show photos of people and brighter colors. Get reactions to these from your stakeholders and future learners, making clear that these are just look-and-feel ideas, not the actual images you expect to use.

As you create your boards, consider the message delivered by the visual style. For example, one trend in corporate elearning is to use bright cartoony people or stock photos of adults who are showing comically extreme emotions. Designers are trying to inject fun, but the images could also say to learners, "We think you should be treated like a child."

If your client has explicitly asked for one of these potentially problematic styles, you could obediently create a mood board showing it, but also create a more subtle, "adult" board. Then see which one the learners actually prefer. In my informal surveys during workshops, participants prefer graphic-novel style images over childlike cartoons or over-acted stock photos.

Don't be afraid of text

If you're creating elearning and your development budget is limited, consider creating a text-only prototype. After people complete the challenge, ask them if they noticed the lack of images. If the challenge is interesting, people often don't notice or care that there were no pictures, and you might consider using text for the final produced scenario.

Often, it's the client who expects images and bling and who assumes that the learners will reject text. If this is the case for you, you might have the client observe when you test the prototype on learners, so they can hear for themselves that people actually don't care.

There's more discussion of this in the chapter on producing your materials. For now, you're creating a bare-bones prototype and shouldn't spend much time on images.

2. Prepare for questions from the SME and client

If you've been applying the ideas in this book, your activity might be different from what the SME and client are used to. As a result, you might want to prepare some responses to their likely concerns.

For example, if you suspect that your client or SME will worry that you're unfairly "throwing people into the activity without preparation," you could plan to describe what studies on productive failure have found, as we saw earlier in the chapter on creating a stream of activities. You'll also plan to point out the optional help that you provide and explain why you provide it that way.

3. Have the SME check the activity

Have the SME check the activity before you show it to the client. That way, the client can be reassured that the content is correct, so they can focus on how the activity works.

It's often best to meet with the SME in person, or at least online. You have two goals for this meeting:

- Have them correct the content
- Get their reaction to how it works

If your activity is substantially different from what they're used to, you might first show the SME a similar example from another project. Assuming that you're using the stream-of-activities approach, also make clear that there's no information presentation before the activity, because that's likely to be a new and possibly alarming idea.

Then have them go through your activity as the learner. Your main goal is to have them experience for themselves the following realizations:

- They can figure things out without a preceding information dump.
- It's more engaging to jump right into a challenging activity.
- Feedback that shows the consequences is more memorable.
- They feel like their intelligence is being respected when they're allowed to pull the information they need.

- They're confident that they can go directly to the next activity without plodding through an extensive information presentation.

If there are issues with the content, the SME is likely to focus first on that, so if possible, edit the prototype right there during the meeting. Once the SME is happy with the content, they'll be able to focus more on the functionality.

Be sure to keep expectations in check. For example, you might say, "The finished activity will have photos" if that's what you're planning, but keep the SME from assuming the finished activity will be loaded with bling. You're probably spending more of your budget on creating challenge rather than special effects, in contrast to what the SME might be accustomed to.

If the SME has a severe allergic reaction to some aspect of your design, acknowledge that you've heard their concern but avoid promising to change it until the client has seen it.

4. Get the client's reaction

Once the content is accurate, go through the same feedback process with the client, showing them model activities from other projects if necessary, pointing out the lack of an information dump, and being prepared to respond to their most likely objections.

If you're lucky, the client will say, "Let's see what the learners think." If you're less lucky, the client will insist you make changes before the user test. If these changes are extensive, such as turning the activity into an information presentation and quiz, try to persuade the client to let you first test the activity on learners.

The learners should have ultimate authority, for many reasons: they vastly outnumber the client, they know best what they like, and they're the ones who are going to have to use your materials.

5. Make sure no one else needs to approve it

During the goal-setting meeting, you asked (I hope!) if there was anyone else who needed to be included in the planning and analysis. You did that to avoid any surprise vetoes later.

Now is a good time to ask that question again, because you're about to invest a lot of time in creating materials. For example, your client might want to involve the legal team at this point, or add another layer of subject matter experts. Include any new people now to get their early responses, before you waste time producing a bunch of activities that they'll reject.

Your client should be confident enough in your project by now to make clear to any new reviewers that their role is just to provide feedback on the content and functionality of specific activities, not to question the overall approach. You might want to reinforce that message in your communications with the reviewers, describing at a high level what has already been decided and making clear you want their feedback on the accuracy of the content and how the activity works.

6. Test it on learners

One activity or several?

Once the SME and client have approved the prototype, you have a decision to make. Is it worthwhile to test just this one activity on some learners, or should you prepare a few more?

If your activities are going to be short, one-scene questions, consider preparing a few more prototype activities. That way, the learners aren't asked to give feedback on one 30-second question, and they can experience the "stream of activities" effect. You'll need to work with your SME to get the details you need, using the same techniques you used to create the first prototype.

How many testers? Alone or in groups?

You don't need a big crowd. Five people might be a good number, as long as they're representative of typical learners.

Of course, this depends on a lot of factors, such as the cost of the project, how different it is from previous projects, and the cost of possible failure. You'll want enough people to get representative feedback, but not so many that the testing becomes a project on its own.

I've had good luck doing the learner test in small focus groups, even if the final activity is supposed to be completed alone. The debate that comes up can inspire more ideas for improvements than individual feedback.

Approach the test using the same technique you used with the client and SME, although this time you're not going to try to convince the learners that your design will work. You're just going to see if that's true.

Invite critiques

Encourage testers to suggest changes. This is especially important with scenarios, where a weak or fake-sounding story can seriously turn off players. Make very clear that you want their feedback about everything and that you won't take criticism personally.

"But I don't have any access to the learners."

It's unfortunately common for clients to expect training designers to work in isolation from the learners. If this is the case for you, it might still be possible to do the test remotely, such as in a virtual meeting room. This would actually be a good idea if you're testing a webinar activity.

If for some reason you can't get any access to your audience, you might rely on your SME or client to run the prototype test on some learners for you. It can take as little as 10 minutes, so it shouldn't be much of an imposition. And if it does feel like an imposition, use that as leverage to gain direct access to the learners.

Elearning: Consider showing how you plan to produce it

If you're planning to create elearning, you probably plan to use the budget to design challenging, realistic activities, rather than spending most of it on narration and bling. However, your client and SME might expect bling.

To avoid unpleasant surprises, you might add a step to your prototyping phase. After the prototype has been approved by the stakeholders and learners, produce it and maybe a few more activities using the same media you plan to use for all activities. Then have your client and SME try the produced activities. Don't point out the lack of bling; present this as "a test of the elearning."

After they've tried the activities, ask them if they noticed that there was, for example, no narrator or flying bullet points. Usually they don't notice, and you've made your point. If they're concerned about the lack of bling, suggest that you first see what the learners think before making any decisions, and then test the developed activities on learners.

Branching scenarios need special attention

If your activity will become a branching scenario, I'd recommend first showing your stakeholders a functioning branching scenario from another project, so they get the basic idea. Then take your scenario through four rounds of prototyping.

Round 1: Get feedback on two or three typical decision points

First, get feedback on how a typical decision point will work. A decision point is the multiple-choice question with options that we've been obsessing about in this book. Your prototype activity is probably a decision point.

For example, the multiple-choice question in which you have to respond to Ravi's concern about hot widgets is a decision point in a longer scenario. Once you make your decision, you go to another decision point that includes the following:

- The consequence of your previous decision (what Ravi says in response, such as his annoyed question)

- A question asking you to make another decision ("What do you say?")

- Options for that decision

For example, here's one decision point:

> You're meeting with Ravi, a new customer.
>
> "I might be interested in your J-12 widget," Ravi says. "At 79 wiga-bits, it has enough power for spurdling. But I've read that it runs hot."
>
> What do you say?
>
> a) "Our studies show that heat doesn't cause issues for the J-12. Would you like to see the test results?"
>
> b) "Actually, the J-12 has only 60 wigabits. If you're going to be spurdling, I'd recommend the K-77."
>
> c) "Are you referring to the *Widget World* review?"

When someone chooses option a, they see the following decision point.

341

"I'm not surprised that **your** studies don't show any problems," Ravi says, sounding a little annoyed. "But *Widget World* does rigorous, independent testing, and they found heat issues. What can you tell me about the heat?"

What do you say?

a) "The J-12 does run warmer than some other widgets, but if I remember right, the *Widget World* testers didn't see any impact on performance. Is there another reason you're concerned about heat?"

b) "It's true that the J-12 gets a little warm, but if you're going to be spurdling, you'll actually want the K-77. It's also one of the coolest-running widgets in the industry. Can I show you the specs?"

c) "All widgets generate heat, thanks to the transmogrification of inductability. However, that heat doesn't affect performance, and ceramic heat-reducers just add cost. Can I ask what budget you're working with?"

For your prototype, choose a typical decision point and two or three of the points that follow it. It's natural to choose the first decision in the story, but if it contains a lot of backstory or other setup, it won't be typical of other points. In that case, you might start with the second or third decision.

If necessary, describe to the reviewers what happened in the story up to the decision point that you've chosen, and then show them the prototype in whatever format you think will be best for the learners. For example, if you plan to project the story in live, face-to-face training and make decisions as a group, show the client the content that you'll be projecting (in sketch form), describe how the discussion will be led, and show them the consequence of a typical choice, which will be another decision point.

At this stage, you're testing the following:

- How will I display each scene? Is this self-paced elearning, projected to a group, printed on paper...?

- Will I provide optional help? How?

- How will people make their choice? Will they click on it? Will they "turn to page X?" Will they vote? Will I require people to debate each choice?

- When will the consequence and next decision point appear? Will it appear automatically, or will I require people to defend their decision first?

- Once people see the consequence of their choice, will I let them go back and change their mind? Will I always do that, or only for certain decisions?

- Will the consequence include telling feedback? If so, where will it appear? Will it be optional or will everyone be equally "exposed" to it? (My preference is to save telling feedback for the end of the story, unless the learner makes a serious mistake.)

- Will I be keeping score? If so, am I scoring each choice or just the endings achieved? Will I penalize people for going back and changing their mind?

Your prototype should show what you've decided for all of these questions. It should work like a point in the final scenario.

For elearning, you can develop clickable slides. For scenarios used in other formats, produce the prototype in that format, such as printed on paper, and as much as possible recreate for the client and SME how it will be used. Then do the same to test the prototype decision point on some learners.

Round 2: Get feedback on the plot

It's common for designers to jump into writing the story now. However, you should first write a high-level plot and make sure people will accept it. It's extremely hard to go back and change the plot if you've already invested a lot of time writing scenes and dialog.

Write a high-level plot using just notes

Write a high-level plot of the scenario using flowcharting software or entering notes in an interactive fiction tool like Twine. Write the best path first and then the less-good paths, finding ways to connect them. You're just writing notes at this point, not detailed dialog.

As you plot, determine which endings you want and write the plot to reach them. For example, you might have one "best" ending, some "fair" endings, some "poor" endings, and a few quick failures for the serious mistakes. Include ways to get from one path to another. For example, if someone is on a "poor" path, let them make a better choice and get on a better path.

If you don't decide the endings ahead of time and just let the story grow organically, you could easily get lost in the weeds of infinite possibilities.

343

Get feedback on the plot

Show your client and SME your plot as a flowchart and talk them through a couple of paths. After you get their feedback and incorporate their changes, do the same test with learners. This can happen in the same session in which you tested the prototype of a decision point.

At this point, you're trying to answer the following questions.

- Is the plot realistic?
- Does it address a situation that the learners care about?
- Have I covered the most important mistakes?
- Are the decisions too easy?
- Is the story too simplistic?
- Should I provide any optional help during the story or in the feedback?
- Should people be able to go back and change their choice, or should they have to recover by making better choices in the future?

When you do this test with future or recent learners, consider gathering them in a small group and displaying the flowchart. In my experience, they get very involved in critiquing your story and telling you how to make it more realistic, and when they disagree among themselves, you'll get good ideas for distractors. You can get much more useful feedback from learners than from your client and SME, so don't skip the learner test.

A common result of this phase is a significantly more complex and realistic plot.

Round 3: Get feedback on the final story

Now flesh out your improved plot into a real story, adding all the details like dialog. Don't produce extensive media, however; you're still prototyping.

If your final scenario will be delivered or displayed on a computer, consider producing your prototype in Twine or a similar interactive fiction tool that creates easily edited scenarios.

If you plan to produce a printed scenario, test an interactive version of it at this stage. It's extremely hard to change a scenario that's formatted for printing, so make sure the scenario is truly "done" before you convert it to print.

You might want to have the SME go through it first, because they're likely to propose changes to details. Then, once the details are tweaked, have the client go through the scenario.

Then test the scenario on the learners, ideally using the final format. For example, if the scenario is designed to be projected to a group, test it that way.

You're trying to answer the following questions.

- Is the dialog realistic?
- Do people care about the characters?
- Are the choices challenging enough?
- Is anything too obvious or exaggerated?
- Are the consequences believable?
- Does the consequence of each choice provide enough feedback?
- Is optional help necessary?

A common result of this phase is more realistic dialog and more subtle options.

Round 4: Get feedback on the production

Whether your final scenario will be interactive or printed on paper, produce the first few decision points using the same media you plan to use for the entire story, and run this by the client and SME for their feedback.

If this is a high-stakes project, also run a produced selection by some learners. This makes sure that you aren't sabotaging your story with the wrong graphic style or clumsy clicking.

Don't produce the entire scenario yet. You still have another approval step to get through in the next chapter.

Common challenges

Your reviewers over-focus on the look and feel.

- Make sure you're showing them a black and white, "sketch-y" version of the activity. If the final activity will be produced in a visually rich medium, create separate mood boards as described earlier and focus graphic design discussion on those.

- If stakeholders appear to expect more bling than you'll be able to deliver, manage their expectations now. Point out that it takes more time to write realistic practice activities than it does to present information, which leaves you less time and budget for bling. Because the activities are more interesting than information, you also **need** less bling. Creating the prototype should have given you an idea of how long it will take to write the remaining activities, so this is a good time to clarify what's going to be possible.

A stakeholder is concerned about having learners make a decision without first being taught how to do it.

- Make sure you've provided optional help if you think it will be necessary. Point it out to the stakeholder. Did the stakeholder miss seeing it? Should you make it more obvious?

- Consider inviting the stakeholder to observe while the learners use the prototype. Let the stakeholder see for themselves that no one quits in frustration or complains.

- You might also point to the research summarized in *Make It Stick* and cited earlier that highlights the advantages of having people take on a problem before they've been taught exactly how to solve it.

Your SME or client wants you to force a lot of telling feedback on learners because they don't trust them to draw conclusions.

- Acknowledge their concern but encourage them to let you test the activity on learners before you add more "telling." You might have them observe the user test so they can see for themselves if learners can come to the right conclusions without being told what to think.

- I recommend making any "telling" feedback optional, but if a stakeholder is concerned that people won't click, then you might deliver it automatically, after showing the consequence of the choice.

- In a branching scenario, I strongly recommend reserving "telling" feedback for the end of the story. If you insert lots of instructive feedback during the story, you not only interrupt the flow, you also keep the learner from seeing for themselves that they've made a mistake and need to adjust their approach. Branching scenarios are valuable partly because they help people practice recognizing and recovering from mistakes, so it would be a shame to remove that advantage.

The learners say the activity is too easy.

- This is a common problem that can happen because you're too close to the content, the SME underestimated how much people already know, or you didn't dig deeply enough during the analysis phase to understand why the decision is difficult.

- Ask some learners to describe what happens when they're faced with the same problem on the job. Is it a decision with grey areas that requires some practice? If it's not difficult, why do people make the common mistake? Is there a problem in the environment that you missed in your analysis? Does this behavior really need a practice activity?

- Ask the learners to suggest how you could make it more challenging.

- See other suggestions in the "Common challenges" section of chapter 10. Some of the most common issues are asking a question that doesn't require much judgment, writing an over-dramatic scene, and not including enough detail to make the incorrect options more appealing.

The learners say the activity is too hard.

This rarely happens. If you experience, take it as a good sign, and then try the following.

- Ask the learners what would make the activity easier but not obvious.

- Provide optional help when the learners need to make the decision. Make sure the help is easy to access, concise, and contextual, providing just the help that a person needs at that point in the process, not a dissertation about the entire topic.

- If you're linking to a real-world job aid, highlight the section that the learner should use at this point.

- Make sure you've started the stream of activities with easier activities that provide basic knowledge. If your prototype is one of the later activities, you might want to re-test the learners with an earlier, easier activity.

- Check your options. Is it too hard to distinguish one from the other? Are you trying to trick learners with convoluted phrasing instead of writing legitimately tempting choices?

- Is the activity too wordy? Try rewriting it with simpler, more concise language.

The learners say there's too much text.

- Ask if the problem is really the text or the challenge itself. Is the problem itself too hard or boring?

- Consider deleting adjectives, adverbs, and small talk.

- Look at how you've provided any backstory. Could it be optional links, like in the Noah and Brian example? Could you summarize it more?

- Does your audience have a strong preference for another format, and can you provide it? For example, if you replace a text-only scenario with graphic-novel scenes, the visuals show what happens, reducing descriptive text, and you're forced to write concise dialog because you don't have much room for it. Even stick-figure comics like those popular on the web will force you to write more concisely and offer some visual variety.

The learners say the activity is boring, or they provide lukewarm responses to your questions.

- Ask how you could make the problem more compelling. Encourage people to focus on the decision that the activity requires, not just the format.

- Make sure the activity focuses on a real problem that learners care about and that requires judgment. Is it just a disguised quiz question?

- Does the behavior really need a practice activity? Ask if the real-life version of the decision is difficult. What makes it hard? If it's not hard, why do so many people make the common mistake? Is there a problem with tools or culture that you missed during your analysis?

- Could you make the problem more emotionally compelling? Ask your learners for ideas.

The learners say that the activity seems unrealistic.

- Ask for details. In what way is it unrealistic? Is it too dramatic? Does the dialog sound fake? Is the problem set up in an unrealistic way? What would happen in the real world that isn't happening in the activity?

- If the dialog sounds artificial, see suggestions in the "Common challenges" section at the end of chapter 10.

Chapter 14. Outline, produce, deliver, evaluate

You'll finish the workflow

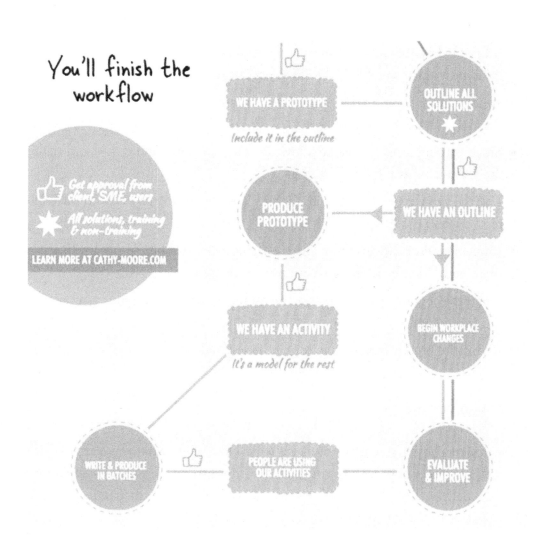

Tasks	Who does it	How long it might take
Create an outline for the project (not a script) Get approval for the outline Write and get approval for activities in batches Make the materials available Evaluate the project	You: outline the project; write and oversee the production of activities Client: approve the outline SME: review and approve activities in batches Everyone: evaluate the project (you'll probably need to initiate this)	This depends on the size and nature of the project.

Big ideas:

- You'll write a concise project outline, not a script or long design document. It briefly describes all solutions you identified, not just training, and shows a timeline with deliverables. The client needs to approve it before you continue.

- You'll write and get SME approval for activities in batches, making it easy to change your approach if necessary.

- Since you've probably created activities that can stand alone, you can make them available as they're produced.

- Use the same types of activities for any assessment instead of a knowledge test.

- Implementation involves not just releasing activities but also coordinating them with the non-training solutions you identified.

- Your project goal is your evaluation measure. Also consider looking at "closer" measurements.

- Refine the project based on your ongoing evaluation.

What you've done

You've designed and tested a prototype activity. Now, using what you learned from the tests, you'll get approval for an outline of the project, design the remaining activities, deliver them or make them available, and evaluate their effectiveness. Yes, all of this in one chapter.

The hard work is behind you now — once you've done the analysis and gotten approval for your approach to activity design, it's all downhill.

What you'll do

You're going to:

1. Outline the project
2. Get approval for the outline
3. Design and produce the remaining materials in short cycles
4. Create the assessment, if there is one
5. Coordinate delivery with other aspects of the solution
6. Evaluate the short-term and larger success of the project

Who's involved?

You'll work with:

- Your client
- The SME (you'll need them a lot; stock up on their treats)
- Whoever is in charge of the technology you'll need (LMS, intranet, email list...)
- The person responsible for developing the final materials, if that isn't you
- Learners

1. Outline the project

I hope you've already described to the client how the activities will work together. Now that at least one typical activity has been prototyped and approved, it's time to get approval for the final structure of the project.

You're going to create an outline, not a design document. "Project Charter" is a good name for it, because that's what it is: a high-level description of what will be done, who will do it, and when it will be done. It's not a detailed list of content or a storyboard, because you're going to write the content in small batches. You're not writing it all right now.

I recommend using just basic word processing software to do this. The document should probably include:

1. The business goal that was identified at the beginning.

2. A list of the high-priority actions that the project will address — for example, "This project will help Region X customer service reps do the following: " followed by a short list of the highest-priority actions.

3. The action map, showing how the actions, activities, and other solutions support the goal.

4. The map might be enough, but if it isn't, include a high-level description of each behavior and how it will be supported, whether that's through an activity (such as, "A customer raises an objection about heat") or non-training solution like a job aid. You might use a chart like the one shown on the following page.

5. The prototypes that have been approved, plus any additional prototypes for different activity types, so stakeholders can quickly see how they'd work. If necessary, make clear that the activity stands alone, and the required information or support will be provided during the activity, not before.

6. Some indication of how the activities will be sequenced. If the learner's path through the material is linear, you could just list the activities in the order they'll appear. If people can choose among different paths, you might use a flowchart to show this. If people can freely choose activities in any order, make that clear.

7. If you're proposing a non-traditional approach, such as not having a training event and instead just making the activities available on demand and online, you might want to mock up an example of how that would work. For example, you could create a mockup of the intranet page that would host the activities and briefly describe the marketing campaign that will encourage people to go there.

8. A concise implementation plan showing when deliverables will be completed and how the activities will be coordinated with the non-training solutions, making clear who's responsible for each item. This should be easy to scan, so each person can quickly find what applies to them and when it's due.

Relate the activities to specific behaviors

If the action map isn't specific enough for your client or they prefer text, you might consider using a table like the one below to show the behaviors you're targeting and their associated solutions.

On-the-job action	Practice activity	Other changes
Quickly identify the weight impact of a specific grade and amount of loribdenum	A customer needs to know how much weight 150 bartles of 90-filot loribdenum would add to their product	Update the existing smartphone app to make it easier to figure weight given grade and bartles
Ask open-ended questions to uncover the customer's current and future performance requirements	A customer says they want the K-76 for low-speed spurdling

A customer plans to use the J-12 at high altitudes but doesn't volunteer that information | In hiring, prefer candidates who express a desire to use consultative selling |
| Close or reassign each customer ticket in the CRM within 24 hours of the initial contact | Not applicable | Have the CRM software send a reminder at 6, 16, and 23 hours for each ticket that is still open |

Make clear who's responsible for what

In addition to describing at a high level what you plan to do, your outline also includes what other people need to do.

For example, if an existing job aid needs to be improved and that aid belongs to someone else, make sure your implementation plan says that the job aid owner must do X, Y, and Z by a specific date.

Also make clear that activities will be delivered to the SME in small batches, and that the SME needs to respond within a certain time frame for the project to stay on schedule.

Show how you plan to use supporting information

Make sure you show in the outline or prototype activities whether the supporting information will always be available, or whether you plan to fade it out so people need to eventually rely on their memories. For example, you could use a graphic like the one below to show how help is gradually taken away.

This isn't a conventional design document

The outline isn't a 28-page single-spaced design document describing and justifying every bit of content, which you might have been taught to create. It's just an outline, and it describes the overall solution, not just the content of the training. For simple projects, it can be as short as four pages.

We're avoiding the mega-thorough design document for several reasons.

- Many clients seem to prefer outlines, at least in my experience.

- Our prototype activities have already made clear what we're planning to do, so we don't need to waste pages describing it.

- The individual activities will be written and approved in small batches, rather than all being written now. This makes it easy for us to change our approach if necessary.

- The longer the document, the longer it takes for the client or SME to approve it. A concise outline with clear examples can be turned around quickly.

- An outline is more flexible. If you invest a lot of time up front in describing what you plan to do, you naturally resist changes to your plan. You don't invest as much time in an outline, making it less painful to change directions if necessary.

"But where are the learning objectives?"

The actions you list at the beginning of the document are, basically, performance objectives. If your client is traditional, you might label them "performance objectives." That's usually enough.

However, if your client or boss insists on seeing school-style learning objectives that describe knowledge, you might expand your outline to include the enabling objectives for each behavior, or include the enabling knowledge as sub-entries in your action map.

For example, in the outline, you could list the behavior "Immediately put contaminated sharps in the sharps container" and, indented below it, list the enabling objectives, such as, "Describe the hazards of leaving contaminated sharps exposed." Your solution will still focus on achieving the performance objective, but your client will be reassured that you're not ignoring "knowledge transfer."

Avoid big surprises

If you're proposing a significantly different approach to the "training," I hope you've already made that clear during the analysis and prototype phases. For example, the stakeholders shouldn't find out from the outline that there will be no training event and you're just planning to make activities available on demand.

If you're not sure that your new approach has been clearly communicated, meet with your stakeholders, show them what you're thinking, and listen to their concerns before you take the time to formalize your plan in the outline.

2. Get approval for the outline

Your client needs to approve the outline, since it acts as a project charter. Whether the SME and everyone else involved needs to approve it as well probably depends on your situation. Once the outline is approved, you can begin work on the rest of the activities.

If you've been including your stakeholders during the planning, analysis, and prototyping phases, nothing in the outline should be a surprise or cause controversy. The main challenge at this point is when a stakeholder says, "Hey, we should have Mary take a look," when Mary is someone who could veto major aspects of the plan. That's why I suggested earlier that you explicitly ask, "Who else should we include?" at both the kickoff and prototype stages.

3. Design and produce the remaining materials in short cycles

Using your prototype as a model, it's time to write and produce the remaining materials for the project.

Write in batches

You might be used to writing everything at once. Instead, I strongly recommend you write the activities in small batches of three or so. You'll interview the SME about only three activities, write those activities, and send them to the SME for approval (or meet with the SME for their feedback, depending on the complexity and the SME's preferred method). While the SME is reviewing one batch, you're writing the next.

I recommend this approach for several reasons:

- **You'll probably get faster feedback from the SME.** It's often easier for a busy SME to discuss and review three activities in a spare moment than to clear a big chunk of schedule to discuss and examine everything.

- **You can easily change direction if necessary.** For example, the feedback for one batch gives you an idea for how to improve the activities, so you decide to rewrite the first batch and use the new approach for all remaining batches. If instead you had written everything and then gotten the feedback, you'd spend an inordinate amount of time rewriting it all or, more likely, abandon the idea to improve it.

- **You can discover that some activities aren't necessary.** During the SME interview for one batch of activities, you might discover that some future activities you were planning aren't necessary. For example, you and the SME might decide that the current batch of activities helps people practice enough, so a future batch of activities won't need to be written.

- **Activities can be produced as they're approved.** You can start making the first activities available to learners while you're still writing and developing the rest. This gets you valuable feedback from the field and gives your client the quick solution they're probably looking for.

Keep activity drafts simple

It seems common for training designers to over-engineer their activity scripts. For example, elearning scriptwriters will painstakingly create columns showing what appears on the screen, what the text says and when it appears, what each button does, and so forth, forcing the SME to puzzle through a complex and almost always redundant document.

Your SME has seen your prototype, so they know how the activities are supposed to work. Instead of describing the functions of the activity in painful detail over and over again, rely on the prototype to make it clear. That lets you create a simple text document for your activity drafts, ideally using Word or a similar program that tracks changes.

When I was designing a lot of custom elearning, a one-scene mini-scenario could be formatted like the following (fictional!) example, in a simple text document. The prototype activity had already made clear that the text appears on the screen, the options are clickable, and that if "Try again" is included in the feedback, it's clickable. No reviewers had trouble understanding this type of document, and we sent it to the developers as well.

[Show two similar food stands at a fair in the sunny countryside. One has a vat of bubbling grease and a sign saying, "Pork skins fried while U wait." The other has a closed plastic drinks cooler and a sign saying "Sushi."]

You're at the county fair. Your kids are off watching the pig race, and you're hot, tired, and hungry. There are only two food carts. You want to be healthy. What do you do?

A. Buy the sushi.

B. Buy the pork skins.

C. Buy nothing because fasting is good for you.

Feedback:

A. Six hours after you eat the sushi, you begin vomiting. Three days later, you finally stop. Your doctor explains that the sushi was probably poorly refrigerated and contained zygodread. "You should have bought something hot that was cooked right in front of you," he says as he hands you the prescription for an expensive antibiotic. "Was there any pork skin? I always buy that if it comes right out of the fryer."

B. While you enjoy your hot, crispy pork skins, you hear a young woman tell her friend, "There's no way I'm buying that sushi again! Last year there wasn't ice in the cooler, and the sushi was full of zygodread! I've never been so sick in my life!"

C. An hour later, the pig race is finally over. Your children run to you, screaming, "THAT WAS SO FUN! PIGS ARE SO COOL! WE HAVE

TO BUY A PIG! BUY US A PIG! WE WANT A PIG!" You're so weak from hunger that you relent and buy a pig, which 20 minutes later you have to sell again at a loss, because it won't fit in your car. Try again.

Make your questions very clear

Clearly highlight any content that you're guessing at. I use bright yellow highlighting in Word and add a direct question to the reviewers. It might look like this:

b) "Since you'll be spurdling at a high altitude, you'll want the P-09." Arno: Is this right?

It's also helpful to give the SME very clear guidance, such as by saying, "Please check this for accuracy and make any changes by typing directly in the document. Please also look for any dialog or scenes that seem unrealistic and suggest how they should be changed."

Should you skip the text stage and have the SME review an early production version?

Some designers create their drafts in their production tool. For example, if they plan to create slide-based elearning, they'll have the SME review the slides in PowerPoint or in the elearning tool.

I resist this for several reasons, including:

- If you go to the trouble of laying it out on a slide, you naturally resist changing it, and change should be welcome at this stage.

- Reviewers can over-focus on the layout instead of the ideas and content.

- It's hard to track reviewers' changes in most slide-based tools.

- Working with slides all the time reinforces the idea that slides are the natural format for training, and we're trying to get beyond that.

However, it makes sense to put the activity in a non-linear tool if you're creating something complex, like a branching scenario. Consider writing the scenario in a tool like Twine or BranchTrack and either interview the SME as they go through the scenario or have the SME use the software to enter their comments directly in the file. It's extremely hard to write and edit a branching scenario as a Word document, and PowerPoint isn't much better, since you have to manually fix any changed links.

Produce activities as they're approved

If you have the SME approve activity drafts in batches, at some point you'll have your first batch of activities that are ready for production. Consider producing those now, before all the other activities are written or approved. This gives you several advantages:

- You'll find out early in the process whether there are issues that no one noticed during the prototype phase.

- You'll probably find better ways to do some things. For example, you might discover a more efficient way to provide optional help than you used in the prototype.

- If production will take longer than you predicted, you'll find out early on, when you still have a chance to adjust the delivery date or the production values.

Don't sacrifice good activity design for bling

Your budget is probably limited, so you'll have to make hard decisions. Something has to go. Often the showdown is between time spent on analysis and design vs. the cost of bling. You can guess where my vote goes.

Our job is to solve the performance problem. Bling doesn't solve problems. Of course, we need our materials to look smart and appealing, but "appealing" doesn't mean dragged down by a ponderous narrator, infested with flying bullet points, and glittering with fake games.

If you're applying the recommendations in this book, you'll design more activities than information. Your job is no longer to make boring information somehow interesting, so you should experience less pressure to provide bling. The information you provide could be just the real-world, bling-free job aid.

Obviously, some information is better presented as a graphic, so of course you'd use a graphic. Other information needs animation, so you'd use animation. My point is that you're not tossing in "eye candy," which are irrelevant visuals added to "spice things up." Research suggests that while learners rate those activities more highly than basic text versions, they actually learn less. You're also not using narration unless it's clearly required, such as to explain a complex graphic.

I could write an entire book about media, but luckily other people have done it first and with far less ranting than I'd use. For elearning, a classic reference is *Elearning and the Science of Instruction*, by Ruth Clark and Richard Mayer (2008). It summarizes research that shows how we can use media to support and not interfere with learning. Ruth Clark has also published a more recent book that covers some of the same ground but also includes recommendations for face-to-face training: *Evidence-Based Training Methods* (2014).

If your budget is limited, most of your effort should go into analyzing the problem and designing contextual practice activities that help people solve the problem. That's where you provide a return on investment. Comparatively little of your time and budget should go into creating slick materials. You're aiming for **challenging activities**, not shallow, flashy clickfests.

What about scenarios?

Your client might assume that learners will reject text-only scenarios. This isn't necessarily true. I've confirmed this over and over in my live scenario design course.

At one point, I send everyone without any preparation to an old-school branching scenario that has no pictures and a downright hideous layout. People immediately get sucked into solving the problem. When everyone is back in the virtual room, I ask if anyone cared that there were no pictures of the people in the story. The overwhelming majority of people don't care, and some comment that pictures would detract from the story — they preferred to imagine the characters themselves.

If you tried the Zeko language-learning scenario described earlier, did you even notice that there was no picture of Ludo, your guide? Did you care?

However, images do appear to make a scenario more engaging, according to some research.[4] If your budget permits, you might include **relevant** images of the characters, showing their **realistic** expressions to help carry the story. Since stock photos tend to be irrelevant and over-acted, you might take photos of colleagues instead.

---

[4] See Ruth Colvin Clark's publications, including *Evidence-Based Training Methods* (2015), for summaries of research about the effect of media.

However, don't promise to include eye candy, and question any assumptions that the images need to include detailed backgrounds, such as office scenes. The more detailed your images become, the more likely it is that someone will reject them as not representing their workplace.

Give learners control, to a point

If you're creating self-paced online activities, I strongly suggest you let learners do the following.

Let them control the pace: Everyone should be able to move through the materials and process new ideas at their own pace. For example:

- Don't force them to stare at a screen for a set period of time.
- Let them easily go back and see something again.
- Let them pause, rewind, and fast-forward audio and video.
- Don't use audio when a self-explanatory graphic or concise text would be more efficient.
- If for some **legitimate** reason you must rely on lots of audio narration, let people change the speed at which it plays. For example, if you want me to listen to a 30-minute audio lecture (and your reason had better be excellent and the lecture extremely relevant), let me select a playback speed, or provide the lecture in a format that I can play through a variable-speed app, such as a podcast player.

Let them choose the information they see: People are notoriously bad at deciding what they need to learn, so I'm not saying, "Let them skip stuff that they think they already know." What I'm saying is this:

- Let them see for themselves what they already know or don't know by starting with activities. If I think I already know the stuff in the course but have trouble making a good decision in the first activity, I'll see that I don't actually know it.
- Let them "place out" of sections when they prove they can make good decisions. If you throw me into a couple of challenging activities and I'm able to make good choices without looking at the optional help, let me skip the rest of the activities about that topic.

- In all activities, let them pull the information they need during the challenge, rather than forcing everyone to sit through the same information, as we've already examined.

Let them choose the path to take, if applicable: You've carefully ordered the activities so people learn basic skills at first and then build on them in later activities. In that respect, you don't want people to jump around unless they can prove that they've already mastered the earlier steps. However, if some sections of the material could be learned in any order, let people start with the section that's most important to them.

Talk like a marketer, not a trainer

In all your communication with learners, make it about them, not you and not the content.

For example, avoid the common practice of listing trainer-style objectives on the first screen of an online course or in the description of the training. Instead, speak directly to the learners using "you," and very briefly list what "you" will be able to do thanks to the project. The list could be a casual version of the actions from the map that matter most to the learner, worded in a way that highlights the benefits to them.

For example, here's one action that we're going to help call-center workers practice. How inspiring is it to the learner?

> Instead of immediately referring a difficult call to management, apply the Insta-Empathy Intervention Model to calm the caller and resolve their issue.

It's not inspiring at all. It's even a little repellant because it seems to care more about the managers than the learners. That statement was meant for us and our stakeholders and should stay in our weird little world.

How could we rewrite the action so it inspires our audience? Here's one possibility:

> Easily calm an upset caller and resolve their issue quickly.

If I were a call-center worker, which I was for one memorable day, I'd be far more motivated to learn that skill.

4. Create the assessment, if there is one

It's common for training events, and especially elearning, to conclude with a knowledge test. Since we're abandoning the school model, what will we do instead to see if people learned?

If you "need" an assessment, the simplest approach is to produce some of your activities as assessment activities. These are exactly the same as your practice activities, with the following changes:

- You remove the feedback and any "try again" options
- You remove any optional information that the learner should have memorized

For example, we could turn our much-abused Magda activity into an assessment with some easy changes. The decision screen stays the same, because learners can look at the job aid or SOP in real life. There's no reason to test them without it.

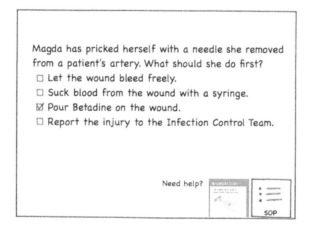

The feedback screen, however, has disappeared. The learner makes their choice, and the system or grader will quietly determine if it's correct or incorrect.

I'm not saying you should repeat an activity they saw earlier. I'm suggesting you use the same format you've been using when you create new "assessment" activities, but remove the help.

Face-to-face training

If you want to conclude a live session with an assessment, you could do something as old-fashioned as distribute a printed test. **Each question is a realistic practice activity** like the kind we've been focusing on, and the learner marks their choice.

Online

Since our practice activities are essentially multiple-choice questions, you could use any test builder to create an online assessment. **The questions and options are the same kind that you've been using to create practice activities.** They're not knowledge checks. The only difference is that the learner doesn't get any feedback.

Branching scenarios as assessment

Just like shorter activities, a branching scenario could be used as an assessment.

The simplest approach is to design the storylines carefully, and then give each ending a score. For example, people who arrive at the best ending get a score of 2, a fair ending is scored 1, and a poor ending is 0.

If going through the story efficiently is also important, such as when learners need to diagnose a problem quickly, you could assign points to each decision as well as to the endings. In this case, the lowest score is the best score, because it shows that the learner took the shortest path. Your best ending should also have a low score, such as 0, and the worst ending should have a high score, such as 10.

In this approach, if I take a slightly inefficient path, collecting a point for each of six decisions, but end up at the best ending, my assessment score might be 6. My more efficient colleague might end up at the same ending with a better score of 5. Our over-confident colleague who takes an even shorter path but ends up seriously mis-diagnosing the problem gets a failure score of 14.

"But we need to test their knowledge."

If your client and SME participated in setting the goal, analyzing the problem, and identifying the behaviors to be changed, they're unlikely to insist on a knowledge test. They understand that the goal of the project is to change what people **do** so the organization's performance can improve in a measurable way. If somehow they've forgotten that, you might want to remind them.

The concern about a knowledge test might come from someone who wasn't involved with the project, or it might even be a voice in your head. The answer is the same: The goal is for people to apply their knowledge on the job, to change what they do. The types of questions you've written show not only whether people know something, but also whether they can make good decisions with it. The questions go **beyond** a knowledge check, and that's a good thing.

5. Coordinate delivery with other aspects of the solution

The non-training aspects of the solution might have been put in place while you and your SME worked on activities. If those fixes have run into issues, you might wait until they're resolved before releasing your share of the solution.

Since you've probably designed activities that are mostly self-contained, "delivery" might not involve a training event. For example, instead of publishing an online course and assigning it to people, you might instead make an intranet page of activities available and encourage people to try them out when they want to practice.

Whether you're about to deliver an event or just make some materials available, you'll need the support of the learners' managers and others in the organization, just as you need for conventional training. The main advantage that you have over conventional training is that your client is probably more committed. By setting a goal and participating in the analysis of the problem, they naturally become more invested in the project and could become good evangelists for it. You've probably also created much more appealing activities, making the training easier to "sell."

Consider starting small

Your activities might be very different from what your organization is used to, so you might want to roll them out to a representative subset of your audience first. Let the learners go through the activities, and then use the assessment and quick evaluation measures described below to get an initial sense of the success. Then you can tweak the project as necessary before you make it available to more people.

6. Evaluate the short-term and larger success of the project

You've planned for evaluation from the start by setting your business goal. Your top-level evaluation is whether or how much the goal's metric improved.

However, if your goal is big and slow, you won't know for some time if your intervention seems to have helped. As a result, consider finding some smaller, closer measurements you can use in the shorter term.

Closer measures

Here are some ideas for ways to see more quickly if your project is effective.

- **Assessment.** We've already looked at how to design these using the same types of practice activities (not knowledge checks). Traditionally, the assessment happens after a training event. If you're not using an event, you might look for other ways to find out who's using your activities and consider sending them some assessment activities, maybe positioned as a fun challenge and not as, "Take this test so we can identify how you're deficient."

    You might also want to challenge the idea of an assessment happening once, after an event. Since your activities are mostly self-contained, you can send them to learners spaced days or weeks apart. These can be practice activities, to help reinforce learning, but some of them could be assessments: "Do our learners still remember how to choose the correct last name when addressing Hispanic clients? Let's send them an assessment activity and find out." The end users see this as a practice activity, while you treat it as an assessment.

- **Feedback from learners.** Be careful with this one. Learners could easily say that they liked the activities and feel more confident about doing their jobs and then fail to apply what they've learned. If everyone still expects you to design this sort of evaluation, you might check Will Thalheimer's book *Performance-Focused Smile Sheets* on how to design more effective "smile sheets."

- **Feedback from managers.** Because you did a thorough analysis, you should be able to go to managers with clear descriptions of the behaviors your training is designed to elicit and ask them if they're seeing those behaviors improved in their trained team members.

- **Learners' choices.** If your learners are using online activities, another option is to look at their choices in aggregate. Are their choices improving as they go through the materials? Are there any common mistakes? If you let people try again and explore other paths, as I think you should, you'll see many "mistakes" that were done on purpose, but you still might be able to see overall patterns that will help you determine if people are learning.

- **Site analytics** (statistics about website traffic). If you provide online activities on demand, the popularity of each activity or the relative time spent on it will give you an idea of what the learners think they need or what their pain points really are. The same applies to any site that provides supporting information, such as a virtual job aid or knowledge base: Analytics will tell you which information is most frequently accessed, and any social tools you provide on that site (upvoting, comments, likes, etc.) will also give you useful feedback. Your IT or marketing department will be able to help you get these measurements.

- **Lower-level indicators.** If your end goal is a change in business performance, there might be other metrics that are closer to the performance problem and that are updated more often. You can check these for quicker feedback about the possible effects of your project.

For example, one of my favorite metrics for software training is the number of calls to the help desk about the software. You could check the help desk calls to get quick feedback about your project's effects.

The Success Case Method

Changes in your goal's metric and other performance measures will suggest whether your project is having an impact, but it won't give you detailed feedback about which aspects of the project worked and which didn't. For that, you might use the approach described by Robert Brinkerhoff in his book *The Success Case Method* (2003).

Briefly, Brinkerhoff has you do a quick survey to identify some people who seem to have learned a lot from your project, as well as some who weren't as successful. Then you'll interview people from each group to figure out how you could improve your materials. This gives you more valuable information than the usual broad but shallow survey.

You can also write up your interviews to create case studies to share with your client and other stakeholders. Your evaluation includes not just a change in metrics but also detailed information about what worked to create that change, delivered as memorable case studies in addition to statistics. This helps your project stakeholders see how well the project has performed and, importantly, shows others in your organization how you work. You're not the "turn this into a course" person anymore.

The survey looks for changes in behavior

The Success Case survey isn't your typical after-training smile sheet, and unlike a smile sheet it's useful even if you never have a training event. It doesn't just provide averages but helps you learn in detail from specific successes and non-successes.

A smile sheet is distributed immediately after an event. In contrast, in the Success Case Method you wait to send a survey until people have had a chance to implement the changes supported by the project. This could be months, depending on your project.

Your survey asks about the behaviors that the project was intended to support. Below is a typical question from *The Success Case Method*. Notice how it focuses on one behavior, which in the action map might have been recorded as, "Complete a development plan."

> Which of the following best represents the extent to which you have used the development planning process tools?
>
> a. I have completed a development plan that has since been put into action with a positive result.
>
> b. I have completed a plan, but it has not been put into action yet.
>
> c. I have started a plan, but it isn't complete yet.
>
> d. I intend to develop a plan, but haven't started yet.
>
> e. I have no intentions of developing a plan.
>
> — Robert Brinkerhoff, *The Success Case Method* (2003)

Brinkerhoff recommends sending the survey to a large enough sample to get 40 to 50 responses.

Interview a few of the respondents

One goal of the survey is to identify who you should interview to learn how well the project is working. Brinkerhoff suggests many ways to determine who to interview. For example, if your main goal is to find out what's working and what isn't, you might interview six of the highest-scoring people and six of the lowest.

Each interview can take 30 to 45 minutes, plus the time needed by the interviewer to write up what was said. They can be conducted in person or over the phone.

For people who were successful with the project, the questions address five categories:

- What elements of the project did the person use?
- What results did they get?
- What was the impact of those results, such as their value?
- What was helpful?
- Any suggestions?

When the interviewee was unsuccessful — they didn't change what they did on the job — the interview is shorter and the questions focus on two categories:

- What barriers did they face?
- Any suggestions?

Your report tells stories

When you summarize your findings using the Success Case Method, your report goes beyond statistics to tell stories of individual cases. For example, you could describe how one person used the materials to solve a specific problem, detailing which materials they used and how well the materials worked.

Brinkerhoff doesn't usually write up cases about unsuccessful participants but says that sometimes these stories are the best way to show the effects of issues in the organization. Because training requests are often a response to issues that can't really be solved through training, you might decide to write up some non-success cases that make that clear.

Your report summarizes the apparent impact of the program and includes stories from your interviews. You might also want to address something that's often forgotten in the typical backward-looking evaluation: What additional value could you get from the project? Could it be adapted and expanded to a larger audience? Could some aspects be improved so more people are successful?

Brinkerhoff includes several examples of survey questions, interviews, and final reports in *The Success Case Method*. I highly recommend the book.

The future

In this book, we've described a reactive approach to training design: A client comes to us with a request, and we respond to that request. I focused on that because that's where most of us are starting from.

However, as you get more comfortable in your expanded role as a problem-solver, you might become more proactive. For example, you might see a performance problem and offer to help solve it without being asked. You might decide to raise your profile in the organization so you can help solve meaty problems and take on bigger challenges.

Common challenges

The client still wants a one-time training event when you think that's not the best solution.

- What is the client really saying? Are they saying, "After going through the analysis with you and seeing for myself that there are many ways to solve each aspect of the problem, I have still come to the conclusion that a training event is the best solution?" Or are they saying, "I have a gap to fill in an event" or "My boss wants a course?"

- If you've been applying the recommendations in this book, your client participated in the analysis of the problem and you helped them see alternate solutions. You included any additional stakeholders that might veto your work. When you created the prototype, you explained how, for example, on-demand activities would put the training in the workflow, while an event would be quickly forgotten. If you've done all this and your client still thinks an event is the best solution, you're probably stuck producing an event. In that case, you might use the Success Case Method to evaluate the project. If non-success cases point out that the event format was a problem, make sure to include that finding in your report so the client can see the effects of their insistence on an event.

- If the client wants an event for purely logistical reasons, try to find a way to help them while also helping solve the performance problem. For example, if you've been asked to provide a one-hour session at a company gathering for a problem that can't be solved in one hour, you could propose a one-hour kickoff session that launches a larger program. Then follow the session with on-demand activities, regular lunch sessions, or some other more in-depth solution that's spaced over time.

Stakeholders take too long to respond to your outline or activity drafts.

- If you've followed the recommendations in this book, your outline makes clear that people need to respond within a specific time to stay on track. Have people forgotten what they agreed to? Can you find a polite way to point out the calendar again?

- If the SME has too much on their plate, consider finding an additional SME. Position it as, "It's helpful to have as many perspectives as possible" or "This is a lot of work for one person."

- If necessary, adjust the delivery date or turnaround times in writing and get approval for the changes.

A reviewer can't picture the activity that's described in your text document

- Make sure the reviewer has a working copy of the prototype to refer to. Consider walking them through a couple of activity drafts and showing how the drafts relate to the prototype.

- If the reviewer still expresses concern about not being able to picture the activity, consider inserting images in the text document, such as mockups of the screen, slide, or job aid.

- Some designers who are creating slide-based materials deliver the activity drafts as slides. However, this makes it harder to track the reviewer's changes and can encourage them to respond more to the look than to the content. The result can be good-looking slides that have ineffective content.

A reviewer approves the draft but then wants to change things after production.

- If this happens often, consider having reviewers formally sign off on drafts. Make clear that a signoff means, "I've carefully checked this, I've made all the changes to the content that I think are necessary, and I've answered all questions" and not "I glanced over this and it looked okay."

- When you write your drafts, highlight any content that you're guessing at. I use bright yellow highlighting in Word and add a direct question to the reviewers. A draft isn't officially approved until all yellow highlighting has been addressed.

A stakeholder wants you to create a knowledge test.

- Create some assessment questions using the same type of practice activities we've focused on in the book, testing not only knowledge retrieval but also the application of that knowledge. Often the stakeholder will see for themselves that a person couldn't correctly answer the question without knowing the relevant fact.

- If the stakeholder rejects that type of assessment and wants you to ask abstract questions to be answered with isolated facts, ask why this is important. If the learners really do need to memorize a ton of information, it could be hard or inefficient to produce practice activities to test it all, so you could legitimately need fact checks. However, if the learners don't need to memorize a ton, ask why it's important to isolate their knowledge from the application of that knowledge. As they try to answer this question, the stakeholder could see for themselves that a pure knowledge test isn't necessary.

You can't tell if the project worked.

- Have you sent out a survey and completed interviews as described in *The Success Case Method*? It's not a huge undertaking and you're basically guaranteed to get helpful information.

- Has there been any change in smaller metrics related to your goal metric? For example, if you have a big metric like "employee turnover" that could be affected by many things in addition to your project, identify closer metrics as described in the chapter on goal setting and look for changes there.

Conclusion: What you've done

Here's what I hope you've done through this book.

- You convinced your client to analyze the performance problem, fix what they can fix, and apply training only when it will work.
- If training was part of the solution, you designed challenging activities that help people practice making the decisions they need to make on the job.
- You let learners pull the information they needed and draw conclusions from the consequences of their choices, showing that you respect them as intelligent adults.
- You made the practice activities available in the most effective format, whether that was as a training event or on a more flexible, on-demand basis, and you included spaced practice.
- You evaluated the success of the project by looking for improvements in the performance of the team or organization, not just "I liked it!" feedback.

I hope you've achieved this happy ending:

> *Your client respects you as a performance consultant, not a training order taker. Your subject matter expert is proud of their contribution to the project. Your learners are enjoying your challenges and confidently using what they've learned to solve problems that they care about. Your organization is seeing measurable improvements in metrics that matter.*

Thank you for trying action mapping, and please see my blog at cathy-moore. com for more ideas and updates.

Appendix 1: Job aids for action mappers

Summary of the entire workflow

See an interactive version and download the image and Word versions at map-it-book.com.

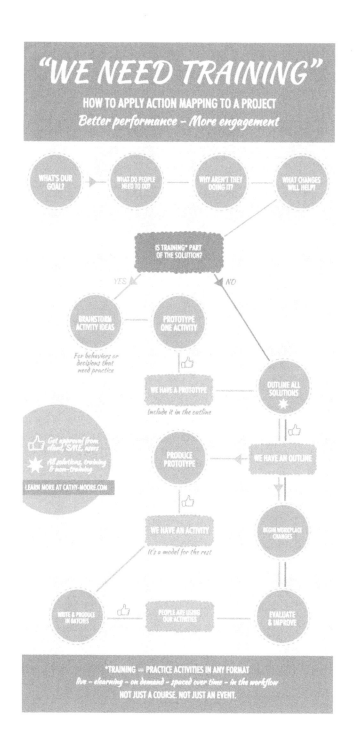

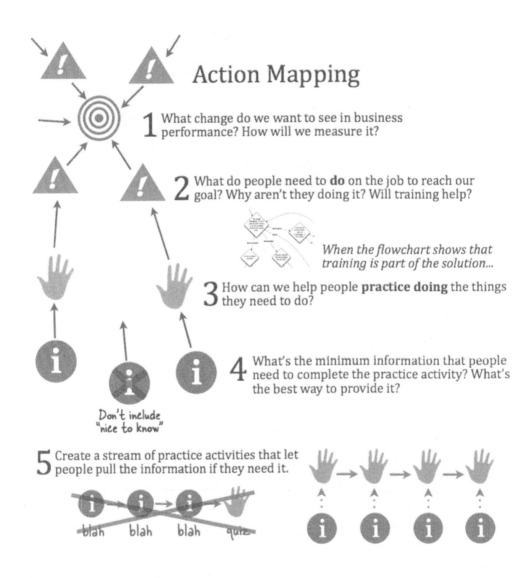

Action Mapping

1 What change do we want to see in business performance? How will we measure it?

2 What do people need to **do** on the job to reach our goal? Why aren't they doing it? Will training help?

When the flowchart shows that training is part of the solution...

3 How can we help people **practice doing** the things they need to do?

4 What's the minimum information that people need to complete the practice activity? What's the best way to provide it?

Don't include "nice to know"

5 Create a stream of practice activities that let people pull the information if they need it.

blah blah blah quiz

Appendix 2:
Common concerns about action mapping

Here are some common concerns you might hear from clients or colleagues about action mapping, with some ways to respond to them.

"Action mapping takes too long."

Action mapping might look like it takes a long time because in the story about Harold's sharps safety project (chapter 2), I went into a lot more detail in the action mapping version. I used more detail because you're probably not familiar with the model, not because Anna actually spent more time than Tina on her project.

However, Anna **did** spend more time analyzing Harold's problem. In action mapping, instead of a five-minute handoff of content, we have what could be a two-hour meeting to analyze the problem.

But once we've had that meeting, we start saving significant time.

We don't create useless training

A two-hour discussion can save hundreds of hours of work and impressive amounts of money. I've seen people realize that they were about to create the wrong training for the wrong audience and change their project entirely. For example, one client avoided the following:

- Hundreds of hours spent designing a workshop
- Thousands of dollars spent on internal and external labor to design and produce the workshop and related material

- Thousands of dollars in travel costs to send hundreds of employees to the workshop

- The labor costs of thousands of hours of employees' training and travel time

- Continuing damage to the business because the workshop didn't solve the problem

Other action mappers have significantly trimmed their project costs as they identified better ways to solve parts of the problem. These types of solutions include:

- Adding a bit of information to a software screen

- Making the log-in process easier

- Creating a quick-reference PDF

- Adding a field to a form

- Rewriting a wordy policy so it's actually understandable

- Having a colleague sit with a new employee for half an hour to show them the ropes

- Creating an easy-to-read summary of the information and emailing it to everyone

Action mapping guides the discussion with the client, helping them see for themselves that a course might not be the best or only solution.

We reduce production time

If we do end up designing training, we often design more efficient, targeted materials that take less time to develop.

Let's revisit Harold's hospital project and compare how Tina and Anna spent their time creating an online course.

Tina

Tina spent most of her time in three segments:

- Writing a detailed script for 130 slides and some quiz questions

- Producing the slides

- Checking everything: the narration, the click-to-reveals, the timing of the flying bullet points...

Tina's approach also introduced a delay, because it took Harold awhile to read the lengthy script and send his feedback.

Anna

Anna's time was broken into shorter segments with more variety:

- Helping the client analyze the problem
- Identifying job aids and other solutions that could help
- Prototyping a few activities
- Creating an outline
- Writing and producing the activities in small batches
- Staying in touch with the client, improving activities, and producing additional activities

Compared to Tina, Anna spent more time listening to the client and writing activities. She spent significantly less time producing the material because she didn't "need" narration or bling — the activities were interesting on their own and had far less information presentation.

In addition, Harold responded quickly to her requests for feedback because he only needed to read short activities in small batches.

Your time savings depend on the nature of the activities

In Harold's material, the decisions were quick and the consequences clear. As a result, it wasn't hard for Anna to write activities with Harold's help.

However, other situations require more nuanced questions. For example, in practice activities for skills like leadership, we need to provide backstory and subtle clues. The "right" answer may lead to a consequence that's only slightly better than the "wrong" answers, requiring careful writing. And sometimes the best way to create a realistic challenge is to write a branching scenario, which can take a lot of time.

So, it's likely that you'll spend longer in the writing phase of an activity-driven project than you'd take to write a traditional one. It takes longer to come up with challenging activities that let people experience something for themselves than it does to just tell them what to think.

However, production time is usually reduced. For example, for face-to-face training, you won't need to design a lot of slides because you're not going to be presenting much. Instead, you might create a handout that guides activities and distribute a job aid.

In elearning, you won't have to find ways to make information slides more "engaging," because you'll use far fewer of those slides. And if you see a branching scenario in your future, don't worry. Interactive fiction tools like Twine help you produce branching scenarios in less time than you'd need with slide-based tools.

Finally, because you analyzed the performance problem, you very likely reduced the expected amount of training from "They have to know everything!" to "They just need to practice these three things." Instead of spending the client's budget on a broad information dump, you'll invest it in some highly focused activities.

We use learners' time more effectively

By creating more efficient solutions, we reduce the amount of time that people spend in training. If you have thousands of learners, that's a lot of time saved.

If our analysis shows that improving tools or procedures will solve the problem without training, then people don't have to be "learners" at all and can just keep doing their jobs. If we do design formal training, the time that people spend in the training can be significantly reduced.

Let's compare those two online courses again, this time looking at the learners' experience.

Tina

When people take Tina's course, they all slog through the same 130 slides of information. If they rely on the narration, this takes them as long as it takes the narrator to read the script. If they read the transcript instead, they'll finish faster, and that's probably their goal: get to the end as soon as possible.

Regardless of their job role or pre-existing knowledge, everyone goes through the material at roughly the same pace, and everyone is "exposed" to all 130 slides. A receptionist and a surgeon have the same experience.

If at the end someone is interested in learning more, there's nothing more to learn in the course. They've been exposed to all the required information.

Anna

When people use Anna's materials, the amount of time they spend depends on several factors.

First, in some jobs, people have only limited exposure to sharps, so they're given fewer activities and spend less time in the material. A receptionist and a surgeon take different paths.

Second, people who already use correct sharps-handling techniques will answer more questions correctly, finishing sooner than those who make mistakes and have to try again or complete remedial activities.

Third, people who are more interested in the material will experiment to see the consequences of different choices in the activities, or they might try a different job role. They choose to explore more deeply, and they're rewarded by seeing different consequences or challenges.

"It's not in my job description."

If action mapping doesn't appear to fit your job description, you're not alone. This is a common concern that comes in several variations, including:

- "Everyone expects me to produce training on demand."
- "My boss thinks my job is to provide training and nothing else."
- "My job title literally is Course Producer."

If you work as an in-house training designer

If your job is to create training for others in the same organization, you might be in a good position to change expectations. Here are some options to consider.

Just start doing it

When a colleague hands you content and says, "Please turn this into a course," gently take control of the conversation.

As shown in the story with Anna and Harold, politely accept the content that they think they're just dropping off, and before they can get away, ask questions that show your interest in the problem that caused them to "need" a course.

Since they probably weren't expecting an in-depth conversation, get them to agree to a meeting. Say you'd like to get together with them "to make sure I understand what you need." If you can, get them to commit to two hours, but you might need to start with whatever you can get.

This meeting becomes the goal-setting and analysis phase of action mapping, and it starts with you committing to a goal that the client cares about. This helps win their cooperation with the rest of the process. Anna's conversation with Harold is an example.

The activities in the courses I offer help people practice this conversation, and in the chapters on each step of action mapping you'll find suggestions for specific things to say. My point here is that you can simply start changing how you talk to people without seeming to step out of your job.

Show them cool activity examples

If you find examples of good activities that you think would help your organization, share them with clients and potential clients. And when someone says, "I want a course like that!" you're on your way.

Since the new activities are different, explain that the process used to create them is a little different, too. That leads to the action mapping meeting described above.

The **serious drawback** to this approach is that you're tempting them with training when it might not be the best solution, so use it with caution.

Teach action mapping

Some people set up a short training session for clients or colleagues and show them how action mapping works. This can lead to the model being adopted as "the way we do it here."

A less formal approach is to blog or otherwise share with colleagues how you complete an action mapped project, showing what you do at each stage, describing your challenges, and explaining your decisions. As people see the process and its results, its use could spread.

Help create an L&D mission statement

If your job description appears to be "provide whatever the client asks for," you might check your department's mission statement. What does it say? Does it even exist?

A mission statement should not only identify what your department does and who you do it for, it should also make clear what you don't do and who you don't work with. Unfortunately, your department's statement might promise eternal servitude. As Shlomo Ben-Hur points out in *The Business of Corporate Learning* (2013), it's common for L&D departments to put themselves in purely reactive roles, laying out the welcome mat by promising to be "responsive to business needs."

If we never prioritize or even define "business needs," we're promising to say "yes" to any request from any person in the organization who claims to have a need. This is so wasteful that it actually breaks the original promise to support business needs. No business is served by a department that throws expensive training at unexamined problems.

> *Good learning leaders know how to cull. They have to get rid of the less than critical in order to concentrate on what is most important and focus resources accordingly.*
>
> — *Nigel Paine in The Learning Challenge: Dealing with Technology, Innovation and Change in Learning and Development (2014)*

Your department's statement should make clear that your mission is to achieve the organization's goals by analyzing and solving performance problems. If your mission statement is instead a variation on "we'll do whatever you want" or doesn't exist, you might open a discussion about it with the people who can change it.

If you work for an external training provider

If you work in a firm that only develops elearning or other training, you face a bigger challenge.

If your employer tells potential customers something like, "Let us produce your courses!" then clients rightly expect you to just produce courses. If your employer isn't interested in supporting any type of consultation, you're kind of stuck.

That doesn't mean you can't apply some action mapping techniques. For example, you might do some reverse engineering to try to identify the business goal that the materials seem intended to reach. You can also look at the materials from the perspective of, "What behaviors do they seem to want?" and clarify your interpretation in a phone call with the client. That can lead naturally to the question, "Why aren't they doing it already?"

While you're not in a position to say, "The course you want to us to create is a waste of money," you can at least identify the highest-priority actions required and approach your work as activity design rather than information design.

Some people in this position find satisfaction in the creative challenge of doing the best job possible under these constraints. Others leave. (If you leave, consider positioning yourself as a designer who cares about results, not as a course producer.)

If your employer markets a higher level of services, saying something like, "We design training that really works," you have more wiggle room. You might show your boss examples of good activities that would look great in the firm's portfolio. Suggest that the best way to design such activities is to change how you talk with clients, and take it from there.

If you're an independent designer

If you're an independent training designer and your clients expect you to produce courses on demand, look at your marketing from a fresh perspective.

Do you position yourself as someone who improves performance, or as a "course designer?" Do you attract clients by listing business benefits like better performance on the job, or do you focus on how engaging your training is? Do you describe your design process and clearly include analysis in it?

In your portfolio, do you explain the strategic reasons you designed the sample the way you did, or do you just present the sample? Do you describe the performance analysis that went into it, or do you just talk about the tool you used?

When you make clear that you analyze the performance problem and create targeted solutions, you'll attract clients who want that. As your roster fills with those clients, you can turn down work from the people who just want "a course."

You might also consider making your own private mission statement that clearly specifies what you do, who you do it for, what you don't do, and who you don't work with. Every time a prospective client calls with a need, compare their need with the boundaries you've established for yourself, and be prepared to say "no" (politely, of course). Use the time you saved to go after clients who are a better fit.

No matter where you work: I'd argue that it IS your job

No matter where you work, if you're supposed to design training, your real job should go beyond that label.

Imagine that you've gone to the doctor. "I need some antibiotics," you say. "Please write a prescription for 10 days' worth."

"Sure," the doctor says, scribbling on his prescription pad. "Here you go."

Is that a good doctor? Of course not. A good doctor would ask about your symptoms and try to solve the underlying problem.

That's what training designers should do, too. We shouldn't create a course just because someone wants one. We should ask about the symptoms and try to solve the underlying problem.

Shortly before I wrote this, I attended a session that Patti Shank led at the Learning Technologies conference in London. At one point, she asked us if we thought instructional design qualified as a profession. The slide that was showing then listed the characteristics of a profession, and on the list was, "Has a code of ethics."

My answer to Patti's question is no, instructional design isn't a profession, because we don't have a code of ethics. Creating courses on demand is as unethical as prescribing antibiotics on demand, yet it's so widespread that it has become the standard in our field.

It's hard to fight the status quo, but that doesn't mean we have to give up our integrity.

"The client or SME won't want to be involved."

Many clients and SMEs view training as a product that they order and we create. As a result, they're not expecting to spend more than the bare minimum of time "checking the information to make sure it's right."

Part of the solution lies in suggestions I made in the previous section. For example, if you teach action mapping to colleagues and clients and it becomes "the way we do it here," you're changing your organization's culture and your clients' expectations. I've heard of several people showing their stakeholders a short slideshow to describe how the process works and how everyone can benefit.

Even if you just change how you respond to the hand-off of content, you've started to adjust people's view of your role. But you still have to convince them the new approach is worth their time and energy.

Show them how they'll benefit

The most important step is to **help the client see what's in it for them.** That's one reason why the first step of action mapping is to identify a performance goal. It puts the focus on solving a problem that the client and SME care about, and it ignites their hope that you could help them reach that goal.

Thanks to your goal, the client no longer sees the project as "They're developing a course for me" but "We're going to fix this problem." Fixing the problem could bring any number of additional benefits for the client, such as, "People will stop calling me with complaints," "I'll finally feel like my team is moving forward," "We'll be able to focus on our mission," or "I'll prove to those nay-sayers that we can do it!"

Based on my own experience and the (many!) comments from designers in my workshops, your client probably hasn't analyzed the problem deeply. They might just be following the lead of everyone around them when they assume that training is the solution. Or they might be too close to the problem, trapped in it themselves, and grabbed the idea of training as a drowning person grabs a life preserver. Either way, they should quickly see the advantages of looking objectively at the problem once you make clear how they'll benefit. You'll see more specific suggestions in the chapter on setting goals.

Getting buy-in is so important that I strongly recommend that you include the client and SME in the needs analysis, which conventional instructional designers might do on their own, if they do it at all. Once stakeholders see for themselves that many causes of the problem are easy to fix, they get more excited about the solution.

It also helps to show the client and SME examples of the types of activities that you think will be helpful. Wait to do this until you're sure that training is part of the solution, but do it as soon as possible, to win their enthusiasm. Since the SME is going to invest a lot of time helping you with the activities, you want them to feel inspired and proud of their involvement.

New client? Treat them right from the start.

If you've just won a new internal or external client, someone involved in the project might pressure you to deliver whatever the client is looking for, regardless of whether it's what they actually need.

"We need to establish a good relationship with them," the stakeholder might say. "Just this time, give them what they want without asking questions. Later, you can do it right." How well do you think this works?

"Sorry, in this scenario, later never comes," writes Edmond Manning in the Allen Interactions blog.[5] "Challenging the status quo ... is exactly how you prove your value."

> Yes, it's difficult to be the person who stands up and says, "We could create this course in three weeks, but no one will learn from it and you won't see any behavioral change." It's a provocative stance; I understand that. But how much worse is it for your professional credibility to remain silent? Your silence cheats the company out of a great opportunity to improve performance cost-effectively.
>
> — Edmond Manning, Allen Interactions

"But no one cares about business impact."

This common claim seems to be more of a dysfunctional belief than a fact. Unfortunately, you're likely to hear it from colleagues, or even from clients or your boss. Here are some ways to challenge that belief.

If it's true that "no one cares" whether we have any impact on the business, why do so many surveys show that leaders think we aren't worth keeping around? For example, in 2012, a survey found that "more than half of line managers believe that employee performance would not change if the company's learning function were eliminated," writes Shlomo Ben-Hur.

> It would be nice if we could dismiss this as "just one survey," but the reality is that over the past ten years research has repeatedly shown that the proportion of business leaders who report being satisfied with their learning function's performance has steadfastly remained around 20 percent.
>
> —Shlomo Ben-Hur in The Business of Corporate Learning: Insights from Practice (2013)

---

[5] Manning, Edmond. "Five Tips to Battle E-Learning Project Constraints." Sept. 15, 2015. info.alleninteractions.com /five-tips-to-battle-project-constraints

If business leaders didn't care about the impact of our work, then they wouldn't say they were dissatisfied with us. Instead, they truly wouldn't care. We'd be the pets of our organizations, kept around because we're cute or just out of habit, never expected to do anything for our room and board.

Instead, business savvy helps us succeed: "Business and commercial awareness is perceived to be the number one factor contributing to the success of an L&D professional," the Chartered Institute of Personnel and Development found in a global survey in 2014.[6]

So according to research and my own experience with clients, a fair number of people actually do care about our business impact. Then why is it so common to hear, "No one cares?"

When you notice that people are clinging to a self-limiting belief, it can be interesting to ask, "How do they benefit from believing that?" My question to learning and development people is, "How do we benefit from believing that none of our clients cares about the business impact of what we do?"

What do you think? What are the rewards for that belief? Here are a few that I can think of.

- We can focus just on creating "fun" training and getting happy smile sheets. We can be creative and free!

- If we're tired or out of ideas, we can work on autopilot, just doing whatever the client tells us to do, since that's all they want, anyway.

- We can work alone, basing our design on the content we were given. That way, we don't have to talk much to other people, who can be so difficult and inefficient.

- Our responsibility ends when we deliver what the client asked for. We can't be held accountable for training that doesn't work because we never promised that it would.

- We don't have to learn things that we weren't taught in instructional design school, like "What's a 'key performance indicator?'" or "How do we measure change management?"

- When we feel unappreciated, we can say that it's because our field is unfairly marginalized by bean counters. We help people experience the joy of lifelong learning, but the bean counters don't care!

[6] CIPD and Towards Maturity. "L&D: Evolving Roles, Enhancing Skills." Research report. April 2015.

By believing that no one cares about our business impact, we get a seemingly easier job plus the martyrdom-enhanced satisfaction that we're doing noble but unappreciated work.

As jobs go, that might sound nice, but I'd argue that an "easy" job can quickly become frustrating, or at least it did for me and for many designers I've heard from. And I also doubt that training that's based on one client's possibly rushed decision will nobly improve anyone's life.

We could say that it's our leaders' fault for not communicating strategy or for treating the learning function as a course factory, and maybe that's true. Or we could not waste time on finding blame and instead change the situation ourselves — by learning the strategy, gently turning requests for courses into requests for improved performance, measuring our impact, and telling everyone about it.

To quote from pop psychology, "You teach people how to treat you."

Then we can flip my question around: "How do we benefit from believing that our clients care, or can be persuaded to care, about our business impact?" What do you think? What are the rewards for that belief?

Here are some ideas:

- We naturally respond to training requests in a way that encourages people to respect us as problem solvers, not order takers.

- We discover what makes our organization healthy or unhealthy, which helps us make it a better place to work.

- We enjoy the seriously fun challenge of designing realistic practice activities, not just delivering information.

- We notice performance problems and offer to help solve them before they're brought to us, raising our profile and giving us meaningful projects that make a difference.

- We show that we're responsible and proactive, which makes us good candidates for advancement, or more appealing to other employers if we decide to leave.

- We find more meaning in our jobs, because we see how our work improves the lives of our colleagues.

Designers who adopt action mapping and its focus on changing performance tell me that it makes their jobs more satisfying. The process "helped me find value in my work again," one action mapper wrote recently. Action mapping "changed my work world" another designer wrote. "I used to hate my job," another designer told me. "Now I love it."

"This isn't how I was taught."

If you have a degree or certification in instructional design, you probably studied theories and techniques that all shared the same goal: to get information into people's heads. From what I can tell, many degree programs still teach the school model and don't prepare designers for the business world.

"Instructional design is instructional design is instructional design," one degree program director was quoted as saying in an April 2015 article in *Learning Solutions Magazine.*[7] "People think K-12 must be so different from corporate, but teaching six-year-olds and adults is not that different."

By now, it should be clear that I couldn't disagree more.

The goal of children's schooling is to put information into kids' heads. The only performance problem is, "They don't know this," and it's such a simple problem that no one analyzes it. The only solution is knowledge transfer, and the only measurement is a test.

In contrast, the goal of corporate learning design is to **change what people do.** The performance problems are complex, caused by issues that go well beyond simple ignorance, and they need careful analysis. Our goal isn't a good test score but improved business performance. We're in the business of changing behavior, not just transferring knowledge.

A degree program in workplace learning design should show how to analyze messy performance problems, identify the training and non-training solutions, and create sustainable behavior change.

If you think a degree or certificate will advance your career and you'd like to work in performance improvement rather than education, I'd suggest that you look for a program that gives you real-world practice with business clients. A program with a separate track for workplace professionals might be best. You'll find recommendations for programs in LinkedIn discussions and in other forums for instructional designers.

---

[7] Collier, Lorna. "Online Degrees and Certificates for Instructional Designers: What You Need to Know." Learning Solutions Magazine. April 13, 2015. Accessed April 22, 2015.

Summary

When you use action mapping, you'll probably spend more time analyzing the problem and writing activities than you would if you used the conventional approach.

However, you're likely to save time and money in the end. You'll avoid creating training when training isn't the right solution. You'll spend less time creating information presentations. People will learn more efficiently and probably more effectively.

You'll need to help your clients and SMEs adjust to the new method. By starting with a goal that they care about, you can help them see what's in it for them and win their cooperation. You might also find that you like your job more.

I think it's unethical for us to create training on demand. Instead, we should **solve the problem** that inspired the training request, because that's what improves the performance of our organizations and justifies our paychecks.

If you do just one thing...

Identify the biggest challenge you'll face when changing how you work. How will you respond to that challenge?

Appendix 3: Checklist for strong learning design

Version 2

Download this checklist as a PDF:

blog.cathy-moore.com/2011/07/checklist-for-strong-elearning/

This tool will help you evaluate a training project and identify ways to make it more powerful.

The checklist is designed to evaluate materials created for **adults at work,** such as self-paced short courses or activities used in face-to-face training. If you're in academia or teach children, this checklist isn't intended for you.

If you use action mapping as your design approach, you could refer to this checklist to make sure you stay on track.

How to use the checklist:

1. For each item, judge the current state of your material and mark the corresponding spot on the spectrum.

2. When you've rated all the items, look down the spectrum column and identify marks that you'd like to move to the left, toward a more action-focused approach.

3. Rework your materials and evaluate them again.

Action-oriented materials	Spectrum	Information dump
The goal of the project is to change performance in a visible, measurable way.	| - - - - - - - - - - |	The goal of the project is to transfer information into people's brains.
Objectives used to design the materials describe visible, on-the-job behaviors that are necessary to reach the project goal ("sell," "lead," "encrypt," "schedule," "design").	| - - - - - - - - - - |	Objectives describe knowledge ("understand"). If behaviors are described, they're behaviors that happen during a test ("identify," "explain," "define").
The format of the materials (webinar, PDF, etc.) is determined by the type of activities and users' needs.	| - - - - - - - - - - |	The format of the materials is determined by tradition, the LMS, or what's most convenient for the client.
The materials feel like one immersive, challenging activity or a series of activities with little interruption.	| - - - - - - - - - - |	The materials feel like a presentation that's occasionally interrupted by a quiz.
The authors appear to respect the learners' intelligence and previous experience.	| - - - - - - - - - - |	The authors appear to doubt the learners' ability to draw conclusions and assume they have no experience.
Activities make people practice making decisions like the ones they make on the job.	| - - - - - - - - - - |	Activities are quizzes, trivia games, or other knowledge checks that don't happen on the job.
Activity feedback shows people what happens as a result of their choice; they draw conclusions from the result.	| - - - - - - - - - - |	Activity feedback explicitly **tells** people "correct" or "incorrect"; they aren't allowed to draw conclusions.
People can prove that they already know material and skip it.	| - - - - - - - - - - |	Everyone is required to view every bit of information regardless of their existing knowledge or performance on activities.
Reference information is supplied outside the activity in job aids; people practice using the job aids in activities.	| - - - - - - - - - - |	Reference information is delivered through the course or training; people are expected to memorize it or come back to the course for review.
Characters are believable; they face complex, realistic challenges with emotionally compelling consequences.	| - - - - - - - - - - |	Characters seem fake (e.g., preachy or clueless); their challenges are minor and are presented as intellectual exercises.
Visuals are used to convey meaning.	| - - - - - - - - - - |	Visuals are used as "spice."
Photos of people show humans with realistic expressions. Illustrations appear intended for grownups.	| - - - - - - - - - - |	Visuals of people are stock photo models who are over-acting or childish cartoons.
In elearning, audio narration is used only for: - Dramatic realism (e.g. characters' voices in a scenario) - Explanations of complex or rapidly-changing graphics - Motivational messages and explanations from people who really exist (e.g. CEO, subject matter expert)	| - - - - - - - - - - |	Audio narration is used to: - Deliver information while displaying simple, static screens - Redundantly read text on the screen - Lecture people about what they should or shouldn't do
The writing is concise, uses contractions, and sounds like a magazine (Flesch Reading Ease score of 50 or higher in Word)	| - - - - - - - - - - |	The writing is wordy and stiff; it sounds like a textbook or insurance policy (Flesch Reading Ease score of 49 or lower in Word)

Appendix 4:
Summary of the scenario design process

First, read the book!

This entire book is about scenario design. If you want to design scenarios, please read the book. This appendix is just a summary of the techniques.

The process

Here's a summary of the process described in this book, which you've read, right?

- **Write a project goal.** Identify how you'll measure success for the project as a whole.

- **List what people need to do.** List the specific, observable actions people need to take on the job to meet that goal. Prioritize those actions.

- **Ask, "Why aren't they doing it now?"** For the high-priority actions, ask, "Why aren't they doing this now?" or "What might make this difficult?" First consider the environment (tools, systems, and culture), to avoid assuming that the problem comes entirely from a lack of knowledge or skills.

- **Note the solutions.** Note the non-training solutions you've probably discovered from the above discussion, and identify the behaviors that will probably benefit from practice activities.

- **Choose a format for each proposed activity.** Identify the best format (live, elearning, etc.) for each activity idea and the best time for the person to use the activity (such as right before performing the task, in short sessions spaced out over time, etc.). If the skills addressed in the scenario are complex or controversial, determine how you'll provide a debrief or other way for people to discuss issues and see the larger picture.

- **Choose an activity to prototype.** Pick a typical behavior that will be addressed with a scenario activity. You'll turn it into a prototype decision point. It can be a standalone mini-scenario or one decision point in what will become a branching scenario.

- **Interview your SME for the prototype activity.** Get the understanding you need to create a believable question, tempting options, and realistic consequences for those options. Capture the common mistakes and why people make them in addition to the best choice and what makes it difficult to make. Consider asking the SME for a story about a particular time this decision was made.

- **Write a stem.** The stem is the setup and question for your decision point. Use the insight you got from the SME to recreate the real-life issues that tempt people to make the wrong choice.

- **Write the options.** Include the common mistakes that the SME identified and make them sound like good choices.

- **Write unique feedback for each option.** Show the consequence of the choice by continuing the story. You might also provide instructive feedback ("You should have done X"), possibly as an optional explanation, but first show the consequence.

- **Identify the minimum supporting information.** Decide what is the minimum information the player must have to make the decision in your prototype.

- **Determine a format for the info.** Decide when and in what format you'll provide the minimum supporting information. My usual recommendation: Put it in a job aid, if that's appropriate, and have people refer to the job aid when they're considering the question. Don't present the information before the activity; let people pull it if they need it. Also provide a snippet of the information in the feedback to reinforce or correct each choice.

- **Create and test the prototype.** Create a mockup of the prototype decision point and test it on the SME, client, and group of learners. If the prototype is a decision point in a longer scenario, describe the bigger story that the question is part of, but don't write it yet.

- **Write the project charter.** Write an outline describing all the solutions to the problem, including the non-training solutions, and listing at a high level the activity ideas. Include the prototype decision point and, if appropriate, mood boards showing how the material might be produced. Get approval before continuing below.

Branching scenario: Additional steps

Here, you divert into a few extra steps if your prototype decision is part of a branching scenario. Once your prototype and project charter are approved, you'll:

- **Identify the story endings.** You might have one "best," some "fair," and a few "poor" endings. Decide in general what decisions a person would make to reach each ending.

- **Write a high-level plot as a flowchart.** Use notes only; don't write a script. Use software like Twine, a whiteboard, or a flowcharting tool to show the structure of the plot (I use Twine because I can complete all remaining steps in it, it's flexible, and it's free). Consider writing the best path first and then filling in the less-good paths. Consider connecting paths so players can realize that they're heading toward a bad ending, make a better choice, and end up on a better path. This helps them practice recognizing and recovering from mistakes.

- **Get feedback on the plot.** Consider including future learners in the review. You'll probably need to describe what happens, since you've written only notes. Make sure the plot is realistic and complex enough to be challenging and useful. Most first drafts are too simple.

- **Fill in the plot with details.** Once the plot is complex enough and approved, flesh out your notes to turn them into a story.

- **Write debrief questions as you flesh out the plot.** You've probably chosen a branching scenario because the skill to be practiced is complex and full of grey areas. Help people see the big picture and process what they've learned by asking thought-provoking questions during a debrief.

- **Get feedback on the complete story.** Again, consider including learners in the review.

See chapter 13 for detailed questions to consider at each review.

All types of activities: Write and produce in batches

At this point, you've gotten approval for the prototype activity, all activity ideas, and, if appropriate, the look and feel you'll use for production. Now you'll write the activities in small batches, send them to the SME for feedback, and produce them as they're approved.

You'll avoid these mistakes

Below are the most common mistakes I see scenario designers make. I like to think you won't make them, because you've read the book. Just in case, avoid doing the following.

- **Skip the analysis:** Assume that the problem is a lack of knowledge and training is the answer. Don't ask the questions in chapters 4, 5, or 6. Write generic, irrelevant scenarios as a result.

- **Answer "What do they need to do?" in broad terms.** List actions like "follow the ethics policy" or "communicate effectively" instead of breaking them down into specific, observable behaviors. As a result, get no useful understanding of why people aren't doing what's needed, and struggle to write realistic scenarios.

- **Don't identify the common mistakes.** Just ask the SME what people should do; ignore what they shouldn't do and why they do it. Write too-easy questions as a result.

- **Tell, tell, tell:** Dump a lot of information on people before you "let" them do the scenario, so you exercise only their short-term memory. Then, immediately tell them what they did wrong, rather than letting them draw conclusions like the adults they are. (You won't do this because you've read chapters 11 and 12.)

- **Start writing a branching scenario without plotting it first.** The story takes on a life of its own, runs down weird alleys to crash into surprise walls, and is impossible for reviewers to see clearly. You need to plot it first to make sure learners will practice what they need to practice, and reviewers need to "see" the plot, literally, to give you useful feedback.

- **Produce activities about difficult grey areas with no discussion or debrief.** Just put some scenarios on the LMS and expect people to change without any discussion or other processing. Instead, help people see the big picture, discuss grey areas, and share their experiences.

Questions to answer

You might have been trained to never question the client's choices. Now that you've read the book, you know that effective solutions require lots of questions of all sorts. Here are several of them all in one place.

Questions to answer before you write a word

- What's our goal for this project? What are we currently measuring that will improve thanks to our work? (chapter 4)

- What do people need to do (not know) to meet our goal? Write specific, observable actions. (chapter 5)

- Why aren't they doing each thing? What makes each task hard? Will a practice activity really help? Can we fix the problem some other way? Do this analysis for each high-priority action, not just once for the project as a whole. (chapter 6)

- Which actions are we targeting with scenarios? What should be the core challenge in each scenario? (chapter 7)

- In what format (elearning, live, etc.) should we provide the scenarios? Ignore for now what the client thinks they want and focus instead on what will likely work best given the characteristics of the job and audience. (chapter 8)

- Which action will we use for our prototype scenario? What makes it hard to perform in the real world? What are the common mistakes people make, and why do they make them? What are the consequences of each mistake? (chapter 9)

- Do we need a branching scenario or a mini scenario? A combination? If we're using a branching scenario, what is the best ending? What are the not-so-good endings? First identify the endings; don't write the whole thing! (chapter 9)

Questions to answer as you write a prototype decision point

- What details will we include in the stem? How can we recreate the real-world issues that make the common mistakes seem like good choices? Do we need to provide a backstory? If so, how will we provide it? (chapter 10)

- How should we write the options? Have we covered all the common mistakes? Should we ask people to defend their choice? (chapter 10)

- How should we provide feedback? Should we just show the consequence, or do we need to tell them things as well? Should the feedback display immediately after the choice, or will we show it later? (chapter 11)

- What do people need to know to make the decision? How will we provide that information? Is it really necessary to force everyone to sit through a presentation first? How can we provide the information optionally, in the activity itself? Should we display the information in the feedback? (chapter 12)

Questions to answer during the prototype phase

- If you're creating a branching scenario: Write a high-level plot. (Just notes! Not a script!) Walk some testers through it. Is the plot realistic? Is it complex enough? Do you want to score it? How?

- For any prototype decision point: Is the stem detailed enough to make the question realistic and challenging? Are the options subtle, or did people easily see the best answer?

- Did people look at the information you provided before making a decision? Did they need more information? Less?

- Did people appear to learn from the consequence of their choice? Did they show any surprise? Did they disagree with the result or the options? If so, would it be useful to let this disagreement occur, so learners will discuss the scenario during the debrief and think more deeply?

Bibliography

Allen, Michael. *Michael Allen's Guide to Elearning: Building Interactive, Fun, and Effective Learning Programs for Any Company.* San Francisco, CA: Wiley, 2003.

Ben-Hur, Shlomo. *The Business of Corporate Learning: Insights from Practice.* Cambridge, UK: Cambridge University Press, 2013.

Bozarth, Jane. *Show Your Work: The Payoffs and How-To's of Working Out Loud.* San Francisco, CA: Wiley, 2014.

Brinkerhoff, Robert O. *The Success Case Method: Find Out Quickly What's Working and What's Not.* San Francisco, CA: Berrett-Koehler Publishers, Inc., 2003.

Brown, Peter C., Henry L. Roediger III, Mark A. McDaniel. *Make It Stick: The Science of Successful Learning.* Cambridge, MA: Belknap Press of Harvard University, 2014.

Clark, Ruth Colvin. *Evidence-Based Training Methods: A Guide for Training Professionals,* second edition. Alexandria, VA: ATD Press, 2015.

Clark, Ruth Colvin. *Scenario-Based e-Learning: Evidence-Based Guidelines for Online Workforce Learning.* San Francisco, CA: Pfeiffer, 2013.

Crandall, Beth, Gary Klein, Robert R. Hoffman. *Working Minds: A Practitioner's Guide to Cognitive Task Analysis.* Cambridge, MA: The MIT Press, 2006.

De Bruyckere, Pedro, Paul A. Kirschner, and Casper D. Hulshof. *Urban Myths about Learning and Education.* London: Elsevier, Inc., 2015

Dirksen, Julie. *Design for How People Learn*. Berkeley, CA: New Riders, 2012.

Fowler, Susan. *Why Motivating People Doesn't Work...and What Does*. San Francisco, CA: Berrett-Koehler Publishers, Inc., 2014.

Kahneman, Daniel. *Thinking, Fast and Slow*. New York: Farrar, Straus and Giroux, 2011.

Kinley, Nik and Shlomo Ben-Hur. *Changing Employee Behavior: A Practical Guide for Managers*. Houndmills, Hampshire UK: Pagrave Macmillan, 2015.

Mayer, Richard E., Ruth Colvin Clark. *e-Learning and the Science of Instruction: Proven Guidelines for Consumers and Designers of Multimedia Learning*, second edition. San Francisco, CA: Pfeiffer, 2008.

Maylett, Tracy and Paul Warner. *MAGIC: Five Keys to Unlock the Power of Employee Engagement*. Austin, TX: Greenleaf Book Group, 2014.

Paine, Nigel. *The Learning Challenge: Dealing with Technology, Innovation and Change in Learning and Development*. London, UK: Kogan Page Limited, 2014.

Rock, David. *Your Brain at Work: Strategies for Overcoming Distraction, Regaining Focus, and Working Smarter All Day Long*. New York: HarperCollins, 2009.

Index

Made in the USA
Coppell, TX
17 January 2025

44509941R10230